Crisis and Political Beliefs

# Crisis and Political Beliefs

## The Case of the Colt Firearms Strike

**Marc Lendler**

Yale University Press

New Haven and London

Chapter 4 epigraph from Eric Foner, *Reconstruction: America's Unfinished Revolution, 1863–1877*. Copyright © 1988 by Eric Foner. Reprinted by permission of HarperCollins Publishers, Inc.

Set in New Caledonia type by Northeastern Graphic Services, Inc. Printed in the United States of America by Edwards Brothers, Inc., Ann Arbor, Michigan.

Library of Congress Cataloging-in-Publication Data

Lendler, Marc.
Crisis and political beliefs : the case of the Colt Firearms strike / Marc Lendler.
p. cm.
Includes bibliographical references and index.
ISBN 0-300-06746-1 (alk. paper)
1. Colt Firearms Strike, Hartford, Conn., 1985. I. Title.
HD5325.M912 1985.H375 1997
331.89′2834′0097463—dc20      96-9747
                                          CIP

A catalogue record for this book is available from the British Library.

The paper in this book meets the guidelines for permanence and durability of the Committee on Production Guidelines for Book Longevity of the Council on Library Resources.

10 9 8 7 6 5 4 3 2 1

To Neil and Ranil, who understand the commitment to
justice underneath the bland exterior of procedural failure
and the courage sometimes necessary to preserve it

*Words and concepts had been reshaped in the colonists' mind in the course of a decade of pounding controversy—strongly reshaped, turned in unfamiliar directions, toward conclusions they could not themselves clearly perceive. They found a new world of political thought as they struggled to work out the implications of their beliefs in the years before Independence. It was a world not easily possessed; often they withdrew in some confusion to more familiar ground. But they touched its boundaries, and, at certain points, probed its interior.*
—Bernard Bailyn, *Ideological Origins of the American Revolution*

*No one who does not cheerfully consent to do this [work overtime] need expect to be employed by me.*
—notice written by Samuel Colt

*Let me tell you something. I did nothing at the plant. Not a damn thing. Here, I'm at a meeting, two meetings there, tomorrow who knows where I'll be. I've never been so busy. But it's what I want to do. I believe in it.*
—Colt striker

# Contents

# Preface

During the time I was finishing my dissertation, I was aware that an unusually contentious strike had begun at the Colt Firearms Division in Hartford, Connecticut. It was highly visible in the state (where I was a resident), but there was another reason it caught my eye. I was working on a thesis arguing that people adapt themselves too easily to unjust situations and was exploring the accommodating attitudes of blue-collar employees toward workplace inequalities as my case in point. The pictures and stories from Colt suggested that these employees were somewhat less accommodating. But thesis writing produces tunnel vision, particularly in its final stages, and I put those images out of my mind.

A year later I was teaching a class on the Politics of Powerlessness at Connecticut College and invited two of the Colt strikers to my class. I was impressed, though not surprised, at their depth of commitment to the strike itself. I *was* surprised at the emphasis they put on the development of community among the participants and the satisfaction they took from it. My thesis had attempted to explain how employees reconciled industrial authority with prevailing orthodoxies of our political culture about opportunity, fairness, and individual causality. It became obvious that the Colt strike would provide a rare opportunity to see how the American Dream looked in "nonnormal" situations.

The leadership of UAW Local 376, including Phil Wheeler, Bob Madore, Russ See, Jim Griffin, and many lower-level officers, was very helpful in providing information and permitting me to attend union meetings and talk freely with strikers. Special thanks are due to David Burnham and Arden Passaro, the two strikers who came to my class, and Maria Vicello, who volunteered to help in interviews with strikers whose primary language was Italian. There were a number of nonstrikers with insight and information on the conflict whose help was invaluable, including Susan Howard, Laddie Michalowski, Rochelle Ripley, Louise Simmons, and Meg Whinnem (the daughter of the founder of the union local in the 1930s). Richard Reibeling, chief negotiator for Colt, graciously sat for an extended interview after he had been displaced at the conclusion of the strike.

In order to get differing perspectives, I discussed the strike events and the manuscript with some people who are not professional academics—notably Jon Baker, Jeanne Chisamore, Bob Pesner, Linda Tarlow, and Jay Youngdahl—and some who are—Ron Cohen, Robert Dahl, Peter Hinks, Charles Lindblom, and James Scott, all of whom provided helpful comments. As has happened before, I began by imagining this book to be a debate with Jim Scott's views on hegemony and opposition; I ended by moving closer to his views than the ones I held originally. I also want to acknowledge the contributions to this book my parents have made simply by the example of their lifetime attention and commitment to the arena of public events.

Finally, I had the instructive, if unfortunate, experience of living through some of the book's themes as it was near completion. I argue here (in part) that people's character and basic beliefs are severely tested and even recomposed in times of dislocation. As I was concluding, I was among twenty-six faculty members fired in the "restructuring" of Bennington College. As those events unfolded, and as people on various sides began to create their interpretations which explained or rationalized the school's actions, it became unmistakably clear that crisis does indeed bring out the best and worst in human nature. I share this study, for whatever solace it may be, with my colleagues who were dismissed.

Crisis and Political Beliefs

# 1

## The Times That Try Men's Souls

*Bad weather brought instead to the town a wide-eyed insomnia, a great nuisance of geese, and a wild sort of grim and giddy spirit of dedication to the town's Common Good—a spirit the likes of which the coast hadn't seen since those big sky-watching sea-scanning war-effort days back in '42 after that single Japanese plane fire-bombed the forest outside of Brookings to give the Brookings area the distinction of being the only American shore ever to suffer a foreign attack. This sort of distinction is bound to provoke a certain amount of community feeling; the bombing and the strike, while they exhibited very little in common outwardly, were in a way quite similar in that both had the effect of making the citizens feel, well, just a bit . . . special? No; more than special; let's admit it: it made them feel downright different!*
—Ken Kesey, *Sometimes a Great Notion*

The political thinking of ordinary citizens changes in times of crisis. This is not a revelation; it has been noted often and the reasons are fairly straightforward. When the circumstances that lead people to judgments about the political world are suddenly altered, conventional conclusions no longer carry the protective coloration of hard-headed common sense. There is a greater need for information, a more compelling reason to process it, and a greater urgency (and sometimes, freedom) to think and speak about political developments. Events that in more normal times seem to demand no more than hazy reflection impinge more directly on people's lives. The *quality* of popular thinking in times of turmoil has been a matter for debate; what some see as a more penetrating perception of reality others see as dangerous irrationality.[1] But both of these interpretations stem from the same observation—that "crisis-time" public thinking is likely to take place in jumps and jolts, and is marked (for better or worse) by a greater effort to fit information together in some broadly explanatory way.

Such periods often involve new forms of activity by those excluded from or on the margins of "normal-time" politics. A historian of the Populist movement called them "democratic moments"—times when some set of events has widened the political sphere and impelled the participation of those who in more ordinary times do not venture close to the operations of authority.[2] The enlarged role played by those who are unaccustomed to the exercise of power accounts for the sense of elation that participants almost invariably report. The entrance of new, energized actors on the political stage—particularly when it includes some who were formerly marginalized—makes the study of such times instructive out of proportion to the frequency of their occurrence. Is the movement from passivity to activism accompanied by a similar transformation in political beliefs? Since Stanley Elkins proposed his controversial notions of the "infantilization" of slaves and the creation of an accommodating "Sambo" personality, social scientists have tried to interpret the variety of responses to systems of domination.[3] Most studies of this kind have noted, analyzed, and argued over the surface passivity of the relatively powerless. I will be examining the behavior and political judgments of people living through a period in which the familiar landmarks of inequality are removed. The purpose will be to learn more about the "grim and giddy spirit of dedication" that people develop as they confront the political equivalent of Kesey's bad weather.

### INTERNALIZED INEQUALITY?

Rebellion is an extraordinary event. When a boss tells us to start working, most of us start working. When a cop tells us to move along, most of the time we move along. When an usher tells us to form a line, most of us queue up. We spend a large portion of our lives compliantly acting out roles in authority systems of one sort or another, accepting daily regulation as a matter of course.[4]

Social science has produced a disparate, although increasingly well-defined literature on accommodation, resistance, and the existence and nature of a "dominant ideology." Societies that are vastly unequal in their divisions of valued resources—power, material rewards, mobility, opportunity for self-fulfillment (to list a few of many possibilities)—can nonetheless remain stable, often for very long periods of time. Although periodic popular movements have challenged social, political, or economic inequalities, they are the exception. But stability lacks the observable proximate causes of oppositional movements, particularly those that challenge entire regimes. The mechanisms that produce and sustain even relative social peace are not so easily traceable. That does not mean those mechanisms are either insubstantial or unimportant; it merely means that they are buried more deeply in convention, ritual, and/or ordering principles of perceived fair mutual obligations between those of different status. That there is a question which needs explanation at all takes a moment's reflection, but only that. Even a political theorist as committed to the virtue and value of inequality as Plato knew hierarchy needed some ideological grease to work—thus the Noble Lie, which was offered up essentially as a way to placate a nonprivileged majority on the cheap.[5]

The question at the heart of that discussion is approximately this: do subordinates—those over whom power and authority are exercised—tend to accept as natural, inevitable, and/or just the constellation of forces that sustains their subordination? By temporarily dispensing with subtleties and refinements, I can summarize the central insights that social scientists have provided in explaining quiescence. Those at or near the bottom of a given distribution of power and rewards and whose conduct does not appear contentious can be said to accept such systems either *pragmatically*—because they have no other real options—or *normatively*—because they accept its operation as just. Is quiescence a sign of *ac*quiescence and, conversely, is de facto opposition to specific acts of authority a sign of rejection of the legitimacy of that authority? These questions are usually discussed in close proximity to claims about the role of hegemony in forging political consensus from divergent interests.[6] Do the beliefs and conclusions of disadvantaged or subordinate groups tend to be those of the most privileged classes, and do those beliefs help perpetuate the pattern of privilege?

One exploration of the questions by Barrington Moore was a comparative study of (among others) concentration camp inmates, untouchables, and German workers in the 1918 abortive revolution to see whether they shared any common standards for judging injustice. He concluded that victims in most cases come to regard the structures that created their victimization as inevitable or natural.[7] Subordinates develop a "moral anesthesia" that dulls their sense of injustice. Moore's metaphoric device for explaining unequal authority relations is the social contract. His contract is not that of classical political philosophy, negotiated between equals to create a compact for a new entity called "civil society" or "government." It more properly resembles a peace treaty, describing reciprocal obligations of *un*equals, based on a previously existing distribution of resources. The most pervasive obligations of ruling authorities are safety, sustenance, and noncapricious conduct. "Moral outrage" comes not from suffering itself—it really cannot in Moore's scenario, since a sense of injustice is an "acquired taste"—but from violation of the implicit contract by superordinates.[8] The nature of the demand raised from below is almost always to restore the violated contract. What emerges from Moore is a picture of the overwhelming importance of adaptation and convention in structuring people's sense of justice and in creating cohesion in potentially conflictual situations. His conclusions lend support to those who find a dominant, or hegemonic, ideology to be important in structuring people's beliefs and in maintaining cohesion in potential conflictual situations. Human beings have a "perilous capacity for getting used to things."[9]

But are passive behavior and the lack of public argumentation on the part of subordinate groups necessarily an indication of their real sentiments? A very different approach is taken by some who describe the apparent normative acceptance of harsh social systems as a pose that subordinates strike for public consumption. This position has been argued most comprehensively by James Scott, who investigates the possible existence of a "hidden transcript"—a more oppositional pattern of belief and behavior in which the powerless engage when not confronting power directly. In order to deflect retaliation or to curry favor, the powerless strategically adopt a mask for public discourse— "the more menacing the power, the thicker the mask."[10] The pose thus creates a "public transcript"—an interaction between powerful and powerless in which it appears that the legitimacy of the authority relationship is accepted by all parties. The stability of inegalitarian, hierarchical systems is the product of simple coercion and anticipated coercion reinforced by the dull compulsion of economic relations. "Everyday resistance" goes on in disguised forms: foot-dragging noncompliance, evasion, feigned inability to understand orders, irreverent gossip.[11] The authors of a British study similar to Scott's concluded, "There is a sense in which it is foolish to ask how societies cohere, for the answer is that they do not."[12]

Another interpretation of compliance in situations where resistance might be expected is that people simply do the best they can with the resources they have at their disposal, within the limits of the political and economic environment in which they live. Lack of resistance, lack of resentment, and absence of articulated or imagined alternatives are not matters that need explanation but rather indications that the populace or group at issue has achieved some relative satisfaction and does not think it is useful to invest time into a broader and potentially risky program of challenge to the system. People who face hardship without much complaint are commonsensical utility maximizers who understand that life is tough. Elkins, Moore, Scott, and others have created an explicit dialogue about compliance and resistance. The argument I am describing here is so diffusely omnipresent that it does not seem at first glance to be part of that dialogue. It was made most overtly a part of the dominant ideology debates by Richard Hamilton and James Wright. They argue that most people are interested primarily and properly in such non–"public issue" problems as marriage, personal appearance, friends, and their immediate economic welfare.[13] Any argument that these humdrum concerns are misplaced, or the product of mystification, the authors say, can come only from elitist outside observers unconcerned with the many costs of deeper structural change:

> A much higher level of realism is found in the average person's appreciation of the world. A comment one hears frequently about objectively unpleasant (alienating) jobs is "Someone has to do it." The advanced intellectual has little to say with respect to such realism. . . . [Intellectuals] have a submerged, an unsaid or unspoken, argument: it is that (i) things can be otherwise, and (ii) life will be better when organized in that other way. Once again, ordinary people are ahead of the advanced thinker. They are either denying these two claims or asking to be shown.[14]

Reducing complex questions to a few contending "schools" carries risks, but simplification has the virtue of highlighting areas of difference. Taken together, these "schools" call attention to the many-faceted responses to domination and injustice. But each also makes a definable central claim. Hegemony theory, finding little resistance at times, is drawn to the possibility of mystification and normative consensus as an explanation. The "everyday resistance" advocates ask us to look behind the public interplay of the powerful and powerless; when we do, they argue, we will find what we expected—scorn and ridicule of authority, foot-dragging evasion. Utility maximizers invert that. If inspection finds no discontent or resistance, it must mean that it was the expectation of opposition which was misguided.

EVERYDAY LIFE

The terrain of this inquiry into quiescence and acquiescence has largely been that of "everyday relations." Hierarchy and inequality are routine in most people's experience of them, and even extreme forms of deprivation are confronted largely as conditions of daily life.[15] It is in the course of this daily confrontation that people make judgments about the usefulness, fairness, morality, and, ultimately, the legitimacy of the social system that organizes and explains the inequalities. Certainly one of the lasting contributions of the hegemony debate, independent of any conclusions one might draw, is that it has demanded "an inventory and analysis of everyday life."[16]

The exploration of routine, superficially unremarkable interactions between powerful and powerless has given rise to the "naturalization" argument.[17] Institutional arrangements, over time, tend to acquire a physical quality and gain legitimacy from the simple fact of their continued existence. Even those who are disadvantaged or victimized by a particular distribution of authority and rewards come to regard them less as a product of human decisions or a result of a discretionary ordering of values than as a part of nature.[18] The naturalization argument needs no conspiratorial socializing agents (although it does not preclude them), since it is the institutions and routines themselves which create the argument for legitimacy. Their trump card is the appearance of permanence. Some political theorists have underscored the value (and necessity) of utilizing this appearance as a resource in creating and maintaining political order. James Madison was essentially describing naturalization ("that veneration which time bestows") when he urged that the governing structures of the new republic not be made "too mutable" lest they forsake "that share of prejudice in its favor which is a salutary aid to the most rational Government."[19] Conversely, what John Stuart Mill called the "despotism of custom" is precisely the legitimacy which arises from the appearance of permanence.[20]

Agnes Heller compellingly describes the clash between custom and "free individuality":

> It is a tough world into which we are born and in which we have to make our way. In this tough world, people work, eat and drink (usually less than they need) and make love (usually by the rules); people rear their children to play a part in this tough world and timorously guard the nook they have managed to corner for themselves; the order of priorities; the scale of values in our everyday life is largely taken over ready-made; it is calibrated in accordance with position in society and little in it is movable.[21]

The emphasis in studies of compliance has been on decoding the narratives people create as they "guard the nook" in this tough world and on the meaning of routine in systems of domination. But simply noting accommodation may be deceiving. Elkins was criticized for (among other things) overlooking the possibility that "Sambo" was a mask or a human enactment of the mythological trickster figure of many cultures.[22] Scott, who emphasizes the same themes as these critics of Elkins, points out the potential for bias in appraising the political values of the powerless by studying situations of apparent social peace:

In the short run, it is in the interest of the subordinate to produce a more or less credible performance, speaking the lines and making the gestures which he knows are expected of him. The result is that the public transcript is—barring a crisis— systematically skewed in the direction of the libretto, the discourse dominated by the powerful. . . . In ideological terms the public transcript will typically, by its accommodationist tone, provide convincing evidence for the hegemony of dominant values, for the hegemony of dominant discourse.[23]

The study of powerlessness in a setting of relative stability and in the absence of overt conflict might yield a distorted record, heavily biased toward finding the widespread acceptance of an accommodationist dominant ideology. There seems to be good reason to worry that in "ordinary," routine relations between powerful and powerless, oppositional thinking and behavior might simply lie further under the surface. Here is where the study of "nonnormal" political situations—important in its own right—can provide information about more normal times.

If routine offers subordinates some consoling comforts—at least by shielding them from erratic uses of coercion—and if that might tend to produce a misleading portrait of acquiescence, then a useful place to turn for a fuller picture would be one in which routine is at least temporarily disrupted. People suffer some abuse patiently, then one day a million are in the street, protesting. Slaves pick cotton, then kill a master or join Nat Turner (however infrequently). Women live with what appears to be consensual inequality, then speak out. Everyone who addresses matters of passivity and resistance can do so in a comprehensive way only by acknowledging that both sets of responses exist. Most arguments about quiescence have properly centered on the first set of characteristics. But by turning to the more infrequent second, we may be able to learn more about how suddenly rebellious subjects regarded their lot previously.

It is reasonable to expect that people will act differently in sharply changed circumstances; the issue at hand is whether they also think differently, whether they reassess fundamental values (and what the nature of the new assessment is), and if so, what light this can shed on prior perceptions of justice and fair play. If the understandings people develop and share in these special moments are greatly different from quieter times, it suggests that the break with socially constructed routine itself plays a role in the creation of the emergent values. That would then provide evidence that those routines had helped pattern people's thinking in normal times—the heart of the "naturalization" argument.

Each of the three "schools" of thought about accommodation also draws attention to different aspects of "crisis-time" politics. Although the utility maximizing perspective is by predilection drawn to descriptions of bargaining and incremental problem solving, it is adaptable to times of turmoil. People's goals revolve around satisfaction of near-term needs. Under normal conditions, this exerts a pull away from radical ("maximalist") programs of change, since the costs of conflict would be prohibitively high, and there is a great deal of uncertainty that a better final result would emerge.[24] But Hamilton and Wright allow for rare occasions that "make revolution seem more attractive than reform." The authors point to popular support for the Bolsheviks and other radical parties in Russia in the fall of 1917 as the archetype—an assessment by nonideological citizens that even their immediate welfare was in danger under the old regime.[25] A new configuration of forces produces a new preference schedule—but one which is calculated in the same manner as before. What has changed are the inputs, and when they change, people who are still utility maximizers should be expected to arrive at new conclusions. When things are different, things are different. The matter of changed public expressions in such periods is relatively self-explanatory and non-problematical; all that has changed are the numbers in the equation (of self-interest).[26]

Scott and others who describe the quiescence of the powerless as a deliberate act of deception can also accommodate periods of high-intensity conflict. People do not calculate their interests differently in such a period, or change their views about the fairness of the distribution of rewards or even the underlying legitimacy of institutions; instead they now have the opportunity to say publicly what they had been saying or thinking quietly all along. There is also a public festivity which comes from the fact that people have previously had to suffer humiliation in silence: "It is only when this hidden transcript is openly declared that subordinates can fully recognize the full extent to which their claims, their dreams, their anger is shared by other subordinates with whom they have not been in direct touch."[27]

This is not a transformational process for participants, although it does disrupt the ostensible harmony of the "public transcript." Behavior and attitudes in democratic moments do tell us something about everyday life; they show us the conflict which has been strategically kept out of view previously.

Hegemony theory would not seem to be naturally suited for times of turmoil; it usually is preoccupied with descriptions of how slow people are to entertain oppositional thinking and how limited their imagined alternatives are when they do. But hegemony theory in all but its most conspiratorial forms calls attention to the influence of routine and adaptation on popular conceptions of social justice. Moore described the denaturalization of oppressive structures as a necessary precondition for the development of moral outrage. Aristide Zolberg called such times "moments of madness," when the limits of the "possible" expand rapidly.[28] Writing about the political vortex which accompanied events of such enormous scope as liberation from Nazi occupation, the Paris Commune, and the May–June 1968 rebellion in France, he found a political discourse which verged on poetry. What moved people were "sentiments of liberation" underdeveloped in normal times: brotherhood (his word), cooperation, a broadened sense of community, and a heightened sense of the urgency of political questions. The enormity of the questions confronting people and the suspension of daily routine produced an altered and broadened standard of political justice. Political imagination expanded; previously inadmissible ideas became part of the dialogue of ordinary people.[29] "You awake?" Thelma asks Louise in a motion picture that explored this theme on a personal level. "Me too. I feel a*wake*. Wide awake. I don't remember ever feeling this awake. Know what I mean? Everything looks different. You feel like that, too? Like you got something to look forward to?"[30]

Do ideas about dominant institutions expressed in highly conflictual situations merely reflect a new set of calculations of self-interest, do they represent the public airing of previously repressed (or self-suppressed) views, or do they represent a substantially changed political discourse as Zolberg suggests? If, as is likely, each of these is in some part true, what does each explain, and/or leave out? What, in short, do "moments of madness" reveal about political beliefs in periods of "sanity"?

MADNESS: A METHOD

Democratic moments are by definition rare and evanescent. They should approximate these conditions: daily routines are suspended for at least a short time; that suspension has been brought about by decisions made by identifiable human actors (to eliminate natural disasters); and a situation exists in which authority must be reconstituted.[31] These conditions apply most prominently to national convulsions—revolution, occupation, the collapse of a regime. But the drama of politics in nonnormal settings when dominant institutions of authority have become destabilized can be played out on a smaller scale. What follows is a brief description of one such event.

On April 1, 1985, the contract between the Colt Firearms Division in Hartford, Connecticut, and United Automobile Workers Local 376 expired. On January 24, 1986, the union members went out on strike. What ensued was a dramatic and bitter four-year conflict which included daily interchanges between strikers and strikebreakers, arrests of strikers, strikebreakers, and even public officials, repeated rallies, occasional violence, and a severe test of will for the eight hundred strikers. Ultimately, it included a settlement that was largely favorable to the union: when the parent company put the struck division up for sale, it was purchased by a group of local investors, which included the union in the process. That transaction included a contract agreement that permitted union members to return to their jobs and awarded them back pay in excess of $10 million. The first strikers returned to work on March 28, 1990.

A conflict of this magnitude is an important subject for study in its own right and will be detailed more fully in the next chapter. The union leaders had to negotiate a course around the reefs and shoals of Ronald Reagan's National Labor Relations Board appointees and the increasingly sophisticated management antiunion practices of the 1980s, including the use of "replacement workers," all in a northeastern city with a typically declining industrial base.[32] For four years, the members had to sustain themselves with strike pay, odd jobs, and hope. The company took what it thought was a well-calculated risk in forcing a strike and replacing the strikers; the union leaders and members followed what they knew was a perilous strategy in accepting the challenge. That the union was largely successful was story enough in a decade in which there seemed to be a direct relation between the importance of a labor conflict and the severity of its defeat.[33] The activities and contributions to history of ordinary citizens can easily be lost, particularly in a country where there is such a rigorous distinction drawn between the public and private spheres. One incentive to write about such a conflict is simply to expose it to the light of day and preserve it.

But my interest in this conflict did not stem principally from the chance to record it (as significant as that task is). A strike of this length and intensity seemed certain to provide a rare opportunity to view the despotism of custom in collision with the fraternité generated in passionate battle. Would the narratives that Colt strikers developed as they lived through an unexpected conflict lead to new conceptions of authority, power, and justice? Not every strike—not even very many strikes—would pose these issues. Strike activity is for the most part legal and tightly regulated, and differs little from other forms of interest-group activity.[34] But some easily observable features made it clear that this case was exceptional with a vengeance. The members worked for ten months without a contract, a period marked by nearly continuous confrontation with the company and one during which each side accused the other of major unfair labor practices. Tensions became unbearable, and the union leadership felt it had no choice but to initiate a strike. The company responded almost immediately by hiring strikebreakers, and there were weekly—for some of the active strikers, daily—confrontations between the two groups. The strikers faced prolonged hardship. They also remained highly committed to the union's goals and played an active role in supporting and promoting them, as will be described in Chapter 3. And—although this is somewhat tangential to the central purposes of the book—the strike was largely successful in a period in which very few were.[35]

The attractiveness of this situation for a study of the political atmosphere of democratic moments is that the striking Colt employees found themselves for a protracted period of time in a sharply altered relationship to the institution which was central to their past and future welfare. Their daily lives were disrupted dramatically. As readers will see, they had no trouble naming villains: local management, the president of the conglomerate, the Reagan administration, and a political system which seemed unresponsive. In the end, the task of reconstituting authority proved to be a very literal one, but that is getting ahead of the story. The point at present is simply that this strike provided an opportunity to look at the political thinking of people living through abnormal times.

Perhaps some readers have twinges of suspicion about the applicability of a study of American industrial conflict to the questions outlined so far. Elkins initiated the debate about compliance and resistance with his controversial comparison between the behavior of concentration camp inmates and that of slaves.[36] It was addressed in Erving Goffman's writings about "total institutions" such as slave ships and prisons and has been discussed most directly in Scott's previously mentioned work centering on Vietnamese and Malaysian peasants.[37] Prisoners, slaves, peasants, concentration camp inmates—is there any contribution a discussion of American hourly factory employees can make except under the most paranoid and outdated assumptions?

There are imposing structural differences (that is, differences in kind rather than the more obvious differences in degree) between the form and nature of subjection of the groups mentioned above and American factory workers. Industrial employees are not formally coerced into employment, have some degree of real mobility, and have citizenship rights in the larger society. But these liberties are tempered by other conditions. Blue-collar workers *during the workday* receive and discharge responsibilities in a hierarchical environment which has been called "workplace authoritarianism."[38] This is precisely what has led some democratic theorists to investigate the basis in principle and practicality for extending democracy to the workplace.[39] In addition to the authority relations which are characteristic of the workday, workers remain much nearer to the bottom than the top of American society in the distribution of rewards and view their position with at least some sense of "groupness," even if they are not inclined to draw grandiose or apocalyptic conclusions from it.[40] The question of whether workers internalize inegalitarian work norms has been studied, and the answers have tended to replicate the broader hegemony discussion—pragmatic acceptance based on maximizing favored values in trade-offs; feigned acceptance, real rejection; normative acceptance.[41] If a reader still might not be prepared to grant any resemblance between factory employment and the much more absolute forms of domination, he or she may be surprised in the pages ahead at how often the Colt strikers reach for metaphors from those more starkly oppressive situations to explain their five-year conflict.

The importance of learning about political attitudes in exceptional times is matched by the difficulties in doing so. A textbook setting would require a social scientist to be fortunate or farsighted enough to catch a historical wave when the surf was up and to be forearmed with a questionnaire and a tape recorder.[42] Even then, the participants are likely to be subject to a variety of stresses and might understandably place sating the curiosity of academics low on their agendas. The Colt strikers lived in an unfamiliar atmosphere of superheated confrontation. They moved hesitatingly toward some conclusions, then recoiled; they tried to beat into shape an experience none ever expected. My goal will be to try to follow this advice from Barrington Moore: "So far as possible we need to learn how they viewed their own lives, what they saw and felt as misfortune and good fortune, justice and injustice, and in what terms they explained these matters to themselves."[43]

# 2

## Irrepressible Conflict

*Should, however, the deferential relationship between husband and wife begin to break down . . . behind the morally charged, traditionally legitimate domination is savage force. . . . When there is a revolt from such relationships, as within marriage, the revolt is typically very bitter, simply because previous identification had been so extensive.*
—Colin Bell and Howard Newby, "Husbands and Wives: The Dynamics of the Deferential Dialectic"

*It's like going through a divorce. Let's get it over with. That's what happened here. We were like married for twenty years. Now it's over. I'd rather see those bastards move out. I'd rather work in a car wash.*
—Colt striker

This chapter will provide some historical information on the company and union and an outline of the central issues and events of the 1985–1990 conflict. It has several purposes. One is to provide context for the subsequent events— the financial and competitive position of the company and division, the nature of company-union relations, and the relation between union leaders and members. Another is to substantiate the claim in the last chapter that the conflict at Colt was an unusual, highly charged event for those who lived through it, exceptional even among lengthy labor disputes. With that established, I can turn to the effects this journey into uncharted political territory had on the beliefs of participants.

On the eve of the expiration of the 1985 contract, Colt Firearms employed about 830 blue-collar workers in two plants, at Hartford and West Hartford. The workforce was relatively old, averaging forty-nine years of age and seventeen years' seniority. About one-quarter of the employees were from minority groups and the same percentage was female. For about 10 percent of the workforce, English was a second language; the major foreign-language subgroups were Italian, Polish, and Hispanic. It also tended to be a skilled workforce, particularly in the commercial handgun plant in West Hartford, where there was little mass production. In addition to skill level, the fact that the division manufactured weapons played some role in employees' attitudes toward their work. That was due partly to the nature of the product, which demands a certain level of seriousness. "Guns are something you don't fool around with" was a widespread sentiment. Also, the fact that the weapons made in Hartford were for military use produced a special twist of patriotism—expressions of obligation to American soldiers. Phil Wheeler, union president at the beginning of the strike, said of the prestrike work force, "There is no doubt you had a committed, skilled workforce at Colt that was much different than most places, and I've dealt with hundreds of companies."[1]

Colt Industries, the parent conglomerate, was a *Fortune* magazine top 200 company, with total sales of about $1.6 billion and profits for 1985 of $132 million. The director of labor relations for the division was Richard Reibeling, who was promoted to that position in 1983 and doubled as chief negotiator. Reibeling also acted as spokesperson for the division during the strike. UAW Local 376 was an amalgamated local, representing about twenty plants and five thousand employees in Connecticut. Wheeler came out of the firearms plant. Three months into the strike, he was promoted to UAW assistant regional director, and Bob Madore became president, remaining in that position for most of the remainder of the strike.[2] Near its end, Wheeler became regional director, Madore was promoted to the job of assistant, and a new local president was named.

This is a snapshot of the combatants who were heading into a five-year conflict that dwarfed anything previous at these plants. There is little reason to believe that the ethnically diverse, relatively old, skilled, and highly patriotic Colt employees were already substantially different in their political views from others in the same general socioeconomic circumstances. Certainly Reibeling did not think so. His working assumption—one in which he had a tremendous personal stake—was that age and length of service would lead employees away from confrontation and toward fulfilling individual goals: "Forty-eight years average age [at the start of the strike], seventeen years experience at the company—people have a lot of themselves invested; they're at the stage of their lives where people don't necessarily want to disrupt their livelihood. In our view, the sentiment was not in favor of a strike."[3]

The usual practice in academic writing on workplaces is to change the names of places and individuals in order to preserve confidentiality. This strike was a public, highly visible event and many of the participants were featured by name in newspaper accounts and even on television. Because of that glare of prior publicity, some of the vows of secrecy social scientists take are unnecessary here. It would be pointless to hide the identity or location of the company. But in order to protect individuals, almost all those I interviewed will remain nameless, including many who were featured on television or in magazine articles and who would be more than willing to be known as actors in this drama. The only names of Colt personnel which will appear already have—Wheeler, Madore, and Reibeling. Disguising those three would be clumsy.

The information to be presented is drawn from these sources: open-ended interviews with strikers, separate interviews with key participants who were not strikers, a fixed-answer questionnaire, newspaper accounts, the transcript of a National Labor Relations Board hearing, and the less formal approach of looking and listening at union meetings and on the picket lines. Qualitative interviewing (semistructured tape-recorded sessions) and written, fixed-answer surveys are sometimes held to be in conflict with each other; my purpose in combining them is to provide as comprehensive a view as possible of strikers' attitudes.[4] My investigation of the strike began at approximately the two-year mark.[5]

The bulk of material presented will be taken from those two sources. Other background and informational interviews were important, notably those with Wheeler and Reibeling. Wheeler's interview took place during the strike, Reibeling's after its conclusion, when he was no longer employed by Colt. I spent some time walking picket lines and talking to strikers at a social gathering point near the Hartford plant provided by a hospital workers union local. There was also a strike headquarters—separate from both the union hall and the picketing break area—where a great deal of socializing took place. I went to about twenty weekly union meetings, usually just observing or talking to strikers I had gotten to know. There is a limit to the value of these informal means of collecting information, but they do serve as a kind of dead-reckoning check on conclusions drawn from other sources.

There were several outsiders intimately involved in aspects of the strike. Louise Simmons, later a city councilwoman but at that point a graduate student writing a thesis on responses to deindustrialization, was active in strike support activity.[6] The most important source of additional information was a professional social worker I will call "Barbara Johnson." She was employed by a labor agency which was a subdivision of the United Way and assumed two roles: Mother Teresa and Mother Jones. As an employee of the agency, she was responsible for identifying and alleviating hardship cases. In this capacity, she had extensive contact with strikers, got to know almost all of them personally, and accumulated detailed information. In her Mother Jones role, she was a principal organizer of the Community–Labor Alliance, which coordinated support for the strike and planned many of the demonstrations and rallies. Her background as a professional social worker enabled her to discuss aspects of the strike with unusual insight.[7] Her comments are to be taken as those not of a disinterested observer but of a highly informed and perceptive advocate.

In the next chapter, I will begin to make use of the interview material. I want to mention here a number of additional sources which were helpful as the following account moves toward the present. The strike left a significant paper trail, including well over a hundred stories in the *Hartford Courant* alone, several magazine articles, and even a half-hour show on Connecticut Public Television. The paper trail includes an indispensable eight thousand–page transcript of the hearing before the Administrative Law Judge of the National Labor Relations Board and later (*much* later, in the opinion of many strikers) the decision of that judge. Finally, I found particularly useful two interviews with Susan Howard, the author of the most important *Courant* stories in the first two years of the strike. In many cases, she was the only observer at events who did not have a personal stake in a particular characterization, which gives her descriptions special value. Her insight into the strike was strengthened by good fortune; she had done an undergraduate research paper on the history of union activities at Colt well before these events began.

## THE COLONEL'S COMPANY

Samuel Colt was one of those creative, cantankerous American entrepreneurs—equal parts inventor and blustering showman—who represent simultaneously the values of creative individualism, mass production, and shameless hucksterism. His stroke of genius was to obtain patents for exclusive production of revolving hand firearms. Even the official company historian disputed his claim to have been the sole inventor of the principle; in fact, Colt personally visited England and France to obtain the patents precisely because he wanted to forestall the possibility of competition.[8] He had a clear—if somewhat cold-blooded—vision of a market niche: "The good people of this world are very far from being satisfied with each other and my arms are the best peacemakers."[9] He also was not without a morbid sense of humor about his product. One of his methods of presenting gift weapons was to create a case which looked like a book, and he produced a "volume" in 1861 entitled "Colt on the Constitution, Higher Law, and Irrepressible Conflict." It contained a gun.

Using proceeds from Mexican War sales, Colt built the Hartford facility in 1855. His timing was flawless; he soon became enormously wealthy by selling to both sides in the Civil War.[10] When he built the plant, Colt made some effort to foster a paternal labor policy. A state historian, undoubtedly overstating the case, claimed that Colt was "best known for the humane way he treated his workers."[11] He built a library and educational program for the use of employees and financed Charter Oak Hall, which was intended to become a technical college.

The company's greatest fame and profit came from a weapon produced shortly after the founder's death in 1862, the Single Action Army—commonly known as the Colt .45 Peacemaker. It was the weapon of choice for most of the legends of the American West: Bat Masterson, Wyatt Earp, Wild Bill Hickok, Pat Garrett, Billy the Kid, and the James and Dalton gangs. More important, the U.S. Army made massive purchases of the Peacemaker and later the Colt-developed Gatling gun. Since then, the company's fortunes have been closely tied to military sales.[12] When Samuel Colt died, he passed on all the company's stock to his wife, who eventually sold it to a New York–based financing company. A Colt Holding Company was created in 1901. With wars popping up here and there, the firearms division remained strong. Its workforce increased tenfold during World War I and remained steady in the postwar years. Arms sales were not insulated from the Depression, however, and company fortunes took a sharp downturn until being revived by the arms purchases in the prelude to World War II.

## FAR FROM BEING SATISFIED

The rapid expansion of production and employment during the war itself also brought on the first appearance of organized labor among Colt employees. There had been two departmental strikes during World War I over rates, both unsuccessful, but until the Depression there had been no effort to organize a union.[13] In 1935, after employees had voted 813–153 to disband a company union, the International Association of Machinists (IAM) and the Polishers Union formed a joint council and demanded that the company engage in collective bargaining with them. That was shortly before the passage of the National Labor Relations Act, and recently established labor rights under section 7a of the National Industrial Recovery Act were in hot dispute even within the Roosevelt administration itself.[14] The company refused to bargain, and on March 13, a thousand employees walked out.[15] The strike which followed was a bitter one, marked by clashes between strikers and strikebreakers, the housing of strikebreakers in the plant, a threat by the Senate Munitions Committee to build a government plant to manufacture machine guns,[16] and, a week before the end, a bomb blast at the home of the company president, Sam Stone. The turning point came when the chairman of the National Recovery Administration ruled that the company was within its rights in refusing recognition of the union. Strikers gradually went back to work and the strike ended on June 3 with no concessions of any kind by the company.[17]

By 1940, a greatly increased workforce, a more enforceable law protecting employees' rights to form a union (the Wagner Act), and a union form based on production workers put organizing back on the agenda. Pulling these elements together was a thirty-two-year-old Irish immigrant, Sid Gunning.[18] The IAM began to organize at the Colt plant again in 1940, but Gunning was distrustful of craft unions, and many people remembered the failed strike of 1935, in which the IAM had played a central role.[19] Gunning contacted the United Electrical Workers (UE), which was organizing widely in Connecticut. His account shows that the employees were more than willing to listen:

> Now in order to get this thing really rolling I had [told] the International representatives of the UE that I was going to call a mass meeting outside the plant to see what kind of support we had. Well, I think all of us were surprised. . . . At that time we were working twelve hours a day, two shifts, and we called a meeting at twelve noon, and myself and two other members of the committee came out at lunch hour. And to our surprise, I have never seen a crowd as large in my life. There were probably six thousand people on the railroad tracks.
>
> I asked them that when they returned to work after the lunch hour that they would punch their card. I didn't want to put anyone on the spot to get fired, but if they had the courage of their convictions to really have a union, nobody was going to work until I was assured by management that we were going to have a meeting with that company that very day. I was gratified to see that in the entire plant of six thousand people, nobody went back to work.[20]

This broad show of support led to a successful two-and-a-half-day strike, which resulted in a negotiated contract. In an unusual twist, the National

Labor Relations Board then informed both the company and union that the company could not recognize the union without an election.[21] The UE defeated the Independent Armscraft organization by a seven-to-one margin, and on August 7, 1941, Colt employees became members of UE Local 270.

There was one more important turn of union events in that earlier period which was to play a role in the 1985–1990 conflict. The reader already knows that it was UAW Local 376, not UE Local 270, that went on strike in 1986. How did that come about?

Gunning went into the army in 1943. When he returned in 1945, he assumed the presidency of the local and almost immediately had to deal with the union raiding and purges which dominated the agenda of American labor in the late 1940s. Communists and other leftists had been an important part of the industrial union movement, particularly in the UE. The beginning of the Cold War brought to a head the sharp conflict over their role within the union movement. In some unions that conflict resulted in a purge of Communists and those who supported their positions, but for the UE it meant wholesale raids by other unions. The government provided a very useful tool to the anticommunist raiders by requiring in the Taft-Hartley Act that union leaders sign loyalty oaths. Because the UE leadership, both Communist and non-Communist, refused to sign, the union was not permitted to appear on the ballot in NLRB-sponsored elections. Even as organized labor condemned the Taft-Hartley Act as a "slave-labor" bill, some union leaders made use of the loyalty oath provision to attack the UE as an illegitimate union.

The Hartford area was a major battleground for the UE attackers and defenders.[22] The UE was the largest union in the Hartford area in 1945; by 1951 it would be virtually nonexistent. In early 1948, many of the largest UE locals in Hartford were raided by the UAW and in nearby Bristol by the IAM. The issues which dominated these raids were foreign policy, religion, and "Americanism," rather than labor relations policy, and in most cases, the votes to move out of the UE were very close.[23]

While it was during this period that employees at Colt switched affiliation to the UAW, the process differed in some important ways from the pattern just described. It was the company, not the union members or outside union raiders, that fired the first shot, announcing that they would refuse to sign a new contract with the UE when the existing one expired on July 4, 1948. They gave this explanation in a letter to employees: "Recently we have been alerted to be prepared again to manufacture ordnance material. If our employees are represented by a union the record of whose international leaders and some of its local leaders, past and present, is apparently one of obstructing the national policies and welfare of the United States, we are faced squarely with the problem of whether we will be able to produce these materials as required."[24]

Gunning was not a Communist, nor much of a leftist, but he disliked the internal conflict he saw during the raids and respected the UE for its stand on economic issues.[25] Colt's refusal to bargain created a dilemma for the local and its president: "Here we were facing a situation of the company saying we will not recognize your union, which meant to us that we had to go through a struggle with this company to win recognition. It meant we had to go through a new election. . . . I was faced with a situation as president of the union to whether I was going to take on the company and challenge them for recognition, which meant—and we were confident it meant—that we were going to have to strike that plant."[26]

Gunning and the other local leaders were not interested in a high-profile, principled defense of the UE, even though they thought the attacks on it were more antiunion than anticommunist. Their goal was to preserve a unified local. During May and June, the local leadership gradually moved the membership toward affiliation with the UAW. Because the UE national leadership would not sign the loyalty oaths, the UE could not be a choice when the membership voted on its union preference. In some raided plants, UE organizers campaigned strongly, if strangely, for a "no union" vote. At Colt, no one was so strongly *for* the UE or *against* Gunning to work for that alternative. The vote was 996 for the UAW, 35 for "no union," and two blank. There was no split in leadership, little division among the membership, and no anticommunist rhetoric.[27] As if to underscore that this action was based on local needs and not the national anti-UE campaign, the membership also voted at the same meeting to send a $100 contribution to a nearby striking UE local.[28] A historian studying these events summarized the union-jumping this way: "Gunning joined the UE for bread and butter reasons. He left when those gains were threatened."[29]

These two moments of union history at Colt portray a talented leadership and a unified, active membership. While it is tempting to make broad generalizations about a "legacy" or lasting union tradition as a result, it is also risky. A historian of the 1936 Flint sit-down pointed out that old habits return quickly: "Contrary to the popular mystique, sit-down euphoria and rank-and-file allegiance to the UAW often dissipated concomitantly."[30] I interviewed one employee who had been at Colt during the founding of the UE and another who had been there through the 1948 events. Neither employee mentioned either episode, and when I brought up some of this history, both had only the haziest of recollections. Even Wheeler—much too young to have taken part, but later a colleague of some of the principals—could only say, "I've heard stories all over the lot" about the move from the UE to the UAW. In the hundreds of hours I spent with employees and union officials, there were no more than two comments about the 1940s, and both were about the personality of Gunning.

BORDER SKIRMISHES

Colt went into a period of decline between the end of World War II and the mid-1960s. It had managed the nearly impossible feat of losing money during the war, despite being the sole supplier of machine guns and employing fifteen thousand people to keep up with orders.[31] Throughout the 1950s, the armory was in constant danger of either going under or being moved. That second possibility had and continues to have, in addition to its practical consequences, powerful symbolic significance in Hartford. The armory is topped with a highly visible blue onion-shaped dome with a rearing golden colt (currently lodged in a museum), which any reader who has traveled on Interstate 91 will have noticed. That dome has virtually become a trademark of the city of Hartford, and a threat to move the company has always produced a quick response from many quarters. During the 1950s, ownership of the parent company passed through several hands until a reorganization brought the immediate prestrike ownership into control. In 1964 the conglomerate changed its name to Colt Industries, drawing on the name of its most widely recognized subdivision.

The middle 1960s also brought the escalation of the war in Vietnam and with it a new set of dynamics in the division's market position and labor-management relations. In 1960, Colt acquired the patent for what became the M-16 fully automatic rifle. In 1963 the army placed its first order, and the rifle quickly became standard issue. Colt remained the sole supplier until it lost the contract halfway through the strike. As the fighting in Vietnam grew heavier, business boomed, reaching a high-water mark in 1969 of 2,300 employees and a $22 million profit.[32]

Many of the new employees were young, and a group of "young turks" emerged within the union who were to become the core of leadership and activists in all the subsequent events. The most important of these young activists was Wheeler, who began working at Colt in 1964 and almost immediately won the position of shop chairman. There was a five-week strike in 1967, during which the government threatened use of the Taft-Hartley Act to force the strikers back. But Colt was so profitable at that point that it was less concerned with holding the line on employee benefits than with getting people back to work. The union won large wage and cost-of-living increases, fully financed insurance coverage, a pension increase, and wage bonuses for second- and third-shift workers.

In October 1969 a wildcat strike began when 250 employees walked out of a department to protest both the use of supervisory personnel to test weapons and safety problems that employees claimed were created by speedup to turn out the M-16s. Wheeler, who by that time had been elected president of the local (at the age of twenty-four), called a meeting of the membership, which voted to turn the wildcat into an official plantwide strike. The union did not have a no-strike clause in its contract, and both local and international leadership felt that the plant could be struck legally. When a judge ruled that it could not, the international urged the local to go back. According to Wheeler, "The strike lasted about two weeks. Walter Reuther came in and met with some of us and tried to get us to put them back to work and we wouldn't do it. He sent everyone a telegram, I would assume to protect the international, to go back to work, and nobody went back to work."[33]

But with the ruling that the strike was illegal, the local was in a weak position to continue. "Finally about two weeks after [Reuther's visit]," Wheeler recalled, "we went to Detroit, we met and they convinced us to put everybody back to work. We did that knowing—the company made it clear—that they were going to get us, and they did. They fired everybody."[34]

Twenty-four people were fired, including Wheeler and several others who would play an important role in the 1985 events. With the 1970 contract negotiations coming up, Wheeler called for the early election of a negotiating committee. Then he and the other fired activists ran as a slate "on the basis that we were going to strike the plant until everybody got back to work."[35] That slate won the election by a margin of 10–1. The message was sent and received; everyone was rehired and the contract was settled without a strike.

There was one more strike prior to 1986, one that involved an issue with a past and a future—the possible relocation of the plant. Before the 1973 contract negotiations, union officials learned that Colt had purchased land in New Mexico and was investigating the feasibility of moving firearms production there. A five-month strike that year involved such issues as wages and a limitation on mandatory overtime, but also secured a plan for funded severance pay as a disincentive for the company to move and a public announcement that the company intended to stay in Hartford. Because the 1973 strike had been both lengthy and successful, some employees went into the 1986 strike expecting it to be similar. A striker who was not an activist said that she responded to union leaders' warnings that any strike would be long and difficult by invoking the 1973 framework: "I thought that meant something like 1973. Five months, maybe a little longer. But not this. I didn't think about three years [the length of the strike at the time of the interview]. It still doesn't seem possible."

THE FINAL CONFLICT

Most of this book concerns the 1985–1990 period and the ways in which this country's political and economic institutions and dominant values appeared to people engaged in a protracted battle with their former employer. To do that requires an in-depth examination of how these employees experienced that period and what they concluded from it. But individual experiences are necessarily richly varied, and it should be helpful for the reader—and was absolutely essential for me—to get an overview of the events of that period constructed from other sources. That is not an easy task. There is no simple way to provide an "objective" account of events and facts which are almost all hotly disputed. The *Rashoman* effect is inevitable—interested parties recount even the most basic facts from their own perspective and to their own benefit. At times I will simply have to note competing claims rather than try to resolve them. This book ultimately is about the development of the strikers' attitudes and is not primarily a legal or ethical judgment on the issues involved.

After 1973 three contracts were settled without a strike. In 1982 a strike was avoided only after Wheeler and the other union leadership agreed to extend negotiations for two days beyond the contract expiration. The settlement was a very good one for the employees by any standard, especially that of a recession year. The wage increases averaged more than 9 percent a year for its three-year term.[36] That settlement created the framework for the 1985 conflict. Shortly after the agreement was signed, the company laid off about half the workforce in quick stages as the recession hit the domestic gun market. Colt was doubly affected; the absolute size of the market shrank, and Colt's relative share in the diminished market shrank as well.[37] While the military orders were not directly affected by the recession, Washington was starting to exert pressures to minimize costs. This was the period of public muckraking about expensive toilet seats and screwdrivers. The military informed Colt that it would be subject to a "should-cost" audit and also began dropping hints that it wanted to move away from single sourcing for the M-16.[38] In this period, Colt again publicly raised the possibility of leaving Hartford, pointing to its rising costs and declining business. The city and state responded on cue. Governor William O'Neill made a personal trip to Colt Industries headquarters in New York and together with city officials offered a grant of $1.8 million to renovate the Hartford plant.[39] Colt Industries was also acting in a manner typical of some other conglomerates in that period, treating the profitable firearms division as a "cash cow," draining its resources and reinvesting very little in new technology, equipment, or product development.[40]

The division's market position was only one factor which pointed toward a confrontation in 1985. Colt Firearms still was profitable and remained so every year, including all the strike years but the first. Another significant contributing factor was the new atmosphere in labor-management relations in the country which had been developing in the 1980s. The symbolic turning point was Ronald Reagan's firing of the striking air traffic controllers. Over half of the strikers I interviewed spontaneously mentioned that as the beginning of their own conflict. The high visibility strikes at Phelps Dodge in Arizona, Hormel in Minnesota, Clinton Corn in Iowa, and International Paper in Maine paralleled the Colt case even more closely. In each of these, strikers were almost immediately replaced by strikebreakers.[41] In an economic strike—one over terms and conditions of employment—strikebreakers can legally become permanent employees. If, on the other hand, a strike is provoked or prolonged by unfair labor practices on the company's part, new employees cannot be made permanent and strikers may be awarded back pay. One decisive factor, then, becomes the criteria by which the NLRB on its various levels judges a company to have committed the unfair labor practice of "surface bargaining"—bargaining in bad faith. Reagan employed the fox-in-charge-of-the-chicken-coop strategy in appointing NLRB members (much as he did with the Occupational Safety and Health Administration and the Office of Economic Opportunity). After Reagan appointees formed a majority, there were fewer findings of unfair labor practices.[42] With little chance of being found to have committed an unfair labor practice, management increasingly stonewalled in negotiations and forced strikes for the purpose of replacing the strikers. Strikes had become a tool of management.[43] In all of the strikes mentioned above, the net result was devastating defeat for the union.

At Colt the 1982–1985 period was one of escalating hostility between the union and the new labor relations team headed by Reibeling. The volume of grievance activity was about seven hundred a year, which Reibeling called "a real and concrete manifestation of unhappiness on the part of the union." The union took a major departmental reorganization plan to arbitration and lost. Here are descriptions of the state of labor-management relations by the two principals:

> WHEELER: The labor relations in the plant had been halfway decent—*halfway* because there had always been a lot of grievances but we could always work them out. There wasn't a hostile relationship, up until two, three years before—right after the last contract.
>
> REIBELING: There's no question in my mind that the relationship between the company and the union was adversarial. It was not an easy relationship. . . . It was not in any way a cooperative environment.[44]

Both union and management were and are convinced that their opposite number had planned to force a strike at contract time. The union leadership saw this management scenario: the division and the parent company, feeling that they had taken a beating in 1982 and emboldened by the success of anti-labor strategies elsewhere, were preparing to provoke the union into striking in order to hire a new workforce and eventually decertify the union. As Wheeler put it, "I think they were angry over the fact that we got what we got [in 1982]. I think that the fact that we were able to negotiate an agreement that they felt they could live with at the time, and then with the recession they had problems, they changed their position because they then changed total management. . . . You could see the change in attitude. It got nastier and nastier. You could see what was happening."[45] Reibeling maintains that the union was never interested in any other outcome than a strike, one that did not involve concrete negotiable issues but rather questions of power: "Unless there was a total agreement on the part of the company relative to the union's demands, there was going to be a strike, and what I'm saying is that I believe the union had determined this before any of the negotiating issues were discussed."[46] What is undeniable is the company's determination to drive a very hard bargain. Reibeling said that his contract proposals "all centered around one basic theme, and that was to find ways to control and lower our costs. That was the theme that drove the 1985 negotiations. We told that to the union right at the first day."[47]

That first day was February 18, 1985. The union negotiators were told that the future viability of the Hartford plant depended on union acceptance of substantial givebacks. The two major items the company said were essential were zero wage increase in the first year of the new contract and employee co-payment on medical insurance. Company negotiators also made it clear that these offers were not to be seen as simple strategic lowballing but as the precondition of any agreement.[48] The union wage proposal at that point was 10 percent increase a year, a high-end offer which would change considerably during the nearly fifty negotiating sessions before the strike.

The union leadership, regarding these company proposals as a call for concessions, sent a memo asking the company to open its books to establish hardship, a procedure Local 376 followed when other companies requested givebacks.[49] The company reply, signed by Reibeling, contained the most quoted words of the conflict:

> Dear Phil [Wheeler]:
> I am in receipt of your letter . . . and can only conclude that the pressure of your heavy workload has caused you to confuse us with some other company you are negotiating with. We have no idea why you made the requests contained in the letter. I repeatedly told you at negotiations that *we were not claiming that we were losing money, nor were we basing our proposals on the company's financial position*.[50]

The two parties did not return to these issues during the next fifteen negotiating sessions, working instead on contract language and codification of numerous side agreements—extracontractual practices which had been accumulating for years and which the company now wanted in writing. On March 28 company negotiators, in the midst of these noneconomic discussions, unexpectedly brought a wage proposal to the morning session. When the union negotiators said that they were not yet ready to discuss economic offers, the company withdrew from the session and came back in the afternoon with their "final offer." That consisted of the zero raise for the first year, 4 percent for each of the next two, and employee contributions for medical insurance ranging up to $15 a month. The proposal was titled "FINAL" and ended with a threat to leave Hartford if it were not accepted.[51] The finality of the offer was important to both sides. In over forty negotiating sessions which followed, the company never changed its basic position on those two red flag issues. Reibeling pointed out in public and in his interview that this form of negotiating was a result of the "very aggressive labor policy" of the parent Colt Industries and their policy was that "once a final offer is made, they will not agree to increasing the value of that offer."[52]

With the two sides unable to reach agreement, the union leadership made its crucial decision of the whole five-year conflict. At a meeting of between five and six hundred union members, Wheeler announced that the union would not strike but would continue to work without a contract. Both Wheeler and *Courant* reporter Howard recount that this decision was booed loudly.[53] Wheeler introduced a speaker who had been a union leader in similar circumstances in another company. This speaker addressed company response and employee rights in that setting and mentioned that some union members had been fired for interfering with production.[54] Wheeler then summarized the union's position, which won over some of those who had booed: "If they want us on the street, we'll be in the plant. And if they want a fight, we'll give them one right in their own damned plant."[55]

The union decision caught the company off guard and threw both company and employees into uncharted waters that proved to be more turbulent than anyone expected.[56] The ten-month period in which employees worked without a contract was crucial for the four-year strike which followed; unfortunately, it was also the most contested and least accessible to an outside observer of any of the events of those five years. The heart of the legal charges and countercharges grew out of this period, which some employees called the "in-plant strike," and I will make a special effort to be precise in differentiating facts from claims. The reader will also have to be even more tolerant of unresolved contrasting accounts.

With the increased difficulties of utilizing a strike or threat of a strike as a weapon in negotiation, some unions began to consider alternatives, including negotiating while working past the expiration of contracts. American labor law does not permit "partial strikes"—slowdowns or other means of pressuring a company by reducing production while still on the job.[57] The union denied that a partial strike was taking place in those ten months and said that they were simply giving negotiations a longer try. The union leadership did organize several forms of employee protest activity that were both legal and protected, including lunchtime rallies outside the plant, singing union songs, wearing T-shirts with union slogans on them, and bringing whistles into the plant for use when someone was disciplined.[58] For their part, they described the company as becoming increasingly arbitrary, dictatorial, and vindictive. Twelve people were fired in those months in circumstances which seemed to suggest that they were singled out as activists.[59] The company argued that the union leadership was engaged in the strategy of "running the plant backward": an intentional, organized slowdown of production.[60] Many employees refused to work overtime during that period, leading to more than four hundred three-day suspensions—an extremely serious matter because any further infraction meant dismissal. A union-led coordinated refusal of overtime is unprotected activity. The company claimed that this refusal was orchestrated by union leadership; the union claimed that the company had changed its policy on overtime and was simply being punitive.[61] Other accusations cited alleged illegality. Company witnesses at the NLRB hearing talked about spills, lost gauges, and floods and fires on the shop floor—accidents that seemed to occur with greater frequency in these ten months—and the company brought the FBI in to investigate sabotage. No one was either charged or fired as a result of this activity.

Clearly, the two descriptions cannot be reconciled on many points. But the ruling of the Administrative Law Judge provided a useful framework for understanding the validity of parts of both.

> I find that whatever strategy the Union used in this case, it did not engage in "running the plant backward."
>
> I specifically find that the Union's leadership did not direct, suggest or encourage employees to engage in sabotage or slowdowns, or refuse to work overtime without a valid reason.
>
> However, it does not follow from the fact that the union leadership did not instigate employee misconduct, that such misconduct did not occur.[62]

The legal import of the judge's ruling is that he denied that union leadership encouraged unprotected activity; just as significantly, he observed that it went on anyway. The union may not have adopted the strategy of running the plant backward, but some employees had.[63]

No one denies that the ten-month period was a very difficult, even traumatic, time. It certainly was a time in which "normal" workplace relations were strained to the limit and any hint of shared interest dissolved. Employees themselves will speak to that directly in the next chapter. Here is a description from the testimony of a high-ranking company official at the NLRB hearing which captures both the turmoil and the spirit of defiance among employees:

> What was happening is that the word got around quickly that somebody was being disciplined, and folks left their machines and gathered on either side of the aisle, and whistled and cheered, and shouted, ranted and raved. So we moved the discipline up front to a conference room so that when they were suspended we could walk them out the door and not have that demonstration—that slowdown of the plant. . . . We basically had gorilla warfare out there [sic].[64]

Negotiations continued throughout the in-plant strike, but given the finality of the company's offer, there was little to negotiate. Starting in the summer, the company took in between 200 and 250 new hires, a move which to union members looked like preparations for a strike. Management also declared that impasse had been reached in negotiations, which, if sustained, would have permitted Colt to implement its proposals without union assent. The union filed dozens of information requests, including one for a company newsletter about a golf league. The company saw these as frivolous and did not respond to many of them; the union claimed that this failure to respond prevented a finding of impasse.[65] Gradually, the company began to act unilaterally to limit union time for stewards, suspend payments to the credit union, and withhold information pertaining to grievances.[66] On October 11, the company implemented one of the two controversial contract items, copayment on insurance. By late 1985 the union leadership was being deluged with demands from employees to go on strike, as much because conditions inside the plant had become intolerable as because a strike seemed like a good strategic move. Just before Christmas a bitter dispute broke out when some employees objected to company-sponsored Christmas celebrations inside the plant. More than one hundred employees left the plant at noon, put up a Christmas tree outside, and hung their disciplinary notices from it. Howard said that the Christmas controversy "put them right over the edge."[67] Wheeler said about the December–January period, "We felt that at that time if we hadn't taken them out, they might have gone out on their own and we would have lost the leadership ability to carry out a good strike."[68]

Howard was also present at the Hartford plant at the onset of the strike on the morning of January 24 and recounted her impressions of the mood of the employees as they left work: "People just came out of the plant, just bursting. There was that pent-up energy, like they couldn't wait to get out of the building. They were strutting their stuff; they weren't taking it, they were saying no."[69]

The company almost immediately moved to hire strikebreakers. Since management denied that it had committed any unfair labor practices, it defined the strike as being over unsettled contract issues—an economic strike. It would thus be entitled to replace the strikers permanently. On the day of the strike, employees received a notice informing them that they had until January 29 to return to work; on that day, the company would begin to create a new workforce. If the union leadership's key decision was to keep its members in the plant after the contract expired, management's key decision was to hire new permanent employees, a decision which, as Reibeling said, "immediately, without question, escalated the conflict to a full-scale war."[70] The primary issue confronting the strikers was no longer either the terms of the contract or unfair labor practices but the future of their jobs. The company had told them that unless they crossed the picket line, they were no longer employed by Colt.[71]

In addition to changing the broad goals of the strike and the nature of the legal issues surrounding those goals, the decision to hire strikebreakers made the daily experience of strikers a confrontational one. This strike was not an uneventful waiting game. Strikers were reminded that they had been replaced every day by hostile exchanges on the picket line. To reemphasize the point, some strikebreakers (in this case, former union members) hung a banner out a window facing the picket line listing the number of paydays strikers had missed. The picket lines were spirited, loud, and emphatically, though creatively, profane. (One striker told me he learned how to curse in four languages, and a deaf striker hurled abuse in sign language.) The flavor of the hostility comes across well in this understated exchange in the NLRB hearing between an employee near retirement age who spent nearly every day on the picket line and the company lawyer.

Q: Mr. [name], you spent a great deal of time on the picket line, didn't you?
A: Yes, I did, counselor.
Q: Was [sic] there harsh words exchanged on the picket lines from time to time?
A: From time to time.
Q: Sharp talk was used on the picket line?
A: Sharp talk.
Q: Sometimes people yelled the kinds of things you might not yell at a dinner table?
A: Both ways.

Q: Both ways, yes.

A: Their side and our side.[72]

While the relation between strikers and strikebreakers was not at the heart of the conflict, it often functioned as the flashpoint for tensions. For a strike of this length and passion, there was not a great deal of violence, but there was some. The company alleges that there were five hundred criminal acts, including acts at the work site and at the homes of those working (mostly damage to cars), as well as threats. The head of Colt security testified that he cleaned up ten to fifteen pounds of nails from plant parking lots.[73] Some strikers also had damage to their homes and cars, and two were injured by BB shots. Over a hundred strikers were arrested, although only three were convicted. Wheeler was arrested and charged with assaulting a police officer and inciting a riot, but was acquitted in the only jury trial of the strike. The deputy police chief Donald Higgins, the first coordinator of police work at the Hartford plant, called the strike relatively peaceful: "Considering the feelings in this—considering the fact that they might lose their jobs—it's pretty good."[74]

Even apart from the daily, grinding confrontation between strikers and strikebreakers and the occasional violence, the scope of strike activity went well beyond simple picketing. The purpose of "maintaining operations" (management terminology for hiring strikebreakers) is to weaken or eliminate the economic pressure that a strike can exert on a company. While the Colt division took a large loss in the first year of the strike, the resumption of production meant that the strike could not be won simply by the economic pressure of the picket line. This forced the union to be aggressive about advancing its position in other ways, and an innovative union leadership turned a potential disadvantage into a strength. Picket lines were always larger than was necessary simply to advertise the fact that there was a strike, even in its third and fourth year. One day a week was targeted for a large protest picket, ranging from a hundred to three hundred strikers. The union also worked with a group of supporters in a coalition called the Community-Labor Alliance to plan protests away from the work site.[75] There were demonstrations at the home of a local member of the Colt board of directors, the home of the division president, the New York offices of the company president and the police station on several occasions. Each of these—an illustrative, not exhaustive list—drew over two hundred union members. In addition, on the first anniversary of the expiration of the contract, on the scheduled opening of NLRB proceedings, and on each anniversary of the strike, large demonstrations drew as many as three thousand strikers and supporters. Here is how a policeman at the Hartford plant described the level of employee activity in NLRB testimony:

COMPANY LAWYER [*eliciting testimony from a friendly witness on the April 1, 1986, rally at which there were many arrests, including Wheeler's*]: Do you recall being on duty at the Colt facilities . . . when there was a large rally?
A: There were numerous large rallies. I was at the Colt facilities for a year or longer.
Q: Do you remember any particular large rally that stands out in your mind?
A: I said there were numerous large rallies.[76]

These rallies and shows of union solidarity were important in maintaining the strike and making it into a public issue, but even picket lines and demonstrations would not have led to a successful conclusion if the union had not also had a legal strategy. It is important to understand that the strikers never thought of themselves as fighting a heroic losing battle. They always had a plausible chance of winning, although in the darkest hours of the third year of the strike, it may have seemed like a long shot. The union fought a number of small but significant legal battles, winning the right to picket at the division president's house, returning arrested picketers to the picket lines, and—not so small—having the strike declared a lockout by the state, enabling strikers to collect twenty-six weeks of unemployment benefits.[77]

The Regional Director of the NLRB rejected the union's claim that the company had engaged in surface bargaining.[78] But he later issued two sets of complaints against the company, charging management with making unilateral changes in the contract before reaching impasse, disciplining employees for union activity, interrogating and polling employees about their willingness to strike, and denying the union necessary information. There were variations on each, adding up to twenty-seven violations of NLRB regulations. Two complaints were also issued against the union—against Wheeler for threatening a company negotiator and against individuals for strike misconduct. Strikers knew that if the union were ultimately successful in proving the charges against the company, the strike might be legally defined as an unfair labor practice strike, forcing the company to take them back. They also knew, because Reibeling stated it publicly and often, that the appeal process would likely take several years.

The ruling was announced on September 11, 1989. The judge upheld the NLRB complaints against the company on most counts. At the heart of his ruling was this judgment: "I find the strike was caused by the company's unfair labor practices and was an unfair labor practice strike."[79] The complaint against Wheeler was dismissed. About half the charges of strike misconduct were sustained, and the union was told to post a cease-and-desist notice. But the ruling denied the company the right to fire strikers who had engaged in misconduct.[80] The dating and amount of back pay were left unspecified, although the ruling seemed to suggest a much smaller figure than the union had discussed publicly.

The ruling was the second of two dramatic turns which eventually merged to lead to an end to the strike. The first, six months earlier, was the announcement by the parent Colt Industries that the Colt Firearms division would be sold. The management of Colt Industries had purchased the stock of the company in 1988 in a leveraged buyout financed by Morgan Stanley, changing its name to Colt Holding Company and going private. In doing so, it incurred a debt of over a billion dollars, which necessitated selling off some divisions. The firearms division was a major headache, but it was still profitable. The M-16 contract had been lost at least indirectly as a result of the strike and tighter domestic gun laws loomed on the political horizon.[81] The strike was past the three-year mark when the For Sale sign went up. Madore described the union meeting following that announcement as the most animated and upbeat of any in several years. The situation had been stagnant, and employees sensed that this development might lead to some movement.

The union immediately retained the Cambridge-based Industrial Cooperative Association and the Naugatuck Valley Project, both of which specialize in worker buyouts.[82] They put together a preliminary feasibility study and advised the union to enter a bid. Typically, worker buyouts take place when companies are failing. This one was not, and there were competitors. Eventually the union decided it could not marshal enough resources for its own bid and accepted an invitation to join forces with a bid put together by a local businessman representing a coalition of the union and some old management personnel, along with the Connecticut State Treasurer and Commissioner of Economic Development. This coalition became the most significant bidder even before the union's legal victory. The decision strengthened its competitive hand—with the certainty that any buyer would have to resolve the strike issues and reemploy the strikers, the coalition had a tremendous advantage by having the union already on board.[83]

But before a sale could be completed, there had to be a contract and agreement on a settlement of the strike. After a period of negotiation among the various interests that one investor likened to "trying to nail Jell-o to a wall," the strikers signed a new contract and the sale was finalized. The proposed agreement between the union and the coalition included the rehiring of all strikers, including those fired during the in-plant strike; seniority including the strike years; ten million dollars in back pay (substantially more than the union was privately estimating would be awarded by the judge's decision); three and a half million more to be distributed among employees after the first year the plant turned a profit; no copayment on insurance; distribution of 11.5 percent of the stock of the new company to union members, and three of the eleven seats on the board of directors reserved for hourly workers. At a meeting of over six hundred people chaired by Wheeler (by now UAW regional director), the provisional contract was approved with only two dissenting votes. With this agreement in hand, the investment team pulled together funding from various sources, including twenty-five million dollars from state pension funds, and after a lengthy period of addressing the concerns of all the constituencies involved, created the new Colt Manufacturing Company.[84] Of the old top management team, only Reibeling and the division president left, although some of the union's other main antagonists had left previously for unrelated reasons. The front-page headline and picture in the *Hartford Courant* the day the former strikers entered the plant caught the festive atmosphere: "Joyous Colt Strikers Return to Work." In a gesture which captured the mood, two strike activists celebrated by getting married at the huge victory rally.

Against long odds, and certainly against the temper of the times, the strike concluded with relative success. The purpose here has been to depict in broad brushstrokes the landscape of the world the strikers unexpectedly inhabited for five years. Of course, the only way to understand the motivations of the strikers and the conclusions they drew from this experience is to move from this broad overview to the individual rank-and-file strikers.

# 3

## A Rather Substantial Commitment

*The first burst of enthusiasm is usually not sufficient to enable the strikers to endure losses and sufferings which frequently follow. Therefore, efficient collective conduct requires that group success be placed above immediate personal advantage.*
—E. T. Hiller, *Strike*

[COLT ATTORNEY]: *You were pretty concerned when they told you, well, I'm not going to work any more overtime, correct?*
[COLT SUPERVISOR]: *Well, I was concerned from a production standpoint, yes.*
Q: *You also were surprised.*
A: *Not necessarily.*
Q: *Why not?*
A: *Because of some of the conversations they told me about. Some of the reasons they gave me for not working overtime.*
Q: *And what kind of reasons did they give you?*
A: *Well, sometimes they—a word. . . .*
Q: *What word?*

A: *I'd ask them to work overtime and they'd just look and say "solidarity."*

Q: *And what would you say?*

A: *What could I say?*

—Testimony from NLRB hearing on Colt

It is now time to bring the first two chapters together to learn what we can from the Colt strike about the effects of high-intensity conflict on people's attitudes and values. How did the Colt strikers evaluate American institutions after, and in light of, their experience? Did they come to different conclusions from those reached by most Americans about the fairness of industrial authority or about American society more generally? Was the conflict an eye-opening learning experience or did it resemble normal-time interest-group activity? Did it create any new sense of grievance or injustice, or did it seem more simply to reveal openly long-standing grievances?

It would clearly be unwise to try to draw conclusions about these or other questions directly from the events described in the previous chapter. There is a temptation for those writing about strikes or other forms of collective activity to generalize broadly about the state of mind of individuals involved either by reasoning backward from event to motive or by assuming that the way leaders frame issues is the way participants understand them.[1] In a group of even moderate size—and certainly in a group as diverse as the Colt strikers—there will inevitably be different motives and interpretations of events. No sentence which begins "the strikers thought . . . " will tell us much without verification, and the public declarations of leaders only represent one among many interpretations. A crowd assembles; a leader (even an elected leader) speaks about their grievances; the crowd cheers and acts. But to move from that sequence to conclusions about the views of those in the crowd is to fall prey to an optical illusion. Among the most consistent findings of contemporary social science is that even popular leaders are likely to understand issues differently from those they lead.[2] All we know so far is that these workers took part in a five-year conflict; we cannot infer attitudes directly from that.[3]

## STRIKERS AS LEMMINGS?

I will argue in the rest of this chapter and book that the conflict led the strikers to develop norms in which immediate individual self-interest played a lesser role than cooperation and solidarity, and in which dignity and self-respect became ends and not means to other ends. But before I can reach that point, I have to address a question Reibeling raised publicly during the strike and again in his interview. He claimed repeatedly that most strikers were not actually in support of union leadership or the strike goals, and that the rank and file barely understood the issues and did not want the strike to start or continue. His explanation for the fact that a large majority stayed out for four years was that the union waged a "campaign of violence," which had a chilling effect on the membership, discouraging wavering strikers from crossing the picket lines. Here are the specifics of his case:

> Q: The company was locked in a protracted conflict with [employees] over nearly a five-year period. . . . I assume you must have had some kind of working assumption throughout all this as to what the individual employees were thinking, doing, and feeling about this conflict that they were involved in. Could you outline what that sense was?
>
> A: I would come back to draw a distinction between the union leadership and the rank and file, because I think the union leadership had a very specific agenda and that was not necessarily the same as what the rank and file's agenda was. In late 1985 [during the period after the contract expired] we started hearing about the possibility of a strike. My view, and I think this was shared by others in the company, was that the rank and file was not in favor of the strike.
>
> Q: Did your views get modified any over the long duration of the strike? Did your perception of what you were dealing with in terms of the rank-and-file employees change any during the subsequent three and a half years that it dragged on?
>
> A: I didn't change my assessment of what happened in those first six months because whatever happened, happened, and I believe that violence played a major role in the length of the strike. I did come to view very clearly—and we knew this before the strike—that there was a group of employees that I estimated between two and three hundred that were extremely committed individuals to the union. Those people demonstrated a rather substantial commitment to their cause, but the point I'm making is that it might have been 30 percent of the total work force at best and that the overwhelming majority of the workers did not necessarily share support for the strike, certainly initially.[4]

Did all those who remained on strike for the duration—about 80 percent of those who walked out initially—do so out of "substantial commitment to their cause"? In simpler terms, did the strikers support their union leadership and therefore the goals of the strike? This is not the most interesting question, nor one that bears directly on the theoretical issues outlined in Chapter 1. Nonetheless, addressing that question is a precondition for proceeding with the rest of the story. If Reibeling were right and a majority of the employees had been manipulated into going on strike and coerced into staying there, any claim about lessons learned through the conflict would be dubious. I did not inquire directly about support for the strike. But I do not think that his is an accurate picture. Much of the interview and survey material I will present throughout is clearly inconsistent with a reluctant or even begrudging rank and file. I offer here a few brief but convincing pieces of evidence that the Colt workers were in fact on strike through their own informed free choice.[5]

I had the opportunity to interview forty employees in some depth, and while I make no claim about the representativeness of this group—or, more accurately, while it is at least somewhat overweighted with activists—many of them were well outside the circle of those most committed to the union leadership. In nearly one hundred hours of conversation, not one comment was made that indicated lack of support for the union's defined goals. While I was not asking directly about that, dissension of any magnitude would almost certainly have come up. My questions encouraged people to wander broadly over many issues. Could this be strategic circumspection? I doubt it; some people were openly critical of several other aspects of union strategy, especially the decision to remain at work after the contract had expired.[6]

If the interviews were one forum where resentful comments about the strike might be expected to turn up, the large union meetings were another. Although there certainly would be social pressure to minimize Why-the-hell-did-they-lead-us-out talk, the same generalization holds; if that sentiment had been there in any depth, it would have been impossible to hide in the premeeting buzzing and in the freewheeling interaction which took place between leadership and rank and file during meetings. The leadership encouraged members to ask questions about any aspect of the strike; on several occasions the questions went on for so long that it was the rest of the membership which yelled for people to shut up. The leadership also freely invited outside observers to their meetings and did not try in any way to restrict access to the rank and file. Reporter Howard's description of her experience at these meetings parallels mine.

> They're such an open group. In some unions, people can be hostile to anyone on the outside. They weren't like that. They would sit down with you. They had a story to tell. [Q: Do you mean the rank and file or the leadership?] Both. I would just walk around. Doing the story was like minibooks—each person would have their story.[7]

In spite of this free access, neither Howard nor I heard anyone argue that the union leaders should have accepted the company's final offer in March 1985 or at any other point during the strike. There was plenty of frustration and some shouting and criticism of the leadership, but neither she nor I (and between us, we spanned the strike period) heard anyone say that they wished they had never gotten into the strike. This might mean that we were not hearing the most private of thoughts and conversations strikers had, but it also means at least that it was not a thought they wanted to be made public, even with the promise of anonymity.

In addition to all of these indirect indications that the strikers did not feel misled, there is at least one fairly direct measure. If Reibeling's characterization were largely accurate, it would seem reasonable to expect that the strikers would have been somewhat resentful of unions generally. In fact, even if Reibeling's version were *not* true, it might be reasonable to expect misgivings about unions; after all, whatever their commitment in words, these employees had faced three years of hardship as a result of being on strike, and whether they supported it initially or not, they might have accumulated some doubts about the usefulness of unions.[8] But table 3.1 seems to show just the opposite.

Finally, Colt strikers had a chance to vote against their union representatives if they opposed them. Wheeler moved up to assistant regional director three months after the strike began, and Madore was appointed president. Madore was already closely identified with Wheeler and the strike. In a special election in June 1986, Madore ran for president unopposed. If there had been a significant disagreement about the direction of the strike, an opposition candidate would have emerged. This was not a one-party union; each time Wheeler ran for president he had faced opposition, until his last election in 1984—when these events had begun to unfold. Some of the potential opposition to Madore, of course, had been siphoned off because some employees had already returned to work, but Reibeling's statements about support for the strike were expressly about the majority of those who remained on strike and therefore could have formed an opposition slate. The reason for the lack of criticism of the leadership in open forums, private anonymous interviews, and the 1986 election is that there was no little or no disagreement over basic goals.

THE WAY THEY WERE

Probably the most important conflict in American labor history was the 1936 sit-down strike at the General Motors plant in Flint, Michigan. Its significance rests on the ripple effect of its outcome—recognition of the UAW as sole bar-

Table 3.1  *Importance of Unions*

| If you had to take another job, how important would it be to you that there was a union there? ($N = 117$)° | | |
|---|---|---|
| Not at all (%) | Somewhat important (%) | Very important (%) |
| 7.7 | 22.2 | 70.1 |

°N's in all tables from nonactivist subsample—see Appendix D for explanation.

gaining agent, the breakthrough which led quickly to the acceptance of the legitimacy of industrial unionism. The sit-down also led employees into territory this book is exploring—disruption of everyday routine, direct confrontation with power and authority. Some of those who have written about the Flint conflict take note of the transformation in the outlook and behavior of the participants. Flint's most comprehensive chronicler, Sidney Fine, devoted a chapter to what he called "the sit-down community," in which he described how the employees organized their own political functions, monitored sabotage and alcohol consumption, held classes in parliamentary procedure and labor history, and had their own theater troupe.[9] These are typical of the observations Fine made about that community: "It [the UAW] had discovered that worker morale might be less a problem in a sit-down strike than in a conventional strike, that 'it became a sort of festivity for these guys.'"[10] Further, "a feeling of kinship did develop among the strikers who remained inside the plants for any length of time that was unique in the experience of automobile workers and that gave a special quality to the social organization developed in the plants they occupied."[11]

Fine's "special quality" is another indication of the "sentiments of liberation" that Zolberg says are consistently reported by participants in high political drama.[12] In the Colt strike, the special quality included behavior characterized by large doses of mutuality and burden-sharing, as well as explanations of the events that minimized the role of individual self-interest and drew on collective and even communitarian languages. That might seem at first to be an unremarkable turn for a group of strikers, but it runs counter to at least three depictions of "normal-time" political activity. It is often argued that people address problems by calculating (implicitly, at least) their own self-interest.[13] Even if the problem is understood as one facing a group, there is little incentive for individual members to work for its solution. Instead, each will contribute as little as possible to the group effort, assuming that there is little he or she could add to the collective group effort and preferring, therefore, that other group members do the work.[14] Finally, there is overwhelming evidence of a deep-seated individualism in the American political culture, pervading all classes, and extending even to those who have had a negative confrontation with our dominant institutions.[15] Those reinforcing tendencies might work to undermine any collective sentiments alleged to be natural to unions and strikes. James Q. Wilson extended this analysis explicitly to unions; he cited studies suggesting that the "ideological unionist" motivated by "devotion to an overriding cause" comprised no more that 2 percent of union membership. His overall conclusion was that "purposive incentives no longer seem to be a major impetus for worker involvement."[16]

Factory employment by itself does not generate a sense of injustice. The daily experience of industrial work is not particularly pleasant, but does provide enough rewards—pay, security, friendship, comforting routine—to make the inequality, hierarchy, arbitrariness, and pervasive boredom at least tolerable to most employees most of the time.[17] In fact, the tendency of blue-collar workers to express satisfaction with their jobs is "among the most robust findings in all the social sciences."[18] Based on the strikers' own evaluations of the pre-1985 period, it seems that this finding would fit them also. In the open-ended interviews, I asked people what it was like to work at Colt before the turmoil developed. The answers ranged from restrained endorsement to extravagant praise, and the latter was by far the more prevalent.[19] Here are some representative comments about "life at Colt before," starting with the most critical, which are scarcely damning. These respondents had between thirteen and twenty-eight years of service and represent a mixture of job types and skills:

> I enjoyed it, I was treated well. Never had any problem with anybody. Little bits of dissension occasionally, but that's par for the course. The job I had was monkey see, monkey do. . . . I wasn't totally in love with it.

> Nice place to work as far as atmosphere. Nobody bothered you. How should I put it? It's a job, you know what I mean?

More typical were these enthusiastic descriptions:

> I'd compare it with [names another large industrial employer in town]. [That plant] at that time was strictly like a prison. In other words, you go to the men's room, you have to ask permission. Colt's, at that time, it wasn't like that. I considered it a nice place to work.

> You felt like getting up in the morning and going to work. You really enjoyed it.

> [A leading strike activist]: We were one big happy family. We all got along, everybody helped each other. I enjoyed it.

And a comment which interspliced past and present: "There was a good atmosphere, a lot of people with seniority. It was—no pressure. Nobody bothered me. It was a good job—but you know, it came to an end."


RUNNING THE PLANT BACKWARD

That end came suddenly, on March 31, 1985, when the contract expired. Since this is a study of how people react to the shattering of socially constructed routine, it might seem more appropriate to take the strike itself as the starting point. That is when the employees literally traded one set of daily tasks for another. But the strikers themselves were emphatic that the ten months spent working without a contract were a formative part of the conflict. Several, in response to a question about why they remained on strike, said that those ten months were so traumatic there was no temptation at all to go back in and face similar conditions. That period was one in which power was contested semi-openly and in which the resulting environment was an interweaving of defiance and frayed nerves. Both sets of responses qualify the period as a sharp break with the immediate past; subordination and resistance took the place of pay and work tasks as defining daily experiences.

The confrontational aspects took place with contractual obligations and labor law as a veneer, but without their niceties and conventions. The weapons on the side of management included strict enforcement of rules regarding leaving workplaces, reduced break times and timed bathroom breaks, the increased use of disciplinary procedures, and sharply reduced flexibility in accommodating employees' needs to leave early or to take time off for other commitments.[20] Employees refused overtime in large numbers, sang union songs together inside the two plants and held rallies outside at lunchtime, contested production rates, and took up collections at the plant gates for those fired. Some of the employee activity was clever and highly creative. Employees brought whistles to work and blew them when someone was suspended—"our little protest," as one interviewee called it. The company retaliated by posting a notice prohibiting outward signs of "celebration." An employee responded to that by carving a large wooden whistle and wearing it visibly around his neck. That spiraling sequence of protest and retaliation was typical of the period. As a union steward described it: "When people were disciplined for blowing a whistle, something like that, they would go into the office at one end of the plant. Then they would be escorted out by the guard. When the word got around the shop someone would be discharged, when they came down we were all clapping. Then they fired a guy for clapping."

Turning down overtime was the most widespread employee protest activity and was the target of most of the company's disciplinary action. An employee who refused overtime faced four disciplinary steps: verbal warning, written warning, three-day suspension, and dismissal. Wheeler estimated that by the end of the ten-month prestrike period there had been more than two thousand disciplinary actions, the great bulk for refusing overtime. More than four hundred employees had received their three-day suspensions, meaning that any further refusal to take overtime (or any other violation) would mean their termination. Table 3.2 is a record of disciplinary actions for refusing overtime produced by the union at the hearing before the administrative law judge. It is

*Table 3.2  Suspensions During "In-Plant Strike"*

| Date | Disciplinary actions (N) | Dept. size (N) | Dept. no. |
|------|--------------------------|----------------|-----------|
| 4/29/85 | 11 | 38 | 126 |
| 4/29/85 | 10 | 52 | 140 |
| 4/29/85 | 27 | 58 | 150 |
| 5/2/85 | 22 | 38 | 126 |
| 5/3/85 | 22 | 38 | 126 |
| 5/7/85 | 12 | 38 | 126 |
| 5/14/85 | 16 | 26 | 129 |
| 5/15/85 | 18 | 26 | 129 |
| 6/14/85 | 43 | 43 | 125 |
| 8/12/85 | 15 | 58 | 150 |
| 8/14/85 | 10 | 58 | 150 |
| 9/4/85 | 13 | 58 | 150 |
| 9/18/85 | 10 | 24 | 170 |
| 9/19/85 | 12 | 34 | 184 |
| 10/1/85 | 26 | 32 | 181 |
| 10/2/85 | 23 | 32 | 181 |
| 11/15/85 | 10 | 23 | 352 |

*Note:* List includes both Hartford and West Hartford.
*Source:* NLRB hearing, union's brief, p. 85.

only a partial list, comprising those occasions on which ten or more employees in a single department were disciplined. This table is presented not as a complete record, but as a vignette. It suggests something of the magnitude of the conflict, including an instance in which an entire department was disciplined and several times in which a substantial number of people in the same department were disciplined on successive days. The number *of* the department shows that there were repeated refusals; the number *in* the department shows the degree of participation.

The protest activity varied somewhat by department and job—those who had the most discretion over their workday tasks could be the most creative—and the degree of management hostility varied according to the personal inclination of the individual foremen. But the overall atmosphere was one of confrontation on both sides. The following descriptions by strikers help fill in the blanks and underscore the similarities to the celebration and defiance of the Flint sit-in community:

> You have to understand what it was like. There were firecrackers going off in the shop, whistles, skunk scent in the bosses' office.

There was a lot of solidarity, togetherness. It was like Sally Fields in *[Norma Rae]*, that type of atmosphere. It was kind of a revolution, like during the sixties, during the Civil Rights movement or the same atmosphere during the Vietnam war. A lot of hard feelings, everybody was pumped up. You had the company and you had us. That's when there was a change, it was no longer a big family. Everyone was choosing up sides.

Colt's lawyer drew almost the same picture, albeit for different purposes, when he discussed that period on the public television special on the strike: "The union didn't sit back like Little Mary Sunshine and do nothing. Rather, the union, in an attempt to try and force the company to agree to its demands and proposals, engaged in a so-called 'in-plant strategy' of—and this is exactly what it's called—'running the plant backward,' and that involved refusing overtime and doing other things that are successful in disrupting the company's operations."[21]

The activity was not confined to a few people in or close to the union leadership. Table 3.3 shows the breadth of participation, although readers should keep in mind that these are percentages of eventual strikers, not of the total workforce.[22]

The T-shirts were created by employees who proudly displayed the silk-screening "factory" in their basement. The shirts were garish yellow and carried such slogans as "Colt Labor Relations Stink" and "Colt: The Pride and Spirit are Gone"; they displayed a backward shooting gun as a symbol. One day a week was designated as T-shirt day, although some wore them every day. An employee who wore one of the T-shirts in his interview recalled the T-shirt days: "It was something. You'd look out and see nothing but a sea of yellow. You know they [management] didn't like it, but there wasn't nothing they could do."

The other question addressed by table 3.3 involves participation in the rallies. Employees met at lunchtime and either marched and sang union songs inside the plant or rallied outside. Susan Howard was an observer at many of the outside rallies and estimated that several had as many as two hundred participants at each plant.[23] There was predictably less involvement in this some-

*Table 3.3  Participation in Protest Events During "In-Plant Strike"*

|  | Never (%) | Once or twice (%) | Many times (%) |
|---|---|---|---|
| Wore T-shirt ($N = 125$) | 19.2 | 20.0 | 60.8 |
| Went to lunchtime rallies ($N = 127$) | 34.6 | 17.3 | 48.0 |

what friskier form of protest, but still more people took part "many times" than never at all. These were certainly not people who were accustomed by their background to such events. Nor was any of this risk-free even when it fell in the category of protected activity. Given the disciplines, suspensions, and firings during that period, the degree of participation is remarkably high. The following testimony at the NLRB hearing on an incident during that period points out the kinds of decisions employees faced:

> We were supposed to have a pretty big rally out in front of the shop. And we had it posted all over the board and all over. Everybody knew [the union] was going to have a big rally out front. Mr. [names foreman] came over to me and said, "You're going to work overtime tonight." And I said, "No, I'm not working tonight. I'm going to the rally." He said, "Well, if you go, I'm going to have to write you up." I said, "Be my guest. Do what you wish 'cause I'm going to the rally." And I went to the rally. [Q: What happened after that?] I came in the next morning and I was greeted by [foreman] and [foreman's supervisor], and they walked me out the door for three days.[24]

### DEVELOPING AN INJUSTICE FRAME

*No, it wasn't like slavery. It was slavery.*
—Striker, on working without a contract

So the in-plant strike period was filled with clever, assertive, widespread protest activity. But the memory most employees had of those ten months was hardship and tension, not the elation of battle. The whistles, the cheering of disciplined coworkers, the rallies, and other forms of resistance were rarely the first things strikers mentioned when I asked them to characterize that period. Almost universally, the first answers centered on the anxieties created by management's behavior, and the change from what some called "the old regime." The outpouring of frustration was universal; some respondents rushed to describe that period before I asked them any questions about it. It is hard to convey through the printed word the depth of anger; I will try to approximate it by quoting extensively. Some described the general tension level:

> What it was, they put like a Gestapo in there, writing people up for foolish things— they were violating rules, but silly rules.

> People could not take the harassment, the daily—; it was unbelievable. It was exhausting.

> Hell, it was hell. Sitting on pins and needles. It seemed like someone was fired every day. It wasn't, but it seemed like it.

Others pointed to the use they felt the company made of the overtime issue—to penalize and harass, and in general create a climate of uncertainty:

Aggravation. They'd come up to you at 3:30 and tell you that you were working overtime. They put pressure on everybody, working overtime when they didn't need it.

If they knew you were going someplace, they would ask you for overtime. I don't know how to explain. If they hear rumors you are going to refuse, they would ask. If you ask them if there's work, they would always say, "No work tonight." . . . We're people, not animals. I thought I was going to have a nervous breakdown.

That company wanted a strike, there's no doubt about it. They had no work in some departments and got people in to work overtime. Why was that? [Q: Why was that?] Harassment.

Still others made the "break with the past" theme explicit:

It was hell. Actually, I couldn't believe it. First, let me tell you that when I started at Colt, I couldn't wait in the morning to go to work. Then after the contract was up, all of a sudden they hired a foreman that was very antiunion. They were trying to get us pissed off, trying to get us to lose our cool.

First month wasn't bad, then next month it completely changed. It seemed like they were coming down with a whip and going to make you do things and you wondered what is going on. Same people I had worked with for eighteen years. Just like night and day they changed.

I used to love my job. I couldn't wait to get up in the morning. But in the end it wasn't the same. Very difficult. Tension—couldn't go to different departments. Management was way off base. Have to limit your potty calls. Nobody was allowed to do this or that. Picky about everything. Company putting pressure on them.

[WIFE (BOTH WERE STRIKERS)] There was tension like—you couldn't get coffee. I know people suspended for getting coffee.
[HUSBAND] It wasn't even the same Colt's we've known for years. It was like walking on hot flames.

One interview involved, at times, five people (described further in Appendix A)—a diverse group composed of a young white and a young Hispanic striker and three strikers with more than twenty years on the job, one black, two white. The tone of voice of each was decidedly agitated. One of the drawbacks of interviewing as a means of obtaining information about a situation such as this is that it is experienced collectively but recounted individually. The way in which these strikers built on each other's story may more nearly capture the atmosphere of the period than an individual interview would:[25]

SPEAKER A: Before we worked without a contract, it was a good place to work. Without a contract, it was an asshole place to work.

SPEAKER B: They were making it a real hell for us. It was getting like a Siberia after a while, timing your phone calls, your bathroom breaks. They made me work out of my classification. I'm a committeeman [a union officer], and they were trying to make me look bad.

SPEAKER C: A lot of petty stuff, it mounted up. There was major stuff, but the petty stuff mounted up, too.

SPEAKER D: I used to go home nights, take it out on the kids. My wife said, "What's wrong with you?" I said, "You don't know what it's like to work in there now."

A: I agree with this man.

B: The last ten months, we seen what was going on. We learned a lot. Take Christmas.[26] The last Christmas we were there, December '85, I was putting up a tree, decorating. My boss comes up to me, he says, "[name], you want to put up a tree, do it on your own time." That broke the spirit of Christmas. I got so fucking pissed off, I ripped everything down, everything. Took everything off the wall. To them it's business, that's all it is—business. You got to work like a slave.

Management argued that the tensions were brought about by their need to meet production schedules in the face of covert resistance by employees. In presenting an overview of Colt's interpretation of the whole conflict at the NLRB hearing, the company's lawyer said that the best word to describe the union's version of those ten months was "chutzpah": "Here you have the Union, which does everything possible, lawful, extra-lawful, and unlawful to prevent the Employer from operating its business and then comes in to complain because the Company is not conducting business as usual."[27]

There is no doubt that there was some strategic deemphasis of employee resistance during my interviews. Consider these comments:

We did what we could within our bounds not to work. *You* run the plant, not the foreman. To avoid the scab problem, it was on the fringes of—you have to have solidarity. I stayed with the program, I'll put it like that.

You didn't care if production was good or not. You didn't feel like you could do your best.

They would push people a little further, and sometimes things didn't go just right. If things went wrong, the foreman would say it was our fault.

Or this almost comical one: "In my department, nothing much happened. As far as losing gauges, I don't know nothing about it."

The questions had not been about losing gauges, or about whether any kind of unprotected or illegal activity had taken place. But the answers were denials that it had. That was understandable—the union had an immensely important NLRB decision pending, and the company was alleging that the union's strategy in that period included unfair labor practices such as these. But only a few people mentioned even the protected activity (such as the T-shirts) until I asked, let alone the more legally controversial practice of "running the plant backward." The great majority of comments depicted it as a one-sided war of management against workers, which it was not—the administrative law judge found that "misconduct" had occurred among the employees, although he did not rule it an unfair labor practice. Why, then, do the strikers have such bitter memories about a situation they helped to bring about?

This is precisely the question to which the company's answer was "chutzpah." That seems deficient on two grounds. First, it ignores the role management played in the conflict. This was not a one-sided war of workers against management, either. Second, the company's assessment could be true only if all the strikers were polished, hard-edged propagandists determined to fool the courts and public by cynically pulling on their heartstrings. The descriptions of that period as one of pressure, mistreatment, disruption, and arbitrariness were universal. It is hard to imagine that all the strikers I interviewed— some not activists in any way—would be so good at sticking to a story if it did not reflect their real feelings.

Some employees took little or no part in "running the plant backward," and some may have forgotten that they did. But the more important explanation lies in the presentation of justice. Who was to blame? Who was the wronged party? How could that be communicated? To discuss frankly all the activities of that period would have required a moral argument that some transgressions should be permitted, or that some are greater than others. That is a demanding argument, although ironically it appears to be the position the judge ultimately adopted. Also, in a spiral of conflict, each side can point to the last wrong done to it as justification for its next action. Since the employees were convinced that the original injury was done by the company, they were not inclined to look farther back on the spiral. The company at the hearing insisted on several occasions that the union had "unclean hands." This may have led the strikers to downplay even such perfectly legal, protected, but unconventional activities as lunchtime singing. The narrative in which the employees were the injured party—which they believed deeply enough to motivate a four-year strike—necessitated the memory of a one-sided war.

The employees' belief that they were the wronged party was coupled with a sense that it was a system—an organization of authority—which was producing the wrong. The bulk of factory workers' interaction with industrial authority is confined to foremen, and comments on the exercise of power tend to be comments on a foreman's personality and bedside manner.[28] In this period, employees cast their eyes higher up the hierarchical ladder. Several strikers said that their foreman took them aside after the contract ended and told them that the strict discipline was a matter of company policy, not individual discretion. Structure and hierarchy, always there but usually unobtrusive, were becoming more visible. The management practices they felt created this cauldron of tension were seen not as the product of misunderstanding or misapplication of policy but as the faithful application of a corporate policy intended to injure. People in positions of authority were reduced to their functions; they *became* their roles:

> Friends were—I know of one case where a foreman fired his dear friend. It was terrible. These things were coming down the line from the front office.

> You could see 'em [foremen]. They'd have meetings with their supervisors and—like a bunch of pit bulls. Open the doors and sic 'em.

> My foreman pulled me aside, he said, "This is not my doing." They turned about-face. They got their orders from New York, right from the top.

> I got along good with my foreman and supervisor, but all of a sudden you couldn't talk to them. It's like, they're management and we're workers.

Not only did foremen appear in a role as part of the chain of command of industrial authority, but the top of the authority pyramid became visible as an opponent:

> When management was local, you could negotiate with them. Then it went conglomerate, went to New York. That [CEO of Colt Industries]—he doesn't give a damn about what happens in Connecticut.

> Orders came from New York. These guys here are just little puppets on a string. Whatever [the CEO] tells them to do, they do it.

> I'm very bitter. These are orders from New York. New York knows nothing—doesn't even know what a gun looks like. It's all dollar signs.

They had come to believe that they were faced with a system of authority which was as a matter of course and with some intentionality producing unfair, unjust policies—seeing authority in an "injustice frame."[29] Further, this was due to the decisions of identifiable people within that system. While employees asserted their interests forcefully, they faced an opponent with greater resources. The comforts of routine and stability were gone; by the end of the ten-month period, most Colt employees felt that they had little to lose by striking. One of the twelve employees fired during the in-plant strike gave this sober assessment of the developing tension between solidarity and frustration as he described how others reacted to his firing:

> In all due honesty, fear. I wasn't even allowed to go to my locker. We had people on three-day suspensions—to show solidarity, when a person would come back, they

would have a cake and would sing labor songs. . . . Departments [were] given three-day suspensions and marched right out the door as departments. Halfway through this thing, I think people were doing good at it. Then the fear, the frustration. Everybody just kept saying to the [union officers], "When are we going to walk?" I consider myself lucky because I wasn't in the plant.

After respondents discussed the ten-month period, I asked each of them to comment on the first day of the strike. This is from a woman who had been at Colt for twenty-three years and who had expressed a great deal of pride at being the first female to work in gun repair:

Q: How did you feel when the strike started?
A: If a truck is coming at you to run you down, get the heck out of the road.

## "YOU WOULD HAVE TO HAVE A CAMERA"

Since everyone on every side described the last several months of working after the contract had expired as intolerably tense, it is not surprising that the onset of the strike had its festive aspects. This was so even though the union leadership warned people to expect a long and difficult strike, advising them to avoid making large purchases and to line up part-time jobs. It was not that people did not take those warnings seriously; one striker's spouse worked for the Colt employees' credit union and commented to me that she was struck by how many fewer people than normal had been making withdrawals.[30] But the act of walking out of an unbearably tense situation—at eleven o'clock, in the middle of a shift—mixed together relief and defiance.

One employee I interviewed had been the first out of the Hartford plant and was pictured on the front page of the *Hartford Courant*. He wore the same coat and hat to the interview that he had worn in that picture and said that he was saving them to wear on the first day he went back in—at the time of that interview, a barely visible prospect. His description of that first moment was, "Go, go, go! Everybody came out grinning, 'Yeah!'" Scott's description of "the intoxicating feeling that comes from the first public expression of a long-suppressed response to authorities" seems apt.[31] Here are some other reactions:

[HUSBAND A]: They were hollering and singing, happy.
[WIFE A]: You can't imagine what it was like. The company men were there gawking like [mimics shocked supervisors].

[WIFE B]: You would have to have a camera.
[HUSBAND B]: When they came through and said "everybody out," I mean, everything just stopped right there.

[WIFE B]: I had one foreman in my area, she like to climb under a machine. It was worth it watching her. She didn't know where to go, what to do, just the look on her face.

[STEWARD]: No one knew. We heard the commotion. I told them to turn their machines off. It was a big relief. It was a long time coming. I felt great, I really did, even though I knew tomorrow I wasn't going to have a job. Just the fact that I wouldn't have to wake up tomorrow and listen to the foremen harassing the people.

That is not to say that the employees were unmindful of the seriousness of taking this step. A woman near retirement age who became an impassioned spokesperson for the union remembered the first day as an emotional roller coaster: "Some were walking slow, some were walking fast, some were laughing, some were crying, because strikes are hard, you know. Strikes are not easy."

The employees fired during the in-plant strike were outside the buildings to greet the strikers. One of them offered this interpretation of the beginning of the strike: "Believe it or not, they came out like it was Christmas Day—they were happy. It was like liberating, like out of a concentration camp. That ten-month period had been so emotional. Us guys [the fired employees] who met them there, we were like the heroes. We hugged and it was like, 'We're all together now.'"

It is tempting to freeze the moment at which the strikers walked out and end the exploration there. That was the most clearly euphoric point, when concerns over livelihood and other everyday matters gave way to celebration. Such euphoric moments are attested to repeatedly by observers. A historian who studied the maritime strike in San Francisco in 1934 called this kind of moment a "pentecost," during which workers "suddenly developed an exhilarating sense of power and self-respect."[32] The sociologist Rick Fantasia, who participated in a wildcat strike as a blue-collar employee, described its beginning moments this way: "The tension of the previous twenty minutes or so, caused by a real fear of losing one's job, dissolved into near jubilation as workers enthusiastically greeted co-workers from other departments. . . . Their expressions almost resembled those of school children as they rush out the doors of a grade school on a warm spring day, laughing and jostling good-naturedly."[33]

Catching people in the act of euphoria is part but not all of my purpose. The moods of crowds in those periods are particularly susceptible to the charge of irrationality; and whether irrational or not, their responses are necessarily short-lived.[34] The thrill of a midshift walkout, a sense of extending a middle-finger salute to those perceived to have been mistreating them, and a release from the pressures of the previous ten months all enhanced that morning, helped make it a significant moment. But by themselves, these expressive elements are a very unreliable guide to the values the employees brought to and took from the conflict.

The Colt employees who walked out so enthusiastically had been on strike for two years by the time I conducted the first of my interviews, and they stayed out for more than four years altogether. Euphoria faded quickly in the face of increasing hardship, but "normalcy"—the status quo before March 31, 1985—was not reestablished. The task now is to see what effect these extraordinary times had on strikers' attitudes and behavior.

There is a great deal of evidence which suggests that protracted hardship—and the strike contained plenty of that—is more likely to force people to look for individual solutions than to increase a spirit of collectivity.[35] That is especially true in the individualist American culture, but is also partly due to normal ways of evaluating means and ends. The answer to the question "How do I best get what I want?" is not usually "Solidarity Forever." A lawyer for a group of Youngstown steelworkers who protested plant closings in 1979 and 1980 explained how individual solutions came to take priority in that situation: "As time goes on, collective outrage dims and personal survival takes over. The failure to produce a quick change in the company's decision leads to a mood of resignation and a focus on looking after oneself. The rhetoric of struggle is replaced by a rhetoric of benefits."[36]

At Colt, the "rhetoric of struggle" was in evidence at all points of the conflict, in interviews, on the picket lines, in the pre–union meeting socializing, on television. But rhetoric is a reasonably cheap commodity, and it might be more important to know whether people invested time and energy as well as words in the strike. We have already seen that participation in oppositional activity during the in-plant strike was fairly widespread. I have also mentioned that a few people picketed virtually every day. Table 3.4 shows that voluntary participation went well beyond a few dedicated activists.

Both the high and low ends tell the same story, and confirm the eyeball impressions of many observers. Large numbers of people took part "many times"; only a few never went beyond minimal involvement. Strikers were re-

Table 3.4  Participation in Strike Activity

|  | Never (%) | Once or twice (%) | Many times (%) |
|---|---|---|---|
| Picketed more than required ($N = 124$) | 5.6 | 23.3 | 71.0 |
| Attended other rallies ($N = 126$) | 5.6 | 33.3 | 61.1 |

quired to picket at least four hours a week. In exchange for that, the UAW provided strike pay of $100 per week and medical coverage. Many people took the local union leadership's advice and got part-time jobs; this makes the extent of participation even more impressive.[37] Some people had full-time jobs, making them ineligible for union strike benefits, and even a few of these continued to do picket duty throughout the strike.[38] As the strike went on, involvement declined somewhat (in part because more strikers got jobs elsewhere), and the numbers here do not distinguish between those who continued to go to events and those who went to many early and then withdrew. But special morning pickets drew 250 people three years into the strike, suggesting that participation was sustained as well as widespread. The "other rallies" referred to in the second question of table 3.4 included the broad array of demonstrations the union conducted on and away from the work site. The importance of these is that they went beyond normal strike activity and beyond what people might have experienced in the previous strikes at Colt. The 1973 strike involved mass picketing, but not demonstrations like those at the Hartford police station or at the suburban home of a member of the board of trustees, or at New York corporate headquarters.

Phil Wheeler was arrested on March 11, 1986, and charged with assault after protesting the arrest of another striker during mass picketing. Barbara Johnson described the response, one which gives some sense of the participatory spirit behind the numbers (as well as, tangentially, the creative tactical flexibility of the leadership):

> He was arrested on a morning picket line, about four hundred to five hundred people, purportedly because he stepped into a street. The membership was told to go back to the union hall. They held the meeting up for about forty-five minutes to see if Phil would come in, and he did, to a standing ovation. And when they completed the meeting, en masse, a thousand or eleven hundred [spouses and children attended the meetings] walked to the police station, probably twelve, thirteen blocks and did just a massive rally to protest what had just happened. Bob Madore turned to me and said, "Okay, what the hell do we do now?" So four or five hundred of us milled around the police lobby with our signs.

This is not storming the Bastille or the heavens, but for the strikers it was taking a step or two into unfamiliar territory.

WE ARE FAMILY

What can we conclude from the fact that strikers were committed enough to their cause to put this much unrequired time and energy into it? There are two possible, largely competing, explanations. Reibeling provided the basis for one in an elaboration of his "working assumption" about rank-and-file support for union leadership goals. During the time of the in-plant strike, and in the days immediately leading up to the walkout, he had felt that there was little depth to the support for the union's positions. As strike progressed, he changed that; he came to see a group of two to three hundred strikers as strong union supporters. But since that still did not explain why the large majority of workers stayed on strike, picketed, and demonstrated, he offered this sophisticated "rational striker" analysis:

> I think what happened was once the company started replacing workers that the majority of employees were caught in between and that they were left with no choice but to give overt or tacit support to the union, because their jobs were disappearing. What alternative did they have? The union was very active in promising back pay, very active promising a return to work for them. If their jobs disappeared and they were interested still in working at Colt, they found themselves in a situation of "what alternative do we have?"[39]

Reibeling is arguing that the decision to replace the strikers left those who might have originally opposed the strike (which he believes was the majority) with only one choice if they wanted their jobs back—to support it now. If this were true—or, more precisely if this and only this were true—it would indicate that what had changed were only the external constraints within which the employees made their decisions. Strike activity then would simply be a matter of utility maximization under changed conditions; that is, there would be no fundamental difference in the way people calculated their interests in nonnormal times, only a difference in the result of the calculations. The Colt strikers may have been acting in unison, but that was because it was the best way to achieve individual goals (principally, in Reibeling's scenario, to regain their jobs). The commitment to the strike (in this formulation) was a form of collective instrumentalism.[40]

The alternative explanation for the pattern of strike behavior is that new and different values developed in the course of the conflict, marked by shared interests among the strikers and a willingness to submerge individual goals for the good of the striking "family." These are sometimes called "solidaristic" norms. A sociologist writing about a shorter but in other ways similar strike at the Clinton Corn plant in Iowa in 1979–1980 described the strike culture as containing "a sense of mutuality and sociability" that extended even to a broadened sense of community property.[41] Was this also true at Colt?

Evidence that it was, and that this was an important part of the Colt story, is plentiful both in informal contacts and in the open-ended interviews. Some people spoke excitedly, even fervently, about the emotional bonds developed in the striking community:

STRIKE ACTIVIST: They're [the strikers] a close knit of people. We go to the union meeting, we hug and kiss each other and it's, "We're almost home."
Q: What is it about this group that makes it so strong?
A: Love for each other. I mean love. We feel for each other. You know how you might say "How are you"—"okay"? Now it's different, now you're concerned. Before you weren't. What does that tell you? That's love.

Q: One of the things that I'm interested in is whether the strike has created any sense of togetherness.
A: Not 100 percent, I'm not crazy. But for the most part, we've gotten stronger. It's like the Nazis bombing London. Instead of submission they just got stronger. "You ain't gonna do this to us." There's a warmth. The individual things have been great. Some of the people in that plant are closer than some relatives.

These are comments one might have expected from the most committed. But table 3.5 indicates that their remarks were not atypical.

An account of an intense labor conflict in 1950 indicated that increased sociability might result in part from the new contexts in which people got to know each other: "Several of the strikers pointed out that the picket line gave them an opportunity to know their co-workers more intimately. 'It was fun after a while, and you really got to know the people you used to work with but maybe never knew more than to say "hello." We saw them every day and really got to know them.'"[42]

The Colt strikers spoke informally in many of the same terms, and as the response to the first question of table 3.5 indicates, took the opportunity of the

*Table 3.5  Solidaristic Norms*

Compared to the time when you were working, have you gotten to know other employees better? ($N = 104$)

| No | About the same | A little more | A lot more |
|---|---|---|---|
| (%) | (%) | (%) | (%) |
| 7.0 | 17.5 | 34.2 | 41.2 |

Circle the phrase which best describes your feelings about the other strikers. ($N = 81$)

| Don't know them | Some are friends | We are like brothers and sisters |
|---|---|---|
| (%) | (%) | (%) |
| 13.6 | 33.3 | 53.0 |

In a situation like this, people sometimes try to help each other out. Has that gone on in this strike? ($N = 117$)

| No | Once in a while | A great deal |
|---|---|---|
| (%) | (%) | (%) |
| 6.8 | 23.1 | 70.0 |

strike to strengthen friendships. Among the dulling aspects of factory work is the routinization of relations among employees, and some strikers found satisfaction in getting to learn more about each other. "A lot of people I didn't know, now I know. On the picket line, we talk. Like [name], I didn't know him at all, even though he just lives down the street there. Now he's my *goombah*, we drive down to picket together."[43]

The fact that people enjoyed making new friends of old workmates may seem unremarkable, but it was a profoundly important and valued social element of the strike for many. The strikers realized that in the routinization of workday relationships they had *missed* something. There also was an exhilaration which came from friendships built on the basis of shared hardship:

I've met people that I didn't know.... I've walked on the picket lines. I figure you've been through winter and you've been through summer. You become more friends. Some tell you their troubles.

Working for all those years, you never know their last names. You get to know people on a first-name basis. Today we all know everybody, where they live. Now we're family, we're together all the time. You're walking in the cold, in the rain, in the heat. A strike, to me, brings people together.

People has got closer together that used to just say good morning and good night. A lot of people has learned each other—the feelings, the hurt, the sadness. The best friend I ever had, I never knew her before. I never seen her and she worked right below my department.

Significantly, each of these refers to friendships earned in shared hardship and the pleasures of getting to know people by their first name. The background had changed, from workaday to heat, cold, rain, and "the sadness." That encouraged the strikers to look at each other anew, as whole and real people.[44] The strikers' newly forged ties had significance beyond increased familiarity. The wording of the second question of table 3.5 was taken from some of the interviews I did before the survey, and the answers show the Colt workers reaching for the most "solidaristic" of the offered descriptions of their relation to other strikers.[45] The "brothers and sisters" answer is somewhat sentimental, but was the strongest wording I could think of to differentiate those who merely spent a greater amount of time with other strikers from those whose friendship carried with it an element of solidarity. Even people involved in collective action are not ordinarily motivated as much by broad general principles as by personal interactions within small groups.[46] The answers to this question do not contradict that but suggest that principle and personal ties became intermingled. For an admittedly impressionistic but compelling elaboration, consider the competing pulls of personal friendship and community in these two accounts by strikers. Both were in answer to a question about whether the strike had changed their attitudes toward other employees:

> I had a neighbor who worked with me—years. He went back after the strike [began]. He called me one day and said, "Come on, it's not so bad." I told him, "Don't call my house no more. I don't need friends like you." You got to have some pride about yourself.

> We just like sisters and brothers—we all out for the same cause. Much closer. I have a guy I didn't give a damn about. We fought—awful. Since he out here, we don't even think about it. We're looking for each other to help and get back in so we can fight in the bar again.

Responses to the last of the questions in table 3.5 indicate that the communal values went beyond lip service. Throughout my interviews with strikers, I heard stories of cooperative activity of a very practical sort. A striker who did roofing work fixed another striker's damaged roof and refused to accept payment for it. Several strikers who were skilled auto mechanics helped keep old cars running for others. A striker who was a former hairdresser cut hair for free; strikers who raised gardens brought vegetables to the strike center, where others brought clothes, tires and even a few televisions. The survey indicated at a minimum that people were aware of a large volume of these informal and largely unpaid exchanges.[47] These were supplementary to more organized forms of support for the strikers, which also took on collective form: the union's Christmas parties for strikers' children, collections at union meetings for flowers and funerals, and the hardship fund, handled by Barbara Johnson and four strikers, which carried on fund-raising activities and directed money to those in most immediate need.[48]

The strike was 3½ years old at the time of the survey, which was taken before either of the events that led to the final settlement, the offer to sell and the favorable administrative law judge ruling. Before those, there was a lot of hopeful talk, but no light at the end of the tunnel. That makes the figures in table 3.6 particularly compelling. They describe people who thought of what they were doing less as an act of calculated self-interest than as contributing to a shared cause.[49]

The company had made repeated offers to take people back in as individuals, and some did go back. Practically everyone remaining on strike knew someone well who went back. But as responses to the first question in table 3.6 show, hardly any of those still on strike at the time of this survey had even thought about returning to work.

There still remains the interpretation that Reibeling proposed—that strikers heard the company say they were replaced, heard the union leadership say,

*Table 3.6  Collective Definitions of Interest*

Have you ever thought about going back in as an individual (*N* = 102)

| No, never | Early in the strike | Late in the strike |
|---|---|---|
| (%) | (%) | (%) |
| 91.2 | 5.9 | 2.9 |

What is the *most important reason* you have remained a striker? (*N* = 95)

| Back pay | Want my job back | Respect for other strikers |
|---|---|---|
| (%) | (%) | (%) |
| 10.5 | 41.1 | 48.4 |

*Note:* emphasis in original questionnaire.

"Follow us and we'll get your jobs back," and made the only logical choice. But the second set of answers better fits a group motivated by principles created by the conflict itself. The phrase "respect for other strikers" was also taken from comments during the open-ended interviews, and there may be better phrases to convey norms of solidarity. But the story these answers tell is unmistakable. Both back pay and going back to work as a group were realistic possibilities, of course—they later came to pass. Nonetheless, the most practical reason for remaining on strike (back pay) is the least preferred answer and the most cause-driven (the "respect" alternative) the most preferred. The argument is not that the strikers were gushing sentimentalists but that a new form of rationality emerged, based less on finely tuned calculations of individual self-interest than on collective definitions of interest, a shared purpose, willingness to sacrifice for it, and a sense of responsibility to each other.

Answering questions posed in a survey can be a cost-free way of expressing noble sentiments. People often appear more virtuous when committing themselves to abstract goals than when there are real trade-offs to be made. More people say they vote than vote; more people are environmentally conscious in surveys than in consumer purchases. But for the Colt strikers, talk was not cheap. The reader already knows that they were not just engaging in meaningless we'll-stay-out-as-long-as-it-takes bravado; that is precisely what they did. But what about the expressions of solidarity and collectivity, the values I am claiming submerged impulses toward individualism? Could these be inflated?

I will offer two illustrations of how these values were just as "real" to the strikers as the cash nexus is usually said to be. In the third year of the strike, the company lost its government contract to produce M-16's. This was a significant blow to the company, but it also raised the possibility of a long-term loss of jobs. It posed an interesting dilemma for the strikers, since the economic hardship it worked on the company would continue if they returned to work. They preferred to look at it as a victory and minimized the significance of the loss of future jobs, even when I drew that to their attention. They interpreted the lost contract through a prism of "justice"; in this case, justice had been done. Only two of the fifteen strikers I asked expressed any misgivings at all, and even they saw the positive side as more compelling:

> Well, it's a two-sided thing. But if I have to take a part-time job, I'll survive.

> I hate to see it go, but I look at it this way. At least you're going to make up all our minds, then we turn around and get another job, because if that's how the company's going to react [referring to a potential closing], then they can close the doors five months after we get a contract and say we can't afford it no more, they can close the doors on us.

Other reactions were characterized by celebration, which the respondents sustained even when I pressed them lightly to look at the cloud within the silver lining.

> Everybody's happy. I got drunk. We suffer, now they suffer too. [Q: But what happens when you go back to work?] Then we'll find something else.

> I thought it was great, really. That was the best thing that ever happened. I slept good that night.

> I'm the happiest person in the world. We know it's because of poor quality [by the strikebreakers]. I'm so glad we lost it. [Q: But isn't there another side? If you get back, the contract will still be gone.] It's better they lost it, if the scabs come out. If we don't work, nobody works. That's the way I feel. Close it up. Take it to South Korea. Let 'em deal with it there, not here. If we don't have jobs, I'd just as soon they were gone. Great, I'm glad.[Q: Any mixed feelings?] No. Even if they lost it and a week later we were back, I still would be happy. Let 'em pack and leave.

In any conflict, each side makes use of the resources it has to promote its own position, and the union leadership had been lobbying in Washington for the contract to be canceled. That seems like ordinary hardball politics. But the sentiments expressed above go beyond that; the strikers were prepared to call in an air strike on their own position.

The other indicator of the strikers' commitment to solidarity and cooperative behavior is even more powerful and persuasive. Many talked about the central purpose of their actions as being to gain something not for themselves but for their children or grandchildren, or, more broadly but in the same vein, for the sake of a future labor movement. It is not uncommon for strikers to invoke the future—there is at least that much left of old-style labor movement talk. But a substantial number of strikers meant it quite literally. Those were the people either near, or actually past, retirement age. Their personal stake in the outcome was negligible. Some of the strikers who were most active planned to retire as soon as the strike ended.

> [From an employee of twenty-two years, fired during the in-plant strike]: They're fighting for principle. You got to respect that. I really feel for the people at Colt, they feel that they're fighting for a thing that's over and above them right now. . . . We like to think we're fighting for other people. I'm not going to be around much longer. I'm fifty-one. A guy like [names activist], he's sixty-five. It's my kids and grandchildren. There's always been a labor struggle. You don't win financially. You win a principle.

> [The sixty-five-year-old activist to whom the last speaker referred]: People say to me, "What are you on strike for, why don't you retire?" But I believe in something. I believe that if I don't do this now, how about the younger generation? They'll make pulp out of them.

The willingness of the strikers to make winning a principle the centerpiece of those five years (as the first speaker said) and the willingness to put vast amounts of time and energy into a cause which could not benefit them greatly (as the second speaker did) is the real measure of solidarity as a norm rather than as a tool.

There is another reason beyond age to take the strikers at their word. An older striker, who did not know I was writing a book based on the strike and was therefore not grandstanding for my benefit, sat down at a table with several other strikers at the union hall. He had just been to a doctor and described his serious heart condition. Then he pounded on the table. "This is what keeps me going. I just want to win this son of a bitch. I don't want to give those assholes the satisfaction of me dying before we won it."[50]

Finally, there was a more somber aftermath to one of my interviews. I spoke with a highly skilled employee in his late fifties who interpreted events in much the same manner as the other strikers in this chapter. He was a strong supporter of the union, talked about the national significance of the strike and about future generations benefiting. When I asked him about the M-16 contract and the possible loss of jobs, his response was, "This strike is not going to be settled in my lifetime." At the time, I thought he was just being a pessimist. Many of the strikers combined strategic optimism with tactical pessimism, particularly about the length of time a resolution would take. Unfortunately, I learned that this was not the case with him. He had lung cancer and died two months later. He was a gracious man; I take no pleasure in recounting his death except to reemphasize the seriousness of the commitments the Colt strikers made.

### "CAUGHT UP IN SOMETHING DIFFERENT"

The picture which has emerged so far is of a body of employees who defined their goals collectively and worked to achieve them cooperatively. There was a minimum of "free riding." They participated broadly both in the in-plant resistance and in the rallies, demonstrations, and regular picketing of the strike. They chose not to take the one step which would have put an end to their personal hardship, crossing the picket line and going back to work, even though it was always an available option. They shared tangible goods and mutual self-respect. And they described this all with a language which located the terms of the conflict in pride, dignity, and social justice.

What seems to have motivated many of the strikers was a belief in the rightness of their cause, not in the usefulness of their actions. Scott, Zolberg, and others emphasize the new public language and enthusiasm of democratic moments; that seems borne out in the Colt strike. These are not simply normal-time calculations made with new terms. What this chapter suggests is changed people, not just changed circumstances. I began my description of the conflict by making an implicit comparison with the 1936 Flint "sit-down community." Both were transformative events for those who took part. An explicit comparison illustrates that quality:

> *Member of the Flint Women's Emergency Brigade:* I found a common understanding and unselfishness I'd never known in my life. I'm living for the first time with a definite goal. . . . I want to be a human being with the right to think for myself.[51]

> *Colt striker:* You get up, you go to work every day because that's what you do. Now I'm caught up in something different.

We do not know how representative the woman from Flint was, and I know that this particular Colt striker was not typical. He had been a steward and was one of the most committed activists. Colt union meetings were not revival camps. But the interviews presented in this chapter suggest that being "caught up in something different" was a widely shared experience.

A strong commitment to the goals of the strike also had practical value, of course. It gave people their best chance of succeeding short of what became the morally unacceptable alternative of strikebreaking. The "rational striker" description was not wholly inaccurate. The final outcome suggests that solidaristic norms and a fervent belief in the rightness of their cause led people to act sensibly, even if at great personal cost. Communalism and the language of self-respect might be largely ornamental. The best way to examine that is to see if there was any spillover into other areas of behavior and belief.

# 4

## A General Attention to Public Affairs

*But too much was at stake in Reconstruction for "normal politics" to prevail. As one scalawag pointed out, while Northern political contests focused on "finances, individual capacity and the like, our contest here is for life, for the right to earn our bread . . . for a decent and respectful consideration as human beings and members of society."*
—Eric Foner, *Reconstruction*

*Even this evil [Shay's rebellion] is productive of good. It prevents the degeneracy of government, and nourishes a general attention to public affairs.*
—Thomas Jefferson, letter to James Madison

*You know, before we went on strike, 60 percent of the people voted for Reagan, 40 percent didn't know what their local's number was, and 60 percent couldn't tell you what a union was. Now it's 90 percent voting against Reagan. People learn, people change. It's been fun to watch. Everybody can tell you everything and it's all since the strike.*
—Colt striker

Open-ended surveys provide the opportunity to obtain information on sub-jects which the interviewer may not have thought of as central but which those interviewed do. Strikers were able to introduce or expand on topics I had not considered or to order the importance of issues differently than I might have. Since the fixed-answer questionnaire was not given until the open-ended sur-veys had been completed, I had an opportunity to devise new questions based on the degree of emphasis strikers themselves gave to some concerns. This chapter is based on one such change of plot.

When I talked with strikers informally (that is, outside even the open-ended interviewing format), I became aware that many of them had devel-oped emphatic opinions about the activities of various politicians, in relation both to their strike and to issues they were concerned with more generally. As a starting point, they almost all seemed to know who their own congressional representative was (their living districts were represented variously by Demo-crats Barbara Kennelly and Sam Gejdenson and Republican John Rowland); where he or she stood on the strike (often in nuanced detail); who the Hartford representative was if different from their own (Kennelly); who Connecticut's U.S. senators were (Democrat Chris Dodd and Republican Lowell Weicker) and where they stood, and what the governor (William O'Neill, a Democrat) had or—more usually—had not done. Several of the strikers I talked with could inventory all the Connecticut representatives with some subtlety. These were not union officials, whose business it is to accumulate this knowledge. Some strikers had initiated contacts with their state or national representa-tives to explain the issues of the conflict; many more did so at the urging of the union leaders and the Community-Labor Alliance. There was nearly universal discussion and condemnation of the Reagan administration's creation of an antilabor climate; more than half of those interviewed pointed without solici-tation to the firing of the air traffic controllers as the real beginning of their own conflict.

Should any of this be surprising? The strike was an issue of immediate con-cern for those interviewed; it might be reasonable to expect them to know about relevant stands taken by public officials. It seems intuitively obvious that the strikers would take an intense interest in what politicians did in relation to the strike. But many studies of citizen-government interaction have found that assumption to be wrong. What seems to be a simple connection between problem and demand for governmental action in fact entails several interme-diary links.[1] At least two of the links are more like barriers. One is that for those involved to turn their sights to the actions of public officials, they must con-clude that conflicts within the "private" sphere, as this one was, are appropri-ate for governmental solution. In fact, it has been argued that Americans make such a rigid separation of government and market that they construct different principles of justice and fairness for each.[2]

Another link is that people must have a reasonably accurate picture of the world of governance, and this has turned out to be an even more formidable barrier. One of the earliest and most unpleasantly persistent findings of survey research is that Americans do not possess a great deal of specific information about government.[3] Many people, the weight of this evidence shows, cannot name their congressional representative, cannot name the candidates in elections, do not vote based on issues, and do not understand issues very clearly anyway. People do not participate very much in the governmental process between elections and do not even have a very strong interest in those. Precise and consistent knowledge about governance is confined to a relatively thin layer of political operatives, or at best to an only slightly larger educated elite. The most famous of the articles presenting these findings spoke of a "continental shelf" separating the political knowledge of elites and nonelites.[4] Stephen Bennett, in a study of apathy, summarized those findings this way: "Many people find the subject matter of government and politics to be dull and boring, that there are seldom direct, palpable satisfactions to be gained from political involvement, and that people are much more likely to be concerned with direct, immediate, and concrete personal needs."[5]

This portrait of the level of political concern among American citizens has been analyzed, debated, challenged, and refined. Some political scientists have argued that people have become more sophisticated since the time of the original studies (the 1950s);[6] that the tools of survey research made it impossible to locate the reasonable but idiosyncratic interpretations people might make of the political world;[7] that the role of education as the only source of consistency was overstated.[8] Another line of criticism admitted the lack of detailed and consistent public knowledge, but argued that citizens were not hampered by this from making sensible political evaluations.[9] It is also possible that a major share of the blame for whatever public ignorance exists falls on political leaders rather than citizens.[10] Finally, there has also been a debate about whether these early findings represented a positive or negative feature of our political system.[11]

But the amount of scrutiny and refinement these early claims have undergone cannot obscure the fact that their fundamental point still stands: citizens see politics through a glass darkly. Not even the strongest critics propose returning to the previous assumption—that most people follow governmental matters closely and pay careful attention to the issue positions of candidates before choosing between them.[12] Government and citizens occupy adjacent worlds, according to public opinion literature, and a view from the latter to the former traverses many cultural miles. "Washington, New York and the other centers of American society are, for many people much of the time, on other planets."[13] Everyday concerns preoccupy people and do not lead directly or often into demands on or opinions about the world of governance.[14] Even when daily life turns up problems and hardships, it does not reduce the distance between citizens and government appreciably. Hamilton and Wright summarize the survey data on the normal-time relationship between the two this way:

> Politics is not a high-priority consideration in the lives of most people: most of the population find that the day-to-day routines of life dominate, and that they have neither the time nor the interest for things political. . . . A small fraction of the population (on the order of one-tenth) does not even sense that there are national problems of any consequence, and many of those who do sense such problems deny that they are touched by them in any direct way. Others who are personally affected by what they see as an important problem find that they are satisfied with present government performance in the area, or that the area in question is not the government's responsibility.[15]

Another analyst of public knowledge puts the same conclusion more directly: "Most people are unable to state how government affects their lives at all."[16]

A different political geography emerges from many descriptions of those times when open conflict replaces routine. The gulf between citizens and government narrows, not necessarily because government is viewed as supportive but because the thought occurs and grows that ordinary citizens have something vital at stake in affairs of state.[17] The thrust of this chapter is that such times of unusual and dramatic conflict lead and perhaps inspire people to evaluate government by comparing it to its democratic ideal type: citizen self-rule. Zolberg, touring regime-shaking events in French history, argues that these "moments of madness" changed the relation of citizen and state. "The private merges into the public; government becomes a family matter, a familial affair."[18]

A sense of the immediacy and urgency of politics emerges from some descriptions of unusually conflictual times in American history as well. Eric Foner's overview of the Reconstruction era is filled with descriptions of ex-slaves excitedly participating in discussions of the construction of a new political order; freedmen on the South Carolina Sea Islands following congressional debates; mass absenteeism from tobacco factories and crowded galleries during debates in the Virginia Constitutional Convention.[19] Another historian described those state conventions: "What made them so unprecedented was that men who had only recently been slaves, along with freeborn blacks, were expressing themselves in ways that had only recently been banned, gathering together for the first time, exchanging experiences, discussing the problems they faced in their particular counties, and sharing visions of a new South and a 'redeemed' race."[20]

Lawrence Goodwyn noted some of the same impulses toward wider definitions of citizenship at the heart of the Populist movement and described that movement as a democratic moment in American history: "The kind of personal participation that Evan James [Texas Populist Alliance leader] had felt in 1888 when he summoned 250,000 Alliancemen to meet in more than 175 courthouses—without notifying anyone in the courthouses—pointed to a kind of intimacy between ordinary citizens and their government that becomes less evident in twentieth-century America. To Alliancemen, it was *their* government."[21]

But historical anecdotes can only be suggestive. More conclusive evidence that high-intensity conflict can provide an empowering civics lesson comes from a study of what may have been the *least* normal political situation in post–World War II Western democracy, the May–June 1968 student-worker uprising in France.[22] Comparing surveys done before and immediately after the events, the authors conclude that participation in the protests led people to declare themselves better able to understand politics and government:[23]

> In the earlier year [1967], the future strikers felt more at sea with regard to politics and government than the future nonstrikers did, while in the later year—after the upheaval—the strikers thought that they understood government and politics better than nonstrikers did, and by a fairly wide margin.
>
> One would be hard put to account for these dramatic transformations without reference to the force unleashed by the May upheaval itself. Back in 1967, the future protesters might not have had much confidence in their ability to untangle some of the complex strands of French politics, but in 1968, a few days of demonstrating (and possibly also a few nights of rioting) or a few weeks on the picket line went a long way toward clarifying the situation for them.[24]

When authority becomes unglued, people become more attentive to politics, even if only to learn how to press for their own goals more effectively. The Colt strike was certainly not a convulsive national event as the above examples were (although for those involved, four years of picketing, demonstrating, and doing without their usual income were not trivial). The comments about public officials I heard in informal contacts led me to suspect that this conflict also "went a long way toward clarifying the situation for them." The open-ended interviews and the written survey included questions designed to test that possibility.

MERGING POLITICS AND MARKETS

In the Colt conflict, government was not a direct participant. The ethical underpinning of American labor law is that the proper role of government is to set enforceable rules by which management and labor can fight around competing proposals. The fairness of the outcome is not held to be a matter of public interest, and government should therefore play as small a role as possible. This reasoning was at the heart of the 1938 MacKay Radio decision, which established the right of employers to hire "permanent replacements" during strikes. "The Board [NLRB] has never contended in this case or in any other that an employer who has neither caused nor prolonged a strike through unfair labor practices cannot take full advantage of economic forces working for his victory in a labor dispute."[25]

This is called "industrial pluralism"—set up guidelines, let each side marshal its resources, and let the market determine the winner. The government plays no substantive role in the outcome.[26]

Thus the strikers first had to decide whether their conflict properly belonged in the public sphere and how fair the "industrial pluralist" assumptions about collective bargaining were. That at first might seem trivial; *obviously,* the argument might be, the union members would look for support from anyplace they could get it, public or private. But that implies the politicization of personal hardship, a step which does not come naturally for most Americans.[27] The standing verdict is that the market produces fair outcomes, and to conclude otherwise requires an active and critical judgment.

Colt management, for its part, wanted to leave the decision to the market. Reibeling pointed to a company strategy of actively discouraging governmental intervention.

Q: On the company's part, was there any desire to see any aspect of this discussed by elected officials?

A: No. One of the things that happened is that after the strike began, the corporation more so than the division, it was more involved. What the corporation did not want to have happen—and this is, I think, very real—that they did not want the negotiations to be somehow sidetracked or lost control of, and therefore they wanted the negotiations to take place between the union and the company, and therefore were not interested—in fact rebuffed—certain attempts on the part of some of the elected officials to become involved.[28]

Despite the corporation's efforts, there were attempts by some elected bodies and individual politicians to address the strike issues. The Connecticut State Legislature passed a resolution calling on the company to negotiate; since the company considered its final offer to be nonnegotiable, it understood that to be an implicit criticism. Reibeling said about that resolution that it was passed "in a process that was highly irregular as far as how these kinds of resolutions are handled, and it was very disturbing that that would occur when people didn't really have the facts."[29] At least these elected officials spoke at union rallies: Bruce Morrison and Barbara Kennelly, congresspeople; Irving Stolberg and Thomas Ritter, state representatives; Joseph Harper, state senator; Norvell Goff, Hartford city councilman; and Carrie Saxon Perry, state representative and later mayor of Hartford, who led a rally in singing Woody Guthrie's "Union Maid."[30] Perry was also part of the "Colt 45"—a group of public figures arrested in May 1986 at a sit-in near the Hartford plant entrance as a show of support for the strikers.[31] Strikers mentioned these actions by politicians frequently, but they were still dissatisfied with government as a whole. As the previous chapter indicates, and as any amount of contact with the strikers made clear, they were overwhelmingly convinced that an injustice had been done to them by powerful and wealthy opponents, and they were disillusioned that government provided no mechanism to rectify the injustice. Colt management, particularly corporate ownership in New York, seemed to be untouchable.[32]

In the open-ended interviews, I asked whether a governmental role was appropriate, and the responses were overwhelmingly affirmative.[33] That was true whether the question was about "government" as an abstraction, public officials in the aggregate, or specific officials. The responses did not produce much highly quotable material, because most people regarded it as a truism. Nevertheless, the reasons people gave for bridging the government-market gap are worth consideration. The narrowest construction was that the government had a role to play because about half of Colt's work was for the military. That created an obligation on the part of the government to oversee the quality of the product, which many strikers claimed had deteriorated during the strike.[34] One of the unavoidable (and understandable) dynamics of the interview process was that people were selling the justice of their cause. A call for government to intervene because of military contracts had the feel of an argument that strikers thought might persuade a prying political scientist. But that was interwoven with what seemed to be genuine anger at the way public money became an asset to their opponents. "Congress and the senators, they should get involved. It bothers me that my money has been funneled back to subsidize scabs."

Another argument was that a Democratic governor bore a special responsibility to intervene, either because the Democrats should live up to their image as the party of working people or because (in the words of one striker, but the thoughts of several) "We voted for him after all, and he is supposed to help us." This is fairly standard interest-group reasoning, that constituents have a right to demand a return on their voting investment. The irony is that no political figure, including Ronald Reagan, was as widely condemned by strikers as O'Neill, who, they felt, had done nothing to help them.[35]

Two other widely held explanations about the proper role of government revolved around strikers' beliefs that the purpose of government is to enhance justice. One version was that the strike was an important issue and it is the government's job to deal with important issues:

> A long strike like this, yes. It's in [O'Neill's] state; he is responsible for unemployment.

> It's community isn't it? Do you want people to go on welfare?

> I can't see why not. We've been out for too long. People are dying left and right.

The other variation, primarily adopted by strike activists, went beyond the obligations of government to attend to its citizens' needs and pointed to its duty to produce fair outcomes.

> The way I see it, more government people should get involved, because the strike has gone on so long. It's not just us. If this union is busted—this is a strong union—all unions are gone.

> We work for the state, we pay taxes. If [O'Neill] were any kind of governor, he'd say, "I'm inclined to go along with the strikers have a valid reason for being out."

Government, in this last construction, has no need to maintain neutrality. It seeks to minimize harm to citizens in such areas as highway accidents; it should simply declare antiunion activity of the kind Colt practiced to be harmful. Some of those who were convinced for any of these reasons that the government had a responsibility to become involved also were convinced that it could have shortened the strike by doing so; that is, that public officials could have forced Colt to negotiate. But others offered an interesting blend of support for governmental intervention and skepticism—public officials did have an obligation to become involved, but it would not have made any difference. That skepticism was based on solid evidence. The activity of all those public officials mentioned above had failed to produce a settlement as of the time of the interviews. The problem, as these strikers saw it, was that government, whatever its intentions, could not reach far enough into the private sector to change the behavior of a corporation which had the wealth and will (or, as the strikers saw it, malice) to resist. The following responses—given by those who had already insisted on the responsibility of public officials to make an effort to resolve the strike—are to the question, "If politicians did intervene, would it do any good?"

No. They're [Colt officials] so pig-headed, they don't care.

No. Not at all. The stakes are too high.

I don't think there's too much [public officials] can do.

What *can* they do? I mean, you're talking about the big leagues in New York. These are millionaires. They make up their minds to bust the union—the mayor, the governor, these are little people. [Mayor] Perry, God bless her, she's just a hometown girl with a cowboy hat [a Perry trademark] on.

So the disappointment the Colt strikers felt with governmental performance during the conflict was twofold. Public officials did not respond forcefully enough or in enough numbers to what was felt to be a legitimate public issue. When some did, it revealed that the democratic process did not extend deeply enough into the real strongholds of power—the "big leagues"—to have much chance of success.

THE SHORT ARM OF THE LAW

Until November 1, 1986, the supervisor of police work at the Hartford picket lines was Assistant Police Chief Donald Higgins. About a month before his retirement, while still overseeing the Hartford site, he disclosed that on leaving the force, he would begin working as security supervisor for Colt. The strikers were incensed. The union leadership charged Higgins with conflict of interest and protested at the police station, demanding that he immediately be taken off the strike work. The police and city regarded it as a nonissue, since the union was not alleging some specific act of misconduct. Both the police chief and Higgins himself used the ethic of professionalism as a defense, the chief issuing a public statement saying, "As far as I'm concerned, Donald Higgins will conduct himself as a professional police officer. I'm not going to allow the union to find him guilty without any proof."[36] Shortly after he joined the company, Higgins became part of the Colt negotiating team.

Most respondents brought up the Higgins incident in some form. It pointed toward another arena of political power which was the subject of some reevaluation—the law enforcement apparatus, including police and courts. My ability to interpret attitude changes toward these institutions is sketchier than in other areas. Again I have to rely on comments in the open-ended interviews, and more important, I have no baseline—no "before" against which to measure an "after." Nonetheless, it is an important topic, and one that demands some effort to make use of whatever information is available.

There was a very wide range of attitudes toward the courts and (especially) the police, reflecting at least in part the different experiences individual strikers had with them. Not surprisingly, those who had had physical confrontations or had been arrested tended to be less generous in their evaluations. While there were many sharply critical comments about the role of courts and police in the interviews, it would not be a fair generalization to say that strikers came to see the police and courts largely as instruments of repression or as agents of Colt. A more accurate overall characterization would be this: strikers saw law enforcement as contested terrain, albeit one on which wealth and power bestowed considerable advantages on the company.

The relationship of strikers to police is an inherently conflictual one, and with the element of strikebreakers added, an inherently confrontational one.[37] As described briefly in Chapter 2, there were more than one hundred arrests of strikers, though few convictions. In addition, there was constant tension as a result of the probing of limits on both sides. This was particularly true in the first year, after which a more regularized pattern of acceptable picket line behavior was established. The union leadership never had a strategy of blocking access to either plant. Although there were weekly mass pickets of two to three hundred at each plant, these were intended more to dramatize the strikers' case (and retain internal morale) than to stop anyone from getting in to work.

Still, the interaction of strikers and those going to work[38] was hostile; there was a great deal of taunting and profanity, and a small amount of spitting and jostling in both directions.[39] When the crowds were large enough and the atmosphere tense enough, the strikers and police also inevitably engaged in small scuffles. Here are two strikers' recollections of those encounters. Both employees were highly skilled workers who had worked at Colt for more than twenty years and both had been through other strikes there. Neither was an activist.

> That first year, there were a lot more people picketing. You might be together at the gate, hollering at those people. Somebody might push you, you push them, you might touch their car. You got to stop when they say stop, you might get arrested.

> There was nothing that bad. When you have six or eight cops, and four hundred people, there's bound to be something, particularly when they turn around and start belting women with nightsticks. I think Higgins was hoping for more violence. They couldn't come up with much. Just about everyone in here has a family. You are not going to get these people to riot.

Howard, the *Courant* reporter who spent dozens of hours on the picket lines in those first two years, described those incidents in essentially the same way. "It would be like this. The line would be going along and here's the fence and somebody back here [back of the picket line] would start to push and they'd get real tight and the cops would get real tight against them and somebody would fall down."[40]

The central lesson employees are sometimes said to have learned in their strike-line confrontations with police is that the law is not neutral, that police are the guardians of established order, and that included in that order are the strikers' opponents, the owners of private enterprise.[41] That this reaction was current among the Colt strikers is attested to by this story from one of the leading female strike activists who was arrested and ordered off the picket lines by a judge even though the charges were dropped:[42]

> I have a personal feeling with the police, because the first day we went out on strike, I was pointed out that I had done something to somebody's van. Then I was harassed by one officer saying, "There's going to be a warrant for your arrest." They did arrest me. It's funny, I wasn't scared, only because that's the first time I've ever been arrested. My main concern was how my kids would react to it, because I've always told them you respect an officer, they're there to help you. I was handcuffed and taken down—it was just like a nightmare. And then being in front of a judge who says I should stay home and tend to my children, that to me is—forget it. . . . I was used as an example so that the police could say, "Here's the first woman to be arrested," to let the other women know this is going to happen to you if you stay on the picket line. Actually what it did was, it made the women more stronger.

Her story and conclusion were not unique. But the strikers' reactions to police were episodal, not uniform. They talked about the differences between the West Hartford and Hartford police (West Hartford was better), between younger and older (older was better), and between police behavior in the first year and later. A few of those I interviewed had no complaints about the police at all. Others saw the police presence as something like a boxing referee—to keep apart combatants who would otherwise be tempted to bring out the brass knuckles. A set of rough and informal "rules" was established as the strike went along. No one could cross a street leading to the plant at any point other than the crosswalk; ten cars in a row would be let out of the parking lot and picketers were then permitted to "make a revolution"—a slow but steady circle impeding the next group of cars; insults were permissible, but not contact. The number of strike-line incidents fell sharply after these patterns were worked out although a degree of tension remained throughout.

But acknowledging the necessity of rules is not the same as admitting that those rules are being applied fairly. Most strikers pointed to some aspect of police performance which bothered them, including overreaction, ignorance of the "rules," arrogance, and an unequal tolerance of violations by strikebreakers. These abuses, along with the Higgins story, appeared in anecdotes throughout the interviews. The consensual view was that the activity of the police benefited the company more than the strikers. The consensual explanation for this was that some officers felt free to violate their proper role of professional neutrality and that it took the public protests of the union leadership and the picketers' insistence on strike-line rule enforcement to move them back toward that role. A striker who had the unusual perspective of having been a policeman during a previous strike at a different company put it particularly clearly:

> I picketed in West Hartford and they were fine. I never had no trouble with the Hartford police, but from what I understand, they weren't the nice guy. I used to be a police officer in the Pratt and Whitney strike. I used to work the picket lines in East Hartford. A policeman's there to maintain law and order, he isn't there to take sides. He's only there if the law is broken. That's all he's there for, no other reason. Some policemen used to be what I would call Pratt and Whitney–orientated. I wasn't that way, and the guys knew it. I used to go down there and the picketers would sweep the nails away, let me park. When people would come in, I'd just ask them [the picketers] to move to the side and they'd move. [Q: I assume your orders were to make sure the nonunion people got in.] Oh yeah, you can't stop a person from going to work. And we didn't at Colt.

This view of the police—described here from the other side of the line—is representative of many strikers. The police were "Colt-orientated" (as the speaker above said that most police were "Pratt and Whitney–orientated"), but by inclination, not function. The criticism centered on perceived lapses of impartiality, not on their structural role.

The strikers' attitudes toward the police were based on interactions with a familiar institution under different and demanding circumstances. Their assessments of the role of the court, however, were largely the product of first exposure. I should more properly say "courts," because by far the more common contact was with the NLRB hearing, not the criminal courts. Despite all the arrests, there was only one significant trial, the acquittal of Wheeler. Virtually all the other charges were dropped.[43] But most people I interviewed had seen the labor board hearing, either as a witness or an observer.[44] The union leadership encouraged members to attend, and the response was so enthusiastic that observers had to be rotated so that everyone had a chance to see some of them. The setting was more complex than a criminal proceeding, with no clear plaintiff or defendant. The NLRB had issued charges against both company and union, and the company and union lawyers alternated roles as prosecutor and defense. It was partly for this reason that my question about "the courts" did not conjure up images of a participant in the conflict, and certainly not of an opponent. The framework in which strikers saw the contest taking place in the hearing was company and union slugging it out on a relatively equal playing field rather than courts and law unfairly stacked against strikers.

That does not mean the strikers were completely happy about that contest. One line of both attack and defense that the company pursued was to try to establish employee misconduct, during the in-plant strike and both on and away from the picket line after the strike began. Those strikers who observed the proceedings spoke with feeling about what they felt was the company's effort to publicly brand them as criminals:

> They were talking about picketing [company president's] house. If you heard the testimony that his wife gave, you wonder, is the judge going to believe all this crap? She was a goddamn good actress. She had it that there was a riot, and here people were walking up and down, singing union songs.

> It was unbelievable. Making up all kinds of fake stories. Houses damaged, cars damaged, swimming pools damaged. It was ridiculous. And when they cross-questioned them, it wasn't true!

Of course some of it *was* true—the administrative law judge upheld half of the NLRB charges alleging striker misconduct. But the anger in these comments is real, not the feigned shock of the police chief in *Casablanca* on discovering gambling at Rick's. The hearing was a public forum, and the strikers felt that both the essential justness of their cause and their character as individuals were being maligned:

> It's like we are criminals. It feels real bad. It feels like you want to get your money and get out, not to go back there no more.

> I was humiliated. Put on public display. How dare they come around and impugn your integrity and make you look like a crook or a bandit. That sticks in my craw.

The courtroom confrontation was not one-sided warfare any more than the in-plant strike had been. Some of the union witnesses did not seem overawed by the proceedings, despite the fact that it was a new experience for all of them but the highest officials. They expressed open contempt for the company's attorney and engaged in what Scott called "profanations" of authority.[45] In plainer English, they mocked the lawyer. In the following instances, the question is from the company's lawyer and the answer is from a striker.

Q: Where were you on February 18, 1986?
A: Where was I?
Q: Yes.
A: On February 18?
Q: Yes.
A: I was here in this world.[46]

Q [*Inquiring about a speaker at a union meeting*]: What did this fellow look like?

A: He had hair, two eyes, something like that.[47]

Q: When did those meetings [to organize picket duty] take place?
A: Jesus, man! Not offhand.[48]

Q: Did you ever get arrested for any misconduct on the picket line?
A: I think it was four times.
Q: Do you remember those times?
A: Not all of them, because they were stupid.
Q: And because they were stupid, you don't remember them?
A: Yes. Of course.[49]

A study of a community of striking British coal miners noted the creation and widespread dissemination of a "folklore," or symbols with shared meanings.[50] Two incidents in the hearings resulted in stories which circulated widely among strikers and became capsule summaries of the felt injustice of the entire situation. The first was a ruling that the notes which the company submitted to the NLRB as an accurate account of negotiating sessions were inaccurate and appeared to have been edited. The second was that the union lawyers forced a company witness to admit he had submitted a bill for two slashed tires when his testimony indicated only one had been damaged.[51] These stories were retold by some people who undoubtedly had not heard them firsthand and were used to undercut the company's claim to honesty and credibility. They varied in the retelling. Enlarged versions included the company secretary breaking down on the stand and admitting she doctored the notes; an epidemic of strikebreakers claiming damage falsely in order to receive compensation from the company; and strikebreakers damaging their own cars for the same purpose. In every case, the symbolic message was that the conduct of the strikers' opponents (both company and strikebreakers) was outrageous and would have gone undetected but for union lawyers who were able to use the legal process to ferret out the truth. But the theme of that message is company subversion of an otherwise fair process.[52]

There were additional reservations expressed about the process itself, although none directed at the specific hearings. One centered on delays. The most prominent delay was in the vital administrative law judge's decision; it became a running joke at union meetings for members to ask whether the judge who heard the case had died. But that was only the most talked-about of many delays. "What is taking so long?" was the first response to my question about courts in several interviews. In singling out delays as an issue, the strikers were actually more perceptive than petulant. An important part of recent management antiunion strategy has involved the strategic use of delay. Companies have greater resources to absorb the effect of delays.[53]

The other criticism leveled at the NLRB was that it (and, some strikers said, the whole court system) was dominated by Republicans, and this threatened to tilt the playing field toward business. These are responses to the question, "Now how about the court system? Does that seem fair?" None of these speakers, I should point out, is a union official, for whom these are familiar matters.

> My impression is that it depends on who's in power. The NLRB in Washington is appointed by the president. That is your court of last resort for a working person. With Reagan there are so many obstacles. It's like a steeplechase.

> What's keeping them so long? It's a political thing. If Bush wins, we lost. That's why we got to vote Democratic, otherwise the unions has had it.

> I have a feeling that the courts at the present time have a tendency to lean toward management. If this [the NLRB case] was ruled against the union, I wouldn't be surprised, not based on fact, but because the courts will listen to what management says more so than what the little guy says.

> What takes them so long? But in the same token, you've got to think back and say, all of these same people who were in office now were in office when Reagan broke the air controllers strike. That's when all of our problem started.

These comments do not seem to indicate that the strikers' confrontation with the legal system produced any blinding revelations. In fact, what is remarkable in these comments is their judiciousness and balance. Strikers viewed the courts as relatively fair, certainly by comparison with other centers of political power. But their exposure to the system did force them to think through what the possible biases were, what had produced them, and how they affected the strikers. Their experience with the courts was not particularly disillusioning, but it was educative. Mechanisms of governance stood out clearly and demanded analysis. Politics which is built on and draws attention to contingency and choice rather than an unchangeable landscape of authority became a more common language. While nothing may seem more commonplace to readers saturated in the mechanisms of government, that represents a considerable change for most people:

> Q: What about the courts? Do you think they're fair?
> STRIKER: Everything's great, but how the hell long does it take?
> SPOUSE: It seems ridiculous. You know, I think when this is over, I'm going to go back and read about labor law. It seems insane.
> STRIKER: When the Democrats were in, the NLRB didn't take as long.
> SPOUSE: I agree. I don't like the makeup of the NLRB. I don't think it should be appointed by one particular individual.

The striker was not a union official, and the spouse was not a striker. It is not a great reach to see in these comments echoes of the freedmen Foner describes as keeping careful track of discussions in the Virginia legislature.

STRONG DEMOCRATS

The Connecticut State Legislature passed a resolution on Jan. 28, 1987, calling on the company "to immediately resume bargaining with the Union in good faith" and urging the state congressional delegation to demand that there be no new defense contracts for Colt until negotiations began.[54] A group of strikers spent all day at the Capitol lobbying for the resolution. The group included some union officials, but others for whom this was their first contact with politicians. It also included some strikers who barely spoke English. Barbara Johnson gave this account of that day:

> There were fifty or sixty strikers there. We literally did training in the lobby of the capitol. When they got a commitment, they gave their legislator a yellow ribbon. It made a remarkable statement on the floor, when you looked down and saw a sea of yellow ribbons. It was moving even for people like myself who are politically very involved, but for people—most of these people had never been inside the capitol before—it was just a tremendously moving experience. Because they were a little naive and didn't know you weren't allowed to applaud from the balcony, they stood up and gave a standing ovation when they passed the resolution.[55]

If the descriptions of normal citizen-government interactions detailed earlier in the chapter are at all accurate, then the energy and excitement apparent in this process stand in sharp contrast. The figures in table 4.1 suggest that there was an overall increase in participation of this kind during the strike.

There was both a large decrease in those who never contacted a governmental official and a small increase in those who wrote or spoke to an official many times. Of course, people were being asked to rely on their memory in order to answer the second question, and memories can deceive. In addition, the order of the questions probably suggested to some strikers that I was interested in seeing whether they had been in contact with their representatives more since the beginning of the strike, and they may have been inclined to indicate that they had. In other words, the differences may have been less a hard fact than a story the strikers wanted to communicate. To the extent that either of these biases exist, it actually makes my case more strongly than the figures themselves do. In the course of the strike, it became more acceptable and desirable to seek out public officials. If people saw a story of increased interaction with government as an important one to tell, that is as informative an oc-

*Table 4.1  Political Participation*

---

*During the strike* have you ever written to or spoken to a governmental official such as state representative or congressman? (*N* = 125)

| Never (%) | Once or twice (%) | Many times (%) |
|---|---|---|
| 59.2 | 34.4 | 6.4 |

*Before the strike* did you ever write to or speak to a governmental official? (*N* = 126)

| | | |
|---|---|---|
| 82.5 | 14.4 | 3.2 |

---

*Notes:* emphases in original questionnaire.
These are the questions on which there was the greatest difference between the activists and nonactivists. Here are the figures for the activists:

During the strike

| Never (%) | Once or twice (%) | Many times (%) |
|---|---|---|
| 42.1 | 36.8 | 21.1 |

Before the strike

| | | |
|---|---|---|
| 50.9 | 31.6 | 17.5 |

The difference is probably due to the fact that the "activist" sample is composed of members of the Community-Labor Alliance, which included union leadership. They are much more inclined to contact public officials, both because it is part of their job and because they are more accustomed to doing that. As a tangential but important point, it confirms the fact that subtracting the activist sample actually does correct a small bias.

currence as a conclusion based on having a more precise "before" number would be.

Although there was no space to ask people to elaborate on the nature of the contacts, the interviews suggested what common sense dictates, that nearly all contacts were on strike-related matters. But that does not trivialize the increase in participation. There had always been the potential for interest-group activity on union goals, or, for that matter, other issues of concern to individuals. The existence of hardship alone does not usually lead to an increase in political activity. Political scientists studying the common sense assumption that citizens facing common social problems would turn to the political arena for solutions have found little evidence that this actually happens.[56] The special circumstances of this conflict activated people, not interest-group politics as usual.

I had little doubt that strikers had also become more critical of Republicans, and standard measures of political attitudes demonstrate that. It is not unusual for union members to dislike Republicans and vote Democratic, but the comparisons strongly suggest that the strike had a very pronounced effect on these political evaluations. The figures in table 4.2 may overstate the differences somewhat, for reasons explained in Appendix E, but the differences between the strikers and other Connecticut union members remain ineradicably huge.

There are two themes in this table—the homogeneity of the strikers' evaluations and the anti-Republican direction that they take. The hostility to Reagan was overwhelming. Ten people—more than rated his performance positively—ad-libbed "worse than poor" or some variant of that on the questionnaire. The criticisms of Reagan were both specific to the strike—he created it by firing the air traffic controllers—and more generally linked to a perceived domination of government and law by corporations. In fact, Reagan and Bush became the repository for everything the strikers saw as unequal and unfair, including, for instance, the widely repeated though inaccurate story that Reagan changed the laws to make the permanent replacement of strikers possible.[57] Although the union had supported Dukakis for the Democratic nomination, there was very little enthusiasm for him as a candidate. The most important qualification that he had was that he was not Reagan or Bush. There was a hard edge of class hostility in people's evaluations of Republicans which

*Table 4.2  Political Assessments*

|  | Colt strikers (%) | Other Connecticut union members[*] (%) |
|---|---|---|
| If you voted in the 1988 presidential election, who did you vote for? ($N = 113$) | | |
| Dukakis | 92.9 | 55 |
| Bush | 7.1 | 45 |
| On the whole, how would you rate Ronald Reagan as a president? ($N = 122$) | | |
| Poor | 71.1 | 20 |
| Only fair | 24.8 | 34 |
| Good | 4.1 | 33 |
| Very good | — | 13[**] |

[*] Figures for other Connecticut union members in rounded percentages compiled by the Institute for Social Inquiry, University of Connecticut, $N = 106$.
[**] Taken from final rating poll; highest rating reads "excellent."

went well beyond partisan identification with Democrats and even spilled over into personal desperation:

> Nobody cares about the average man. The Republicans have done it. It makes me laugh to hear him on TV, Bush. The country is going to hell, in plain English. It really stinks to have to say, if we get this guy [Dukakis] in, is he going to help us? It shouldn't be like that. But it is.

> I tell you right now, if Bush gets in, I'm going to Canada. Does that tell you something?

### INFORMED DISAFFECTION

*A lot of these people saw politics as "once a year Barbara Kennelly comes through the plant and shakes hands." For many of the workers, it is not an uncommon reaction that the political person is seen as a person who is famous and removed from them, and it's a very special event. I don't think they look at elected officials as sacrosanct anymore. They've become somewhat more cynical, but more realistic and they don't see their elected officials as being held in some kind of special light that can't be penetrated.*
—Barbara Johnson, interview with author

Johnson's overview coincides with the figures and interpretations in this chapter. To most American citizens, politics is a murky business, one regarded as vaguely distasteful.[58] The strikers saw it through the lens of the conflict which had reordered their world. The task of identifying friends and enemies and acting on that information became an immediate one. At times, the strikers took on tasks which are normally left to leaders—writing to congresspeople and lobbying. Anti-Republican sentiment became invested with images of class which are usually present only in diluted form among blue-collar workers. Such normal cross-pressures as race, religion, and ethnicity diminished, and a workforce otherwise consistent with the Reagan Democrat profile instead uniformly defined the Republicans as the party of the rich—and was cautious in its assessments of Democrats. Said one, "Governor O'Neill, he's done nothing. I always voted for the Democrat, but I don't know if I'm losing faith in politics. That's what the strike has done to me. I wrote a letter to [a TV news personality] about the whole thing."

But while the strikers became more aware of how to press demands on the machinery of government, that knowledge did not work to increase allegiance. Their experience led them to conclude that government and politicians were more responsive to corporate power. While politicians exhibited a range of attitudes toward the strike, most of those who could help did not, and most of those who tried to help could not. From a striker fired during the "in-plant" strike:

> Q: Should elected officials get involved in the strike?
> A: I wrote to all my Congressmen and Senators on this situation.
> Q: What did you tell them?
> A: About my firing situation and what was going on inside there. This was on my own. The union didn't know about it.
> Q: And what happened?
> A: Only Weicker wrote back. They don't care.

While strikers gave credit to various congresspeople who seemed to be concerned, they also generalized that what politicians gave them most often was lip service. Only Hartford Mayor Perry was exempt from this judgment. Some of the strikers combined political activism and disaffection in roughly equal proportions. This is also from (a different) employee fired in the in-plant strike, a former steward: "Look, you're talking to someone who used to drive voters to the polls. Politicians can't say, 'Do this.' But if they make the attempt, people would respond to them. Politicians are—the best way I can put it is, I've met union people, like Phil [Wheeler], who to me are smarter and more articulate and to me, they should be representatives. During a strike like this, you lose faith in things."

But there is no real inconsistency here. The strikers became at the same time more active, more informed, and more critical. The distance between these striking citizens and government was reduced, but familiarity bred, if not contempt, then at least a large dose of skepticism. The last speaker went on to describe his perception of the biases of the political system and the necessity and difficulty of combating them.

> Our strike—the reason why it's so long—it's tied in with the laws in the country. You have to be politically active. We used to have guys at union meetings who'd say, "Let's not get involved in politics." They didn't understand it. Even a good contract, the powers that be can negate the whole thing. . . .
> How many politicians would really be willing to take on big business? Even those who so-called do vote for labor, how many really, bottom line—it's power. It takes thousands of people banding together to take on one corporation.

As Johnson indicated earlier, this is politics without awe. Strikers became fuller citizens, people who understand that there is a link between what government does and the quality of their lives.[59] Alienation may stem from a vague distrust of poorly understood processes or from involvement which fails to achieve ends seen as just. In the case of the Colt strikers, it appears to be the latter.

This chapter has been built around the argument that the world of governance clicked into sharper focus for the strikers and that this represented a sharp departure from normal-time politics. Although increased use of the political system and increased support for the Democratic Party are logically related to strike goals, they are certainly not closely tied—and the point of the brief summary at the beginning of the chapter is that people often miss the logic. Strikers learned to appreciate more the relevance of the public sphere but also found it wanting in important ways. The vision of fairness against which they weighed the actions and statements of public officials was strike derived but not linked only to immediate strike issues. The political geography was redrawn.

But one could draw exactly the opposite conclusion from the evidence. Since the conflict drew these people more directly into the political orbit, and since it seems to have increased their allegiance to one of the two major parties, perhaps the strikers have been roped in more closely to American core values, or what some have called the dominant ideology.[60] Benjamin Ginsberg makes this (general) argument: participation and increased communication actually decrease citizen ability to penetrate ideologies favorable to dominant classes by reducing the likelihood of class-based opposition.[61] Has the increased attention to government and elections tamed the strikers by channeling them into prepackaged avenues for dissent or "civilized" them by narrowing their range of opinion?[62] The answer requires a look at how the strikers assessed American core values, and whether the strike experience created any substantial challenge to those values.

# 5

## Horatio Alger to Robin Hood

*They speculated about the end of the world and the coming of the millennium; about the justice of God in condemning the mass of mankind to eternal torment for a sin which (if anyone) Adam committed; some of them became skeptical of the existence of hell. They contemplated the possibility that God might intend to save everybody, that something of God might be within each of us. They founded new sects to express these new ideas. Some considered the possibility that there might be no Creator God, only nature. They attacked the monopolization of knowledge within the privileged professions, divinity, law, medicine. They criticized the existing educational structure, especially the universities, and proposed a vast expansion of educational opportunity. They discussed the relation of the sexes, and questioned parts of the protestant ethic. The eloquence, the power of the simple artisans who took part in those discussions is staggering.*
—Christopher Hill, *The World Turned Upside Down*

*I have been so impressed with these people. I've gone to a lot of functions, a lot of the demonstrations, taken the trip to New York with them, gone to the parties. These are a*

*dynamite bunch of people. . . . I figured my husband was kind of an exceptional guy—I
know he's pretty sharp—and I wondered why he was in the shop. I've heard some of
the rest of them speak at meetings—these people are downright eloquent.*
—Spouse of a Colt striker

These past two chapters have essentially been about political temperature.
The specific judgments the strikers made in broadening their definitions of
interest and recasting the electoral arena into a class battlefield are not unheard of—unusual, but not unheard of. What is more striking is the vehe-
mence, passion, and unanimity with which these views are expressed. That
temperature was apparent to even a casual observer, and was what led me initially toward seeing this conflict as a transformative experience. The "naturalization" argument suggests that many aspects of American society should look
different to the strikers. If, as that argument goes, stable institutions and daily
routine tend to dull critical facilities and narrow choices to match a narrow set
of "realistic" alternatives, then this most unsettling experience should kick up
some political dust in an observable way.

A historian who saw transformative elements in the heated strikes he studied generalized about such moments this way:

> History has demonstrated a persistent if uneven tendency on the part of working
> people toward the formation of ideas, institutions, and values that have transcended
> time periods and national boundaries and have reflected a striving toward a collec-
> tive affirmation of self. At some moments, this tendency has resulted in an inwardly
> focused, politically passive subculture. In other circumstances, it has led to an ex-
> pansive consciousness, based on a lively sense of class relations and class struggle,
> and seeking to create a more just social order.[1]

Is there any evidence of this "expansive consciousness" among Colt strikers
on issues not immediately related to the strike? Was the conflict accompanied
by a free-wheeling rediscussion of basic principles as Hill describes in the
chapter epigraph? I believe so, and will explain why in the rest of the chapter,
but there is a prior task. There is no good way of judging whether any particular set of beliefs or range of questions is "expansive." The same size box of laun-
dry soap can be regular or king-size. But it is possible to determine what is expanded. What that requires is a baseline—a description of conventional
wisdom and specific patterns of belief on comparable questions asked of others. Then it will be easier to evaluate whether the strike has placed new questions in front of people and whether their answers are regular or king-size.

DOMINANT IDEOLOGY, AMERICAN-FRIED

There are two separable (although not unrelated) allegations which fall under the umbrella of "dominant ideology." In one formulation, a dominant ideology is something like a trick played on everyone else by a dominant class. Since relying completely on force would be impractical, this class promotes a political discourse which explains its own privileged positions as being to everyone's advantage, or, at the very least, unavoidable. The take-off point for these claims is this well-traveled excerpt from Marx in *The German Ideology:* "The ideas of the ruling class are in every epoch the ruling ideas: i.e., the class which is the ruling material force of society, is at the same time its ruling intellectual force. . . . The ruling ideas are nothing more than the ideal expression of the dominant material relationships, the dominant material relationships grasped as ideas; hence of the relationships which make the one class the ruling one, therefore the ideas of its dominance."[2]

A dominant ideology exists here as the product of a relation between classes, as something one class (or dominant group) does to another. It benefits the most privileged, and is intended to do so. The other landmark contributor to that theme is Antonio Gramsci, in whose analysis popular political ideas played a heavy role in the cohesion of class-divided societies. Gramsci's insightful addition to Marx's notion of "ruling ideas" is that a dominant ideology, in order to play its role, must extend promises to subordinate classes and actually deliver on some of them. But the central function of a dominant ideology is still that it "produces a condition of moral and political passivity" on the part of the less privileged.[3]

Some critics of these formulations have pointed out that it is not always clear what constellation of ideas constitutes the suspected dominant ideology.[4] There must be some observable way[5] in which people fit together facts and values to legitimate dominant institutions and political processes. The other rendition of "dominant ideology," found in literature on American public opinion, helps fill in those blanks. In this case, the meaning is approximately, "What Americans generally believe about the fairness of their political-economic system," particularly its underlying (legitimating) principles. Survey-based answers to that question have cross-fertilized the Gramsci-derived version, although the two usages are largely distinct. It has long been a contention of those who study American political culture that there is widespread agreement among people here about fundamental political principles.[6] Survey research has been able to substantiate that claim and make it more specific. While American politics is full of distrust, almost none of it comes from or results in criticism of the fundamentals of the political order and in fact is much more likely to result from the belief that underlying principles are being corrupted.[7] The system is good; only people make it bad. Public opinion analysts have found a dominant American ideology composed of these elements: belief in the wide availability of opportunity, individualist explanations for success and failure, and acceptance of the fairness of unequal distribution of rewards.[8] One writer summarized that package of shared beliefs this way: "Each individual is responsible for his or her own fate in a perpetual competition for rewards against others in society, . . . success in competition for rewards is justly arrived at through the marketplace, and those who succeed owe nothing to those who fail in this competition, especially through the intervention of government."[9]

Further, there is not even a great deal of variation along the socioeconomic spectrum; the least privileged are only slightly more likely than the most privileged to challenge this description of American society. A survey of the unemployed reached this conclusion: "The Horatio Alger ethic is not a middle-class ideology rejected by lower socio-economic groups."[10]

A graphic example of the strength with which people hold to these core values, and one particularly useful for contrast with Colt, comes from a study of the employee-owned plywood cooperatives in the Northwest. The cooperatives are democratically run enterprises, some of which have survived profitably for as many as sixty years. All decisions can be reviewed at a twice-yearly general membership meeting in which each worker-shareholder is permitted one vote. Has this unconventional work environment produced any significant challenge to the dominant ideology?

Despite the highly egalitarian internal organization of the cooperatives—including, for instance, a strong commitment to equal wages—those workers are as supportive of the dominant ideology as employees in conventional firms. In fact, on matters like the general applicability of the principle of equal wages and the right of the public, through government, to intervene in the economy, co-op workers are *more* inclined toward market-oriented "classical liberal" positions. The author's conclusion is that the market is "a more powerful educative tool than the cooperative experience itself."[11]

So Americans of all classes reject proposals for major economic redistribution, applaud the degree of opportunity available, and believe deeply that people create and deserve their own fates. They do so in an "American unison that breathes through every pore of the culture," as one author put it, taking only slight poetic license to characterize support for the dominant ideology.[12] In the last chapter, I pointed to studies showing that Americans typically divide the economic and political spheres rigorously and that they apply different principles of justice to the separate spheres. That can be taken one step further: the public generally prefers the allocations made by the market because of its flexibility and the directness of its rewards.

The link between market and justice underwent a severe test in the conflict at Colt. The ambivalences were illustrated well by the son of a strike activist, in business school during much of the strike. "It's been a tough conflict. It's been a battle of emotions not only between he and I, but between myself—within myself personally. Whereas I've got one side saying maybe this is the way businesses really should be run—they should be run cutthroat—and seeing what a cutthroat business can do to a family by being in a family that's been part of a business that's been run like that. It's caused an awful lot of internal strife within myself."[13]

Looking at the way in which Colt strikers thought about and attempted to resolve these issues, then, provides an opportunity to see whether the conflict has reopened some old and settled questions.

STRIKERS REASSESS

In this section, I have to rely almost exclusively on strikers' answers to the written questionnaire. I did not systematically ask questions in the open-ended interviews about justice in American society. But a fairly consistent picture emerges from the survey: compared with the broader population and even with other blue-collar workers, the strikers were less convinced that the country's political and economic processes were fair, less inclined to see wide opportunity, and more inclined to support economic redistribution.[14]

The greatest difference between the strikers' views and those expressed in other surveys is in the least surprising area—economic redistribution. Redistribution contains several elements which conflict with the individualism of American culture.[15] In principle, economic inequality is just—people should be rewarded differently for different contributions. The existence of a ladder of success is enticing to those who aspire to be unequally wealthy and who are willing, toward that end, to run the risk of being unequally poor.[16] While there is some public sympathy for giving to the poor (except when the question uses the word *welfare*), there is almost none for robbing from the rich. That is true even in cases where respondents felt that the rich attained their wealth unfairly.[17] Part of the explanation is that the vehicle for redistribution is King John, not Robin Hood: "Taking from the rich" implies government intervention in the market, and while people may not always be satisfied with the fairness of market distributions, they are even less satisfied with government's ability to produce fair outcomes.[18] The result of this interweaving of belief and principle is that there is little demand for extensive redistribution of wealth even on the part of those who would presumably benefit.

Table 5.1 presents the responses of strikers to the two questions I included about equalizing wealth and/or income. Regular or king-size? Some comparative information will help. The first question was taken from the Schlozman-Verba study of unemployment. Their published set of responses included only "agree" and "disagree." Of their survey as a whole, only 47 percent agreed that the rich should be taxed heavily.[19] There was not a great deal more support for that idea among blue-collar workers—51 percent agreed.[20] The strikers were much more sympathetic to redistribution. The combined total of those who chose one of the two positive responses is 75 percent, and the ratio of those who "strongly agreed" to those who "strongly disagreed" is about seven to one.

The second question does not appear on the surface to support the claim that the strikers were more likely to advocate economic equality. Only 41 percent agreed that there should be a top limit on incomes, and less than half as many "strongly agreed" as did on the question of taxing the rich. But other polls show Americans to be extremely resistant to leveling wealth by limiting it at the top, perhaps because income is seen as more deserved than other forms of wealth. The Colt strikers are less resistant. In this case, there is no question with the same wording for direct comparison, but there are several which are close enough to establish a tendency. In one survey, people were asked for responses to the statement, "There should be an upper limit on the amount of money any person can make." Only 21 percent chose either "agree" or "strongly agree" (only 3 percent strongly agreed).[21] A question in another survey was "Should there be a top limit on incomes so that no one can earn more than $100,000 a year?" Seventy-nine percent of the respondents rejected the top limit, including 83 percent in the $15,000–$24,999 income group, which would have contained almost all the Colt employees at the time that survey

*Table 5.1  Redistribution*

Circle your feeling about this statement: The government should tax the rich heavily in order to redistribute wealth.

|  | Strongly disagree (%) | Disagree (%) | Agree (%) | Strongly agree (%) |
|---|---|---|---|---|
| Strikers (N = 108) | 4.6 | 20.4 | 43.5 | 31.5 |
| Activists° (N = 49) | 4.1 | 10.2 | 32.7 | 53.1 |

Circle your feeling about this statement: There should be a top limit on income so that no one can earn more than $200,000 a year.

|  | Strongly disagree (%) | Disagree (%) | Agree (%) | Strongly agree (%) |
|---|---|---|---|---|
| Strikers (N = 103) | 16.5 | 42.7 | 26.2 | 14.6 |
| Activists° (N = 49) | 26.5 | 40.8 | 18.4 | 14.3 |

°Strikers who attended Community-Labor Alliance meetings; see Appendix D.

was taken.[22] The strikers were at least a little more likely to entertain reservations about unlimited accumulation.

There is a great deal we cannot know about the strikers' attitudes toward redistribution from these two questions alone, but space on the survey form did not permit more. What would have been especially interesting would have been questions that could have helped explained why the strikers thought as they did. That is not immediately obvious from their answers alone. They might have become more favorably inclined toward equality as a principle, more favorably inclined toward government (the role of which is explicit in one question and implicit in the other), or less favorably inclined toward "the rich." Probably all three contributed; for instance, Chapter 3 indicates some increased support for equality as a principle, and Chapter 4 indicates that the strikers had more use for government and less use for the wealthy than others do. But it is at least safe to say that the two questions show a movement on the part of the strikers toward positive evaluations of economic equality.

LAND OF OPPORTUNITY?

One of the reasons that Americans are not receptive to far-reaching plans for the redistribution of wealth is that they believe that the means by which wealth is currently distributed are fair. People are rewarded according to their input, and that input is the combined product of ability and effort. Both of these traits vary by individual; thus, people get their just deserts. But in order to justify existing rewards, one more element is needed—the wide availability of opportunity. Without that, rewards would be a product of luck at best, and structural factors such as family background at worst. James Kluegel and Eliot Smith found in *Beliefs About Inequality* that, "A clear majority of the American population subscribes, largely unreservedly, to the characterization of America as 'the land of opportunity.'"[23] As table 5.2 shows, the Colt strikers had many more reservations.

What stands out immediately in the responses to the first question is the large number of strikers who felt that there was little chance for advancement. It is the response chosen least in the general population but most by strikers. Fifty-nine percent of the strikers gave one of the two negative assessments about the existence of opportunity, while only 37 percent of the Kluegel and Smith sample did so. The second question, on essentially the same topic, is harder for people to answer negatively; by the inclusion of "America" and the phrase "the land of opportunity"—which many people have recited by rote since kindergarten—the question demands a greater repudiation of valued

*Table 5.2  Opportunity*

How good a chance do you think a person has to get ahead today, if the person works hard?

|  | Little chance (%) | Some chance (%) | Good chance (%) | Very good chance (%) |
|---|---|---|---|---|
| Others* | 11 | 26 | 38 | 25 |
| Strikers (N = 118) | 30.5 | 28.8 | 19.5 | 21.2 |
| Activists** (N = 52) | 26.9 | 30.8 | 21.2 | 21.2 |

Circle your feeling about this statement: America is the land of opportunity where everyone who works hard can get ahead.

|  | Strongly disagree (%) | Disagree (%) | Agree (%) | Strongly agree (%) |
|---|---|---|---|---|
| Others* | 4 | 27 | 56 | 14 |
| Strikers (N = 111) | 9 | 36.9 | 35.1 | 18.9 |
| Activists** (N = 53) | 24.5 | 28.3 | 24.5 | 22.6 |

How much chance does the child of a factory worker have to become a business executive or a professional?

|  | No chance at all (%) | Slight chance (%) | Some chance (%) | Good chance (%) |
|---|---|---|---|---|
| Others*** | 4 | 25 | 30 | 41 |
| Strikers (N = 105) | 15.2 | 39 | 32.4 | 13.3 |
| Activists** (N = 52) | 17.3 | 28.8 | 25 | 28.8 |

*Kluegel and Smith, *Beliefs,* p. 44. They also offered a "no chance at all" category; I combined that with "little chance."

**Strikers who attended Community-Labor Alliance meetings; see Appendix D.

***Schlozman and Verba, *Injury,* p. 107

symbols if one of the negative responses is to be chosen. Predictably, the degree of opportunity is portrayed more favorably in both sets of responses to this question, but the pattern is about the same. There is one anomaly—the slightly higher number of strikers who strongly agreed that there was wide opportunity. Other than that, the strikers were more likely to disagree, both strongly (although both numbers are small) and mildly. The strikers' total negative evaluation was 46 percent, compared with 31 percent in the Kluegel and Smith sample. It would seem that the strikers are a great deal more skeptical about the availability of opportunity; it seems logical to assume that the conflict played some role in fostering these doubts.

The third question in the table places opportunity in the context of class structure and reveals even sharper differences. Seventy-one percent of the respondents in the Schlozman and Verba sample chose one of the two positive answers, while 54 percent of the strikers chose one of the two negative answers. The most striking single response comparison in this question is the "good chance" answer. The most frequent (by a large margin) in the Schlozman and Verba sample, it was the least frequent among the strikers, chosen less than the extreme negative response, "none at all." The fact that Schlozman and Verba did not limit their sample to blue-collar workers is not decisive; they divided it by occupational level, and in the category in which it appears the strikers would have been included, 62 percent chose one of the two positive answers.[24] And if age is taken into account, 70 percent of those in the sample who most closely resemble the Colt strikers felt that the child of a factory worker had either some chance or a good chance of becoming a professional.[25]

It would be shortsighted to overlook the second story contained in table 5.2. On the one hand, strikers have become comparative doubters of the Horatio Alger scenario. On the other, the absolute distribution of opinion is not one-sidedly negative. On the first question, the categories chosen are roughly even. On the other two, the answers fall along a fairly symmetrical bell curve. This confirms the point that Schlozman and Verba emphasize—that economic strain does not lead automatically or directly to a repudiation of the American Dream, and it illustrates the tenacity of the dominant ideology in the face of tremendous personal hardship. It does not trump the story of change, however. That is as real as the remaining ambivalence. By demonstrating the staying power of the dominant ideology, the strikers' responses show its enveloping character; by challenging important parts of it, they suggest that this conflict produced abnormally severe shock waves, capable of reaching into a set of long-standing and virtually unquestioned beliefs about the fairness of American society.

Another interesting twist in these responses about opportunity and inequality is that there is a different relation between the views of the activists and the nonactivists than on other questions. As summarized in Appendix D, the typical relation shows very little difference, with activists slightly to the "left" on some questions. On the questions in this section, however, that pattern does not hold, which is why the activists' responses are included in tables 5.1 and 5.2. The activists' answers are more emphatic than those of the nonactivists, grouping toward the "strongly" categories and away from the center. On the "land of opportunity" question in table 5.2, 47 percent of the activists took one of the two polar positions, as opposed to only 28 percent of the nonactivists; on the "child of a factory worker" question, it was 46 to 29. Many more activists than nonactivists strongly favored taxing the rich—the most "left" of the alternatives—while many more activists strongly *disagreed* that incomes should be limited—the most "right" position. The small number of questions does not permit drawing any profound conclusions, but it does suggest two points. First, those strikers who gravitated toward the Community-Labor Alliance tended to have strong opinions on these general questions, whatever the direction of those opinions. They were more decisive, although not always more decisively critical. The other lesson from the activist sample is the relative disconnection of these ideological dispositions from the degree of involvement in the strike. The conflict as a whole is, I have argued, the reason for the more critical attitude toward the dominant ideology that these answers reveal. Increased involvement in strike activity was not accompanied by a neatly predictable increase in critical views.

The survey questions I have drawn from in this chapter center on the fairness of the class and reward structure in American society. It seems to be undeniable that the strikers have done some rethinking of basic principles on these questions. But it could still be argued that this is a relatively unimportant finding and does not constitute convincing evidence that this was a period of reexamining entrenched beliefs. Since strikes by their nature pit those with fewer resources against those with more, this kind of movement around such related issues as opportunity and redistribution might be expected. The strikers acted as those in any interest group would act, particularly a temporarily unsuccessful one, and gave answers predictably intimating that the deck was stacked against them.

That argument rests on the assumption that there is a fairly tight fit between self-interest and political views on somewhat broader questions related to those interests. The assumption is that it does not require much of a leap for people to generalize from a set of immediate concerns to an adjacent set of political questions; in this case, from a demand for a more favorable division of rewards in their particular case to a sense that rewards are not divided equitably in society as a whole. But if in fact the Colt strikers' political attitudes have moved from particular to general in this way, that is news in itself. The assumed role of self-interest as the overwhelmingly determinative, or even (as a lesser claim) the decisive force in political life has been called into question.[26] It is even more misleading to think that there is some normal cognitive process which would lead the strikers to extend the perception of unfairness about their own treatment to a more generalized sense of unfairness about "class" issues. They *do*—that is the point of the chapter. But that is not an ordinary occurrence.

A number of recent studies of self-interest have shown it to have very little impact on broader questions, even on those bearing a family resemblance. The authors of a book about the Proposition 13 property tax revolt in California found that self-interest played only a narrow role. Those who stood to gain measurably from the proposed tax cut did support it in somewhat greater numbers, but there was little increase in opposition from those who would be hurt most by the cuts in government spending, and there was little generalization effect of the kind outlined above on the part of those who had the most to gain. The measure "failed to produce the other political effects in the California mass publics that might have been expected from it: it did not produce broadly rationalizing attitudes toward government in general, or self-interested activism, or strong anti-government sentiments."[27]

The strikers restructured their vision of American society around themes of privilege and exclusion. It is tempting to see the principal news as a movement to the "left" (relatively speaking) in political attitudes. But that may be the lesser of two stories. To organize events and information around personal (or group) hardship is first to *organize* political perceptions at all. The strikers extended the lessons they drew from their shared personal experience and systematized a view of American society based on those lessons. Some analysts of public opinion, borrowing from cognitive behavioral psychology, have called such a systematization a "schema." One of the early proponents of cognitive therapy defined it as "a [cognitive] structure for screening, coding, and evaluating the stimuli that impinge on the organism."[28] People have to adopt cost-cutting devices to process political information. Schema theory suggests that this is done not on an ad hoc basis but through the maintenance of core evaluations which are retrieved to serve as a filter for new information. The push is cognitive efficiency; the pull is coherence over a range of related questions.[29] Self-interest ordinarily plays little role in the construction of schemas. Blue-collar workers, for instance, always have a degree of group identity based on some of the shared characteristics of factory work and roughly equivalent social and economic status. But under ordinary circumstances, that shared identity, as with other elements of socioeconomic status, has a very narrow reach. Self-interest plays a limited role which is "quite specific to the policies most narrowly linked to the self-interest dimension in question. The effects of self-interest usually extend neither to other related policy issues nor to more general policy or ideological questions."[30]

Various cross-pressures, competing predispositions, and the normal dose of disorganized and inattentive thinking usually limit the potential extension of immediate experience—here, prestrike work-related issues—into a broader belief system. The strike experience traveled further and became more central in evaluating other political questions.

If this portrayal of the relation between self-interest and schematic think-ing is accurate, then the Colt strike is indeed a special case. The strikers did what most Americans do not do—restructured their thinking about "related policy issues" and "ideological questions" around the lessons (as they per-ceived them) of the strike. American society looked different to them than it had before. They perceived exclusion as a group, and this became the impetus to reconstruct the political system and the market as more closed and less kind to those with a similar lack of resources than they had previously believed. Schematization can be understood in shorthand as a lens which people use to look out at the world; incoming information is refracted through previous ex-perience and core evaluations. The strikers put aside their Horatio Alger–col-ored eyeglasses and tried on a Eugene Debs–tinged model.

## ONLY IN AMERICA

In a previous book about factory life, I asked employees what changes they would make in industrial relations if they were given the authority. The nature of the changes they considered seemed to be very limited. Some were highly specific—better parking, more flexibility in job classifications; others were vague—"I'd communicate better." The most far-reaching proposals were for more consultative management. While that particular factory setting may have been unusually benign (only two brief strikes in its history, none in the twenty years before the interviews), the conclusion that workers do not pro-pose extensive changes even when invited to do so appears to be a general one. When blue-collar workers in one study were asked to imagine what "perfectly just and fair" pay differentials for blue- and white-collar employees would be, they offered only "relatively minor variations within familiar parameters."[31]

This unwillingness to propose major changes is not confined to blue-collar workers. It may be another symptom of the narrow American value consen-sus.[32] An author who studied this possibility found that even among those he called "the disaffected"—those severely critical of existing politics—there was little preference expressed for any alternative, nor even any desire to talk about one. He found (within that group) distrust, protest, embitterment, and denunciation of the government on virtually every count, but also a peculiar reluctance to consider any basic change, or to look elsewhere for different principles or methods of governing.[33]

The Colt strikers did not redefine heaven and hell in the manner Christo-pher Hill suggests in the chapter epigraph. It was a smallish strike, not a social convulsion. But they did seem to broaden the range of acceptable ideas beyond the pinched spectrum which is typical of most political thinking in this country, and that resulted in some imaginative rethinking about fundamentals. The raw materials for the construction of alternatives were certainly there. Apart from the simple anger at perceived mistreatment—which seems not, in general, to produce much system-searching—there was exposure to new sources of information. Workers from other publicized strikes, like Hormel and International Paper in Jay, Maine, walked the Colt picket lines; a member of the British Transport Workers union visited the strike; such outside activists as Barbara Johnson and other CLA members were in constant contact with the strikers; reporters, documentary makers, and inquiring political scientists were often in attendance at meetings. All of this is fairly standard "labor solidarity" stuff and is not highly unusual in its strategic dimension of providing practical and moral support for the strikers, but it was an unusual exposure to new ideas for the rank-and-file strikers.

One contribution to the strikers' reeducation was their increased free time and the amount of it they spent with each other; the strike-generated reevaluations of American society were the product of hours of collective schmoozing.[34] The alternatives strikers proposed were not blueprinted counterideologies. There were no committed socialists, for instance, although as we shall see, some strikers gravitated toward European or Scandinavian social democratic themes. But that makes the extent of thinking about alternatives more interesting. They did not come prepackaged. They were the product of strikers dedicated to their cause reflecting on how things might be organized more fairly.

In most of the open-ended interviews, I inquired about alternatives that strikers considered by asking some variant of this question: "If someone gave you the power to change one thing for the better for working people in this country—anything at all, from the biggest to the smallest, but only one thing—what would that be?" What follows is a division of the entire set of replies into definable categories.

There were a variety of individual, hard-to-categorize answers, ranging from "I'd change management" to "The president. Shoot him." Two subsets gave thematically coherent responses that might not qualify as alternatives. The first was a group which answered, "ban cheap labor," by which they meant restricting immigration. A substantial number of the replacement workers were Asian. The strikers were not always reticent about pointing this out, particularly on the picket line itself. Some resentment toward those who "hadn't paid their dues" took a racial form. Bonds of solidarity can be exclusive as well as inclusive; Scott points out that the mutualism of the powerless may not always be a pretty sight.[35] A striking couple—both activists—touched on the racial issue unprompted with remarkable candor and insight:

HUSBAND: New people coming into the country, that's the problem. Whole families of them are scabs, ten or twelve sleeping in one apartment. Don't these people have quotas?

WIFE: We're a little more bitter than prejudiced. They're flashing their hundred dollar bills in front of us when we're picketing, beeping their horns. It can turn to hatred.

There were also a number of people who jumped quickly to a practical and highly relevant legal reform—a change in the law which permitted companies to hire "permanent replacements" during strikes. Actually, rank-and-file strikers who brought this up did not make the distinction between permanent and temporary replacements that the UAW leadership has in promoting legislation to nullify the MacKay decision. While advocating this kind of legislation is a demand for a significant change, given the importance of MacKay in American labor relations, it is probably too closely related to strikers' particular interests to justify calling it a genuine alternative.[36]

Three other sets of responses do warrant being called alternatives. Some strikers wanted to change the power of corporate ownership. Others were explicit about their dislike of the connection between wealth, authority, and power. While they did not propose a game plan for dismantling it, they did single it out for change:

I just wouldn't let corporations run the country like they do. They pay the lawyers so much, the way they pay the politicians. Big money. Root of all evil. You know that. The more money you got, the more power you think you have.

My question is, are these people [Colt management] going to be put in some corporation somewhere in the United States to do the same damn thing all over again? That should be criminal, but it's not. They can do it legally.

These comments are not so much support for specific alternatives as a general populist critique. Several others translated that into a Huey Long–style share-the-wealth appeal:

I know how I feel, I just don't—companies should share instead of corporations making millions and millions of dollars. Those corporations should show more appreciation to the worker. Big corporations, shoving dollar bills in their pocket while the little guy has to make ends meet.

I would want to share with those who produce it. I feel that they're entitled to a certain way of living. I would be willing to take less so that they could benefit by it. Look at Boesky. What's he producing with that wealth? Misery. Are they helping anybody else?

The wording of the questions suggested that respondents think about what could help them in their strike, or what might have made it unnecessary. It is especially instructive, then, that several respondents offered changes which were not specific to the situation of striking. Three of these have a component of labor-management interaction but are not strike-related. They draw from a social framework within which industrial relations are one part:

> That anyone who works for a living, no matter what they do, have enough of a wage to able to support their family. I don't mean with a Cadillac, but at least not to have to worry about a kid going to the emergency room. Why should people have to work and wind up with a living existence worse than welfare?

> I think there should be job security. If you've done a job for two years, I don't think they should just let you go. That's not too much to ask.

> The Supreme Court. They're in there for life. If you got one—which there is— which does not care about the workers, if you don't change that, we're going to be in deep-shit trouble.

Several others left the work site completely to go after other unequally distributed resources.

> I find it heartbreaking when a person like my father who's worked hard all his life gets sick, goes from this hospital to that hospital and dies in Connecticut Valley Hospital [state mental hospital for the poor]. You know why? Because he fucking ran out of money. They took every cent he had. I'd have to have a committee set up, or something to help the old people.

> Health insurance is one of the things. You're covered as long as you're younger and working and I'd like to see everyone, really, have free health care, to protect all of us. Health care is out of reach for most of us.

> You've got to give kids a good reason to be educated. Not just the rich ones, they go into slots for the rich. You've got to give poor people a reason. Education doesn't mean a thing unless you've got an opportunity to apply it. And if you're put into a position where they say, "We don't want your knowledge, we don't want your intelligence, we just want you to do *this* at such and such a time, and then we don't want you anymore," then this is a poor, poor relationship in what is supposed to be a trust-in-God nation. It's really quite a strange attitude.

These statements still contain more distress than plan, though they do envision a semipractical rearrangement of power and wealth. But could any of the strikers actually bring themselves to say that a specific different arrangement, somewhere else, was better? The author of a study of loyalty and dissent talked about the astonishingly strong comparative pride of even the most alienated Americans: "And rereading the depth interviews, in which we did our best to encourage or prod respondents to tell us how they actually felt, I am struck again by the extent to which the idea of America envelops Americans: even among the disaffected who openly call for a change in the system of government there was no intelligible trace of an alternative political vocabulary, of an alternative political order."[37]

In a last subgroup of responses, the strikers named names. The first two were respondents who gave "no replacement workers" as their specific answer, but added a comparative thought about the particularly American character of that proposal:

> Keep the scabs out while you're negotiating a contract. That's the main thing. Make a law in the legislature. In Italy they, Christ, I was there, they put a chain on that building and that was it, not even the owner could go in till you negotiate a contract. That's what we need here in the legislature.

> No scabs allowed. This situation would have never happened if they weren't allowed to hire anybody. And I guess that's what it's about overseas. When everybody strikes, they have to shut down or nothing moves in the country.

Three more strikers looked overseas, but for broader purposes than "anti-scab" legislation:

> You know, I heard that in Europe they have a law where a plant can't just get up and leave. This is not the greatest country, I don't care what they say. There are people out of work, people on the street.

> In Europe, they tend to favor working people more—some people call it socialism, whatever you want to call it. They tell me that over there a plant can't just simply shut the door. In fact they were quite amazed, the people over there, how a plant here can just do what they want to do. American business does possibly have more power than anywhere else.

> Maybe Japan should teach us a little different. If you have profit sharing, then workers will sacrifice. If you try to do what the Vanderbilts and Morgans did, then you got all kinds of trouble.

One lengthy and animated answer from a striker pointed to an alternative which was not overseas, but was perhaps even more out of the ordinary: the employee-owned plywood cooperatives of Oregon.

> What would I do? That's a very—whew! Try to provide a decent living—a better understanding of what people want, if corporations can work with working people

and try to make a change in their plants and let the people make suggestions about how to make better productivity so they can provide a decent living. Because that's what they want, they want to make more money and be productive worldwide. Why don't they ask the working people what they can do to make the corporation a better place to work in? Seems if they're going to spend a majority of their life there, you're going to want to go to the job and be a part of it. You don't want to go there and just punch a clock and just do your job. That's what's wrong—no cooperation or communications. They ought to make public what the company's doing, like the employee-owned company in Portland. The employees do good, they get bonuses. You don't see none of that. It's like—how can I squeeze, how much can I get? What kind of life is it, you know?[38]

DEMOCRACY AS AN ALTERNATIVE

In the midst of his shotgun attack on traditional industrial authority, the last speaker pointed toward a specific, actually-existing alternative—workplace democracy. Despite some movement in the direction of Japan-style consultative management techniques, and despite some vague talk by a candidate for the Democratic presidential nomination in 1988 (Bruce Babbitt) about greater employee participation at work, the daily experience of most blue-collar workers remains that of a subject.[39] Some have argued that employee participation in decision making is not really an alternative; it is paternalism at best, and a conscious managerial antiunion strategy at worst. There is no categorical answer to that charge. At times it certainly is true.[40] Employee participation is least challenging when decision making is wholly illusory (the "suggestion box" approach), is subject to managerial overrule, or exists only in some immediate task-related areas (the "quality circle" approach). It is closest to an alternative model when it cuts into long-held managerial prerogatives on investment and personnel decisions or becomes a vision of employee ownership. In this form, it dramatically changes the exercise of authority and distribution of rewards.

Colt had not experimented with even the most superficial forms of employee participation. Authority was exercised in the traditional top-down method. Reibeling, when asked whether there had been discussion at Colt about various participatory options, indirectly affirmed the company's essentially traditional pyramidical structure:

We worked very hard at trying to put together a communications program for the employees. The idea was that we wanted to make the employees aware of what was going on in the business and try to make them more aware of how their jobs and what they did could affect the business at least from the standpoint of trying to communicate why things were happening the way they were and what kinds of dynamics this set up in the organization. We set up a communications program whereby the employees . . . would come together for—we called them "meetings with the president," whereby the president would sit down and talk with the people about what was going on in the company, really try to break down barriers between the factory workers and certainly the top management and in the process also try to convey the idea that we're all one employee group. . . . That's about the only example that I can recall sitting here where we tried to develop some kind of better communications and certainly a sense of one-company identity on the part of different work groups.[41]

The short answer, in other words, was no. Industrial authority as it has traditionally been practiced has never precluded informing employees of company goals. The meetings he described did not extend any decision-making power to employees and do not sound particularly consultative. One interviewee was a former supervisor who had quit several years before the strike and was married to a striker. He had been an inventor before he joined Colt management and was invited there because he had patented a new handgun safety device. Part of the reason he quit was because he felt that the personal initiative of both white- and blue-collar workers was suppressed. Here is his assessment of the participatory content of Colt factory life:

This company would just as soon you didn't speak English. They want to train you to sit there for eight hours and keep your mouth shut. They want robots. [Q: Can you think of a better way to run a factory?] Could there be a worse one?

The fact that Colt employees were encouraged to punch in and leave any notion of citizenship outside the doors did not make this managerial team especially dictatorial but only typical—typical, at least, of all but the most recent tendencies in industrial relations. What the absence of even lip service to employee participation did mean was that there was no previous language of participation for strikers to draw on as they answered my questions designed to test their support for industrial democracy.[42] There *was* an upturn in the amount and intensity of public discussion of the applicability of democratic principles at one point in the strike. The two organizations the union contacted when it first considered a buyout bid—the Naugatuck Valley Project and the Industrial Cooperative Association—are both strong advocates of democratically run enterprises. From my least formal means of research—listening to spontaneous discussion—this turn of events seemed to create some genuine interest in and argument over the principles of workplace democracy. But fortunately for ease of interpreting the questions on participation, the buyout bid came up just after the meeting at which the written survey was given, and so could not have shaped people's responses.

The questions about strikers' attitudes toward workplace democracy were taken from a survey conducted by John Witte at a plant assigned the pseudonym "Sound Incorporated," which was experimenting with extensive forms of participation.[43] Even a quick glance at table 5.3 shows that the strikers were much more interested in workplace democracy than those at Sound. There are two especially notable categories. One is the whole set of "none" answers. All of the questions show fewer Colt strikers taking that position, and few also in an absolute sense (that is, compared with the other Colt answers). The two questions on which a large number of the Sound respondents felt they should have no say—selection of supervisors and investment of profit—are far beyond the range of even the most genuine "quality of work life" plans, and it is not surprising that so many employees see it as a hands-off arena. But far fewer Colt strikers agree that it should be. The other eye-catching disparity is on the high ("a lot") end of the profits question. The strikers are far less reluctant to demand the right to participate in investment decisions.

Sound Incorporated was a rather peculiar enterprise—the sweeping experiment in employee participation was initiated by the CEO. It was also nonunion. There is some evidence that unionized workers are slightly more interested in participation than nonunion workers.[44] Could this be the reason that the Colt strikers appear to be converts to industrial democracy? Table 5.4 adds another sample for comparative purposes. This one is a unionized Fortune

*Table 5.3  Workplace Democracy*

| How much say should employees have over the way work is done? | | | |
|---|---|---|---|
| | None (%) | A little (%) | Some (%) | A lot (%) |
| Sound Inc.* | 9.7 | 7.6 | 34.0 | 48.6 |
| Colt strikers ($N = 112$) | 3.6 | 6.3 | 40.2 | 50.0 |
| How much say should employees have over the quality of work? | | | |
| Sound Inc.* | 19.1 | 9.9 | 36.2 | 34.7 |
| Colt strikers ($N = 110$) | 3.6 | 4.5 | 23.6 | 68.2 |
| How much say should employees have over selection of supervisors? | | | |
| Sound Inc.* | 40.8 | 15.4 | 23.9 | 19.7 |
| Colt strikers ($N = 109$) | 19.3 | 13.8 | 45.0 | 22.0 |
| How much say should employees have over what a company does with its profits? | | | |
| Sound Inc.* | 50.0 | 17.1 | 22.1 | 10.7 |
| Colt strikers ($N = 114$) | 13.2 | 16.7 | 38.6 | 31.6 |

*John Witte, *Democracy, Authority, and Alienation*, pp. 178–179.

*Table 5.4  Support for Participation*

| Workers wanting say in: | Apex[*] | Sound[**] | Colt |
| --- | --- | --- | --- |
| | (%) | (%) | (%) |
| The way work is done | 83 | 83 | 90 |
| Quality | 83 | 71 | 92 |
| Selection of supervisors | 42 | 44 | 67 |
| Investment of profits | 46 | 33 | 70 |

[*]Thomas Kochan et al., "Worker Participation in American Unions," p. 276.
[**]John Witte, *Democracy, Authority, and Alienation*, pp. 178–179.

500 company that the authors call "Apex." The figures combine the positive responses from Apex, Sound, and Colt.

The pattern of interest in participation at Apex is fairly consistent with that at Sound. The small differences are likely attributable to the fact that Apex is unionized and that a quality-of-work-life program there had already begun at the time of the survey.[45] These two groups of employees are similar in their views on the extent of desired participation, but markedly dissimilar from the strikers. Again, the difference is most noticeable in two sacrosanct areas of managerial discretion, selection of supervisors and the use of profits. These comparisons strongly suggest that the strikers' interest in workplace democracy grew as a consequence of their experience. They had not been subjected to much discussion of these questions beforehand—probably less than many other blue-collar workers whose enterprises had been dabbling in employee participation. There is also no reason to believe that they were idiosyncratically predisposed to workplace democracy before the strike.

As with the redistribution questions, there is little direct information on the mediating judgments which led the strikers to question managerial prerogatives in the way they did. It could have been a simple increased interest in political equality; it could have been an increase in their own sense of worth, both as individuals and as a group; it could also have been a retrospective judgment on the performance of traditional authority in the case with which they were most familiar. Some of the general conclusions that strikers reached—that corporations have too much power, that wealth confers excessive advantages, that opportunity is unfairly distributed, and that real wisdom lies with the common people—are consistent with the interest expressed here for a greater role in the workplace.[46] Some democratic theorists have argued that greater participation in the workplace might lead to an increased sense of responsibility in larger politics and that industrial citizenship would have a "carryover" effect.[47] What happened here seems to have been a reverse carryover. The strikers developed questions about the overall fairness of American society and extended that critical judgment to the workplace. Industrial authority as the strikers knew it and as commonly exists is a classic pyramid. It concentrates decision making and rewards at the top and distributes both downward in a fairly strict hierarchy. The entry cards at the top include prior wealth, family ties, and expertise. It should not be hard to understand how this clashed with the egalitarian values which became typical of the striking community. What began as a conflict with a traditional managerial hierarchy over its reward structure grew to include questions about the validity of the power arrangement and a widely shared belief that it should be substantially altered.

"Workplace democracy or death!" was not a rallying cry of the strike. Neither was a call for European social democracy. The strikers did not offer detailed counterplans, but it might not be fair to insist on blueprints before concluding that strikers expanded considerably the range of admissible ideas.[48] They called for and offered proposals for rearrangements of wealth, power, and authority and in some cases pointed to specific examples or places they thought might serve as models. They wanted to extend the principle of employee participation into largely taboo areas. These are formulations of alternatives, different from the flat, constricted landscape of political discourse pictured by studies of normal-time patterns of belief.

## ORDINARY PEOPLE, EXTRAORDINARY TIMES

Lafayette once remarked to Thomas Jefferson that the evils of slavery were easier to see from abroad.[49] Physical remove sometimes makes perceptions clearer. A contemporary political scientist writing about peasant politics made much the same point about the effects of a changed political environment: "New conditions, new options, new skills and opportunities can create situations in which long-standing practices come to be viewed as arbitrary, capricious, or intolerable."[50] The evidence in this chapter suggests that the Colt strikers came to view some long-standing practices in American society in just that light, or at least were a great deal more likely to than most Americans. Debates about opportunity and rewards which are usually closed were reopened. The strikers' conclusions were not uniformly negative but stand in contrast with prevailing opinion, which tends to be uniformly positive. Some strikers went beyond unfocused criticism and pointed toward some alternative visions. They generalized from their shared hardship to other related issues, a form of schematic thinking which in itself is unusual. Their views are not unrecognizable, but they are distinctive. They are certifiably different from mainstream public opinion, including that of other blue-collar workers, and although there is no ironclad proof, it is only reasonable to assume that they are also different from the views the strikers themselves held before the conflict began.

These are changed people, not just changed circumstances. Neither the utility maximizing nor the "hidden transcript" explanations of political transformation suffice to explain the genesis of this challenge to the dominant ideology. There is no reason to believe that these strikers were not giving their honest appraisal of the fairness of dominant social and political institutions. Looking at answers to an anonymous survey is as close to "offstage" attitudes as one can get without electronic surveillance. If the strikers were evaluating broad questions like redistribution and industrial authority differently, it is because their world, or a large part of it, had been turned upside down. It also appears that these new judgments were not simply new calculations of interest based on the admittedly new conditions. Very few of the beliefs expressed in this chapter had any instrumental value for the strikers. Some combination of breakup of daily routine, different sources of information, increased social interaction with others in the same position, hardship, and activism—all the elements which Zolberg attributes to "moments of madness"—led the strikers to call previously held views into question, look on some aspects of the "old order" in a new light, and propose remedies.

# 6

# Reconstructing the Political Spectacle

*Expressions of self-pity provide incentives to act. This is the meaning of such self-imposed titles as "downtrodden" and "wage-slaves." Self-praise likewise increases the feeling of oppression and swells the desire for self-assertion.*
—E. T. Hiller, *Strike*

COLT STRIKER: *Their pride is there. They're hurting, don't get me wrong. But they will not fall into the company's hands.*
SPOUSE: *They're not crumpled and desperate men like Mr. [company president] says.*
STRIKER: *I learned a lot. I have never seen a lot of people take their spirits and pull them together like these people here.*

At times in the interviewing process, the timing and phrasing of answers—their theatrical qualities—is as informative as the substance. The strikers had a singular story to tell: a responsible group of people wronged by an unjust exer-

---

This chapter owes its title and part of its purpose to Murray Edelman, *Constructing the Political Spectacle*.

cise of arbitrary power held by those with an overwhelming advantage in political and economic resources. But they told it in a variety of styles: some diffuse, some sharply focused, some profane, some pleading. All of the distinctions in rhetorical form were collapsed in the answers to one question: "What do you think it would be like working here without a union?" That the responses were invariably negative is not surprising, but the uniformity of the responses is. The question appeared to take people aback, as though it were the one thing they had not expected to be asked, or as though someone had posed a heretical thought. The responses (reproduced in their entirety in Appendix C) were all brief, none lasting more than a few seconds. Each respondent began with a terse declaration that it was unthinkable, then added a few more words by way of explanation:

> It would be hell, really. It would be like those ten months [before the strike].

> Oh shit. Whew! It would be a sweatshop.

The unanimity of rhetorical form, as well as of judgment, is striking, evidence of the way in which the conflict created its own conventional wisdom. The brevity of the responses indicated that everyone felt a few precise, clipped words would suffice to dismiss the premise of the question. What was so unthinkable about the prospect of working without a union? The central theme was the fear of capricious treatment on the part of the company:

> Buddy, if you didn't kiss nobody's butt, you'd be in a whole lot of trouble.

> I'd be scared. We'd get pushed around and they'd shove you anywhere they wanted. No union, I can't work.

> Unbearable. After you get kicked a few times, you get tired of it.

These are not tales of economic hardship or lack of access to collective bargaining but of the potential affront to dignity. In some other contexts, this might seem to be a relatively narrow-minded affirmation of craftlines ("They'd shove you anywhere they wanted"). Here it draws from the sense of self-respect engendered by the conflict, which made the exercise of arbitrary authority in even petty ways seem unacceptable. The existence of a union creates some semblance of political equality by establishing procedures to which everyone agrees to submit. The lack of rules would mean humiliation:

> I wouldn't, no way. With a union, at least next week, you got a job. It isn't like walking down a dark hall. You got procedures, there's no brown-nosing.

> The foreman would push everyone like a slave. If you don't have no union, you don't have no respect. He'd say "Polish my shoes!" If you don't polish his shoes, they fire you.

Most justifications for unions by members or supporters center on economic fairness and collective bargaining as a form of democracy. Members who are not officers traditionally see unions as insurance agencies. The strikers appear to have dug deeper into the underlying reasons democratic countries have permitted the formation of unions, which openly create a labor monopoly. A market system will treat labor like any other factor of production. Laws permitting the existence of unions (in this country, the Clayton Act and Wagner Act) are the expression of a historical political consensus which mandates that a distinction be made between humans and tools. Employees are allowed to create a monopoly in their labor, while owners are not permitted to create monopolies in trade, because of what differentiates people from property. Feeling that they had been treated as property, the Colt strikers insisted on the importance of unions in retaining their humanity. That accounts for the tone of these responses: the thought of working without a union is frightening. "Without a union, you're like a log rolling down the river, nothing to grab on to."

THIN ICE

That last response struck another theme that was prevalent—the fragility and contingent quality of institutions. Particular orderings of rewards, privileges, rights, responsibilities, and obligations seem to be impressively *there*—"like a rock," as one respondent in my previous industrial research put it.[1] The strike experience seemed to shake that. There was an increased sense of unease about institutions (such as firms) and practices (such as loyalty and reward for effort) which had previously been taken for granted. Life looked more precarious and arguments for its fairness less compelling. Much that was solid melted into air.

This alertness to the fragility of long-standing institutions is strongest—understandably—in the matter of unions and corporate power. The defining image was no longer of a company which would always be there and a union which would always be trying to claim its share:

> Everybody understands we're all in the same boat. Today you might have a union, tomorrow it might not be there.

> Even if we get a contract, there's no guarantees. We can go in and then the doors are closed.

> If they close the door, what am I gonna do? I'm just the little guy. I'm not the guy with the bucks. If they're going to make more money by shutting down for two years, what am I going to do about it? That's what I learned.

It is important to reemphasize that this was an older workforce. Common sense usually leads to the same conclusion Reibeling drew from that fact—that older meant less likely to engage in a crusade. But here age and years of service increased the sense of betrayal for some and undermined the reassuring sense of solidity which long-term employment creates. The two speakers above were in their sixties. This speaker is a black woman near retirement age who had previously talked about growing up in Mississippi where "life was hard":

> I was stunned by the way Colt's treated us. I think everybody felt that way. [Q: Did you feel betrayed?] Yes. We were all shocked when we heard their proposals. For the years we put in, they slapped our faces.

The permanence of the work-related aspects of the strikers' lives was jolted so severely that some invoked the language of natural disaster to describe both the conflict and the response:

> You don't know what's going to happen until the hurricane or tornado hits. Then you find out what people are made of.

> We all pitched in, like a town when a flood hits. Everybody comes and helps and you put everything else aside for awhile.

There was also a perception that any achievements were fragile, and that there was a permeable line between comfort and disaster:

> It's no more, "you get a decent job, a decent living, a house." There is no more of that. You have to fight. Be very, very cautious because corporations have a lot of power now and it's not fair to the average citizen. They can lay low for ten, twenty years, get all the money, and then come down on the American people.

> The average person is three months away from being a street person. I know a beautiful, elegant lady—never worked a day in her life—her husband dies, boom. She's out in the streets. Everybody—you're just walking on thin ice.

## CALCULATION AND TRANSFORMATION

This was in fact a "democratic moment" for the participants. Structurally, it was marked by the breakup of socially constructed routine which had to be reconstituted. It also embodied some of those "pentecostal" elements which have been noted by others studying such moments—hardship, power, and possibility became mixed together in a way which virtually forced people to submit old conclusions to new analysis. The political geography in which those conclusions and judgments were made was sharply altered. Strikers were doing little or no work (certainly none with their long-time employer); they experienced tangible hardship, constant strike activity, conflict, and the appearance of individuals in position of authority as opponents (and of government as a suspected accomplice). They took what amounted to an unexpected journey into a new land, "seeing everything both strange and familiar in a new light."[2]

In this new light, old practices lost those aspects of legitimacy that begin with longevity. The centerpiece of the "naturalization" concept is that people are apt to mistake the product of human decision for what is physical; what is contingent for what is unchangeable. Here, the reverse process took place. The strikers' sense of the frailty of institutions and practices widened. It was a kind of "denaturalization," stemming from what Moore called "holidays from normal society" in which the need for obedience and the obligation to work are suspended.[3] It was at least in part this destabilization of their accustomed political and economic surroundings which led to the more critical inquiry into the fairness of American society.

Each of the three attempts described in Chapter 1 to explain political thinking in nonnormal times corresponds to part of the Colt experience. Looking at the strikers as hard-headed utility maximizers calls attention to the changed circumstances in which choices were made. It is reasonable that people would devote more time and energy to the strike than they normally would to public events, even public events which affect them directly. Reacquiring their jobs required them to become temporary activists, just as Hamilton and Wright pointed out that the old regime's inability to satisfy everyday concerns caused nonideological Russians to look favorably on revolutionaries in 1917.[4] Reibeling argued that otherwise reluctant employees had no choice but to work wholeheartedly for the union's goals once the company had replaced them (the "rational striker" scenario). In other words, one aspect of the five-year conflict was interest-group activity writ large and noisy. Even the prevalent language of solidarity had a practical side to it. Since the union could only force people to picket four hours a week (to qualify for strike pay), there had to be other incentives to encourage people to take part in activity beyond that. A sense of fulfillment and peer acceptance could be substitutes for individual economic incentives.[5]

These attributions of motivation and incentive touch parts of the strike experience but miss others. It is true (to take the last point first) that a language of solidarity was in part responsible for the extent of voluntary activity. But that was true because people genuinely believed (in varying degrees, certainly) that they were working for a cause. The predominant attitude was what Christopher Jencks called "communitarian unselfishness."[6] That strikers thought, talked, and acted within that framework is reasonable, but it also represents a considerable change from a calculation of personal interest.[7] It is more difficult to explain the changes in strikers' views on issues not immediately related to the strike from this perspective. Their new reading of the availability of opportunity and the fairness of existing distributions was not especially useful in furthering strike aims. Both the existence of extended schemas and their content suggest that strikers reevaluated rather than simply recalculated. Finally, what needs to be explained is why people stayed on strike for four years. The rational solution to satisfying daily needs—crossing the picket line to go back to work—was available. The utility-maximizing perspective accounts for some of the prose of the strike, but not its poetry.

James Scott provides one way to understand the poetry: "the intoxicating feeling that comes from the first public expression of a long-suppressed response to authorities."[8] An open challenge to authority builds pride and a sense of elation and can lead to a general conflagration of defiance. It necessarily elicits mutualism, since the hidden transcript is by definition shared among the powerless. Scott's insights help account for other aspects of the Colt experience, although it must be kept in mind that this was a local strike and that industrial authority is not as harsh as the forms of domination with which Scott is concerned. The sense that the employees had endured ten months of humiliation working without a contract was an important reason for the exuberance on the morning of the walkout, and it helped sustain the strike through uncertain times. A watchword of strike folklore was "We've got three things Colt doesn't have—determination, courage, and pride." The primary reason people did not return to work one by one was that it would have violated a moral code more important to them than their individual welfare.

Scott's characterization of "an entire discourse of equality, justice, and revenge" as typical of these periods is consonant what has appeared on these pages.[9] But his focus is on changed public behavior, not beliefs. There is no reorientation of attitudes toward the old regime and no need for it. What has occurred is not transformation but ventilation. The exhilaration that participants feel is the joy in acting authentically: "The acts of daring and haughtiness that so struck the authorities were perhaps improvised on the public stage, but they had been long and amply prepared in the hidden transcript of folk culture and practice."[10]

Here is where some aspects of hegemony theory can help explain the strike experience. This was an intense learning experience for the participants, one which led them to look at American society differently. Burdens which previously might have been interpreted simply as misfortune now appeared to be injustice.[11] The strikers became more demanding of political figures and more homogeneous in doing so. They became less charitable in their estimates of the extent of opportunity available and more likely to call the structure of rewards into question. In some cases, they proposed, or at least entertained, alternatives, including some (such as workplace democracy) in which authority would be ordered very differently than before. In brief, they became more consistent, more insistent, and more egalitarian. These changes are less the public airing of a hidden transcript than the creation of an "emergent culture," shaped and shared by the participants as they lived together through the conflict.[12] What had changed for the strikers were not only the new calculus of preferences and the new freedom they had to air long-standing grievances but also the terrain on which their central life experience was being conducted. In listening to the conclusions strikers reached about industrial authority, the political system, and the importance of class, we are hearing not what they *really* thought (all along), but what they *now* think.

It is important to avoid an oversimplified picture—Colt employees transformed from grinning wage slaves to Eisenstein's heroic workers storming the Winter Palace. The strikers did set out on a journey to new territory but were guided in varying degrees by language, values, and goals typical of more normal times. I have stressed the solidaristic norms because they were new and therefore newsworthy. That does not mean that individual self-interest was absent. It was the congruence of communal impulses (and other "ideological" motivations, like pride, dignity, and self-respect) and more mundane goals of job retention and back pay which sustained the strike for such a long period. The strikers were also reluctant to abandon traditional definitions of fair mutual obligations; that is one reason they downplayed somewhat the creative and original forms of protest behavior during the in-plant strike. All three explanations of how people respond to the times that try men's souls convey important information and correspond to elements of the Colt experience. But any version of the story which leaves out the creative and transformational aspects is incomplete.

CASTING AWAY ILLUSIONS OR CREATING DELUSIONS?

If the conflict at Colt was a high-impact, compressed learning period, what can be said about the lessons that it taught? There is an almost unavoidable temptation to conclude that the strike uncovered the secrets of class; that is, that it has produced an ontologically "truer" picture of reality. That claim rests on the assumptions that the strikers have penetrated the dominant ideology and seen it for the misrepresentation of reality it is and that crisis is an ideal time to see the world without pretense. But the first assumption requires an independent judgment about the distribution of opportunity and the degree of stratification in American society, which has been the subject of endless debate. Some readers will find the more egalitarian norms which have emerged to be attractive and some will not; no one can claim that their preferences are self-evidently less a product of mystification.

The more interesting claim to ontological truth is the second—that the world is clearer when the gloves are off. Here is how this was stated in a case study of an earlier strike: "It is when all hell breaks loose and all men do their worst and best that the powerful forces which control him and society are revealed. . . . It is in these moments of crisis that the humdrum daily living of thousands of little men going to work with their lunch boxes and the prosaic existence of the big man in the top office reveal themselves as human dramas of the utmost significance; more importantly, behavior in such crises tells us the meanings and significance of human society."[13]

I have previously alluded to Zolberg's formulation of these periods as "moments of madness." What he intends by that is roughly what is stated above. His is the madness of the dishonored prophet; these crisis times are the infrequent moments when the prophecies look like common sense. The realities of power and authority relations, the unnecessary way they confine social and political relationships, and the possibility of transcending those limitations are revealed as history speeds up.

The rhetoric which has appeared on previous pages makes it clear that the conflict at Colt was something of an epiphany for the participants, if on a lesser scale than what hit Saul of Tarsus. But political epiphanies have their critics.[14] The authors of the *Federalist Papers,* for instance, would have no trouble agreeing that turbulent times produce a transformation of goals and values, but they saw that dynamic as a malady and a principle fault line of democratic government. One of their festering concerns was that people "stimulated by some irregular passion" might demand changes which they would regret when the passion cooled.[15] Other critics of passion in political crisis shared similar concerns. Thucydides wrote about the defeat of reason and moderation in the civil war in Corcyra; in the overheated atmosphere, people were attracted to extreme positions *because* they were extreme.[16] Crane Brinton compared the popular mind-set in revolutionary periods to a fever.[17] E. T. Hiller extended that characterization to strikes: "For a moment the individual, in resigning himself to collective sentiments, escapes the responsibility of choice in conflict."[18]

These concerns invert the concept of democratic moments—or would use "moments of madness" in a more clinical sense. It is precisely the democratic character of the times which produces the delusion that everything is possible.

Even extended schematic thinking has its critics. In cognitive psychology, "schema" is typically the name for a bias or distortion in perception and is frequently the object of corrective therapy.[19]

## HARDSHIP TO CITIZENSHIP

If we cannot necessarily conclude that the narratives derived from the strike are "truer" than those in everyday life, are there reasons to welcome them rather than just take note of them? I believe there are. American political discourse is cramped and centrist, and at a minimum, different voices enliven the public dialogue. John Stuart Mill in *On Liberty,* at heart a call not merely to *tolerate* but to *celebrate* nonconforming thought, says of those challenging conventional wisdom, "Let us thank them for it, open our minds to listen to them, and rejoice that there is some one to do for us what we otherwise ought . . . to do with much greater labor for ourselves."[20] Even those who see the centrism of the public as beneficial cannot be pleased with the extent to which the causes are ignorance and lack of attention to politics. If apathy and ignorance today are a source of stability, tomorrow they might lay the basis for Perot-style know-nothing movements.

The more thematically consistent political reasoning, attention to public affairs, and mutualism that the strikers developed made them fuller democratic citizens. Hardship and deprivation can suppress a sense of citizenship, as voting participation rates suggest. The American founders were probably right that those without a stake in society, or other resources such as broad education, were less likely to develop a universalist perspective (though sharp differences ensued about whether that argued for inclusion or exclusion).[21] The figures of admiration among submerged people are often real or mythical "bad men," who lash out indiscriminately against the strong and the weak.[22] Scott points out that civic spiritedness may be an unreasonable expectation made of those "whose experience of community has mostly been that of victims."[23] The political world was not of their making, and they feel little sense of obligation toward it.

But the strikers' experience was not limited to deprivation—although there was plenty of that—nor their self-conception to one of victimhood. Their conviction that wealth and power were divided unfairly disturbed but also energized them: "The scabs will pull their money, wave it, and it just reinforces my feelings—they've sold themselves. They've prostituted themselves."

Barbara Johnson, who as head of the hardship fund was reminded for four years of the financial difficulties people faced, describes how hardship coexisted with a sense of accomplishment: "There is the dichotomy between what they've lost and the other side, that they have their dignity, that they have not laid down and passively said, 'There is nothing I can to to impact this, to change this.' There is definitely a feeling among the strikers that they had a choice and they made that choice."[24]

The strike did not turn participants into disinterested Madisonian citizens. The redefinitions of American society which emerged grew from a heightened and lengthened sense of self-interest. But selflessness has proved to be an impossibly high standard against which to measure democratic citizenship, and a difficult one to sustain when there is no shared goal or enemy.[25] There is considerable room for the development of a civic virtue short of assembling in the agora and deliberating the permanent and aggregate interests of the community. A less demanding conception of democratic citizenship is that people "must be able to put aside self-interest narrowly conceived (in which the horizons of interest stop at one's front doorstep) and consider instead what is in their self-interest as members of the political community."[26] In short, rather than expect the public to resemble a collection of impartial judges, we might more reasonably use the image of active and informed watchdogs as the standard to evaluate citizenship.

If there is reason to value the political thinking developed in the strike, it lies in the movement of the participants in this direction. The strikers developed fairly consistent ideas about what they wanted from government, what constituted fair principles of distribution, and what government should do to bring those about. They became more vigilant and active in attending to those ends. What may have begun in self-interest did not stay there. None of the questions and responses presented here fall narrowly into the "what's in it for me" category—they all travel well beyond the doorstep of individual strikers and many beyond the strike events themselves. The strikers developed some out-of-the-ordinary alternatives and invoked a vocabulary of group identity, both of which contribute to democratic dialogue, independent of how anyone might judge their validity.[27] The "babble" of elites and masses speaking in "different political tongues" places few constraints on leaders and can burden them with impossible demands.[28] Thematically consistent public thinking provides the best basis for negotiation and compromise. The strikers moved, to borrow a helpful description, from being *private* citizens to being private *citizens*.[29]

# 7

## A Vernal Morning, and the Day After

*There have always been times in which people pressed beyond existing arrangements without being subordinated to the rule of a priestly caste, times of movement, times of a people led by prophecy. Only in such movements did masses and classes who were otherwise inevitably subaltern manage to reach the level of a historical consciousness, of immediate communication with the universal. In movements of this kind, fishermen from Galilee and Paris workers suddenly rose to the highest possible human dignity attainable.*

—Rudolph Bahro, *The Alternative in Eastern Europe*

The political territory I have been exploring here is not brand new, but it has not been visited often. That is through no one's fault—there are many fewer opportunities to study "moments of madness" than the politics of more stable periods. Most people develop their political dispositions within the confines of familiar landmarks; very few experience the sudden, wrenching rearrangement of political geography as happened here. Outside a relatively narrow circle of political activists, people are generally and understandably more concerned with "making lives" than with "making history."[1] So, too, with polities.

A contemporary political theorist has argued that American politics oscillates between extended periods of mundane interest bargaining and episodic outbursts of "higher lawmaking" characterized by expanded public involvement in redefining basic principles.[2]

What the Colt strikers experienced were not simply hard times. The studies mentioned earlier suggest that individual or collective hardship produces very little challenge to American core values. This study does not dispute that; something much more significant than hardship was the operative factor here. There was a shift in the backdrop against which life tasks were weighed and political values formulated. Many of the strikers had reached an age at which, in Barbara Johnson's words, "They normally would have been looking forward to the successful completion of the work portion of their lives." For all of them, simply "making lives" as before had become impossible.

I began by asking what the political views formulated in such periods might tell us about the greater stretches of political normalcy. The answer will have to be somewhat speculative and include further questions. I will begin by summarizing the changes in political attitudes among the strikers briefly and more broadly than has been done chapter by chapter.

"MADNESS": A SUMMARY

The first lesson of the strike is that the generally distant world of political life came to look more vivid and compelling to the strikers, and government took on some relevance for their personal lives. They saw more reasons for gathering information, for evaluating political figures, and for participating in the process. "Good citizenship" in the abstract is too time-consuming and underrewarding to have much shelf life beyond high school civics class exhortations; paying close attention to matters of policy and elections ordinarily makes sense only for those who practice or study it for a living. The citizenship which emerged during this conflict had a different source than piety or political genes—it came from focused and studied judgment on the roles of public officials in this and similar events and a sense of undeserved political exclusion.

Second, many of the strikers became more suspicious of the market as the best arbiter of distributive justice. In such spheres as the availability of opportunity, the relation of contribution to reward, and the discretionary role of corporate owners, the market began to look unfair. The unfairness was not just around the edges, where many Americans are inclined to locate it, but at its heart. Some had privileged access based on prior wealth and power, and could make the competition inequitable. Others, like the strikers themselves, had played by the rules and were not rewarded commensurate with their effort.

Government intervention to produce a fairer outcome was not only legitimate but a moral obligation.

Third—and this is ironic because the argument that strikes uncover the real nature of capitalism usually comes from the left—the conflict probably made the strikers more aware of aspects of market systems that unions traditionally deemphasize: the impermanence and instability of any fixed pattern of exchange, and therefore the life of any particular company. One analyst of workplace cultures pointed to a wide gap between risk-accepting entrepreneurs and security-seeking employees; this experience seems to have closed that gap.[3] The strikers' increased understanding of the contingent qualities of political and economic events made them more sensitive to the "perennial gales of creative destruction" inherent in a market system.[4] This proved to be important as the poststrike company went through difficult times.

DURABILITY

How long will the moment stretch? A highly publicized miners' strike against the Pittston Coal Company in Virginia overlapped the last year of the conflict at Colt. A political scientist drew the same central conclusion from his observations as I have here, that the most significant outcome was "the personal transformation they [social movements] engender; bright shining moments when democratic imaginations are stirred and people dare to take organized action for group benefit."[5] But he also calls this result the "least tangible." Could such a transformation better be understood as a paroxysm with little lasting significance? What would be left of that democratic imagination in the cold light of day, when the "holiday from normal society" (in Moore's phrase) was over? Democratic moments widen horizons but do not make them disappear. Participants return to face the limitations the world imposes on aspiration. This unavoidable turn has led to an argument that such "explosions of consciousness" leave nothing of lasting value in their wake.[6]

There has been little enough research done on individual political attitudes in high-intensity conflict; there have been almost no follow-up studies that could provide reliable information on the duration of the lessons learned. But it is important to keep in mind that notwithstanding some claims about "class consciousness," these lessons do not come in one tight package, and some changes in political values may prove more ephemeral than others. This will probably be the case in the Colt strike, even though it was a lengthy and extremely important chapter of the lives of the participants. The fierce partisanship, for instance, may well last. Most explanations of party identification suggest that the most decisive moments in partisan affiliation come about when some set of important issues clearly divides the public, with the parties perceived as lining up on opposite sides. That is the point at which party identification is most imbued with issue content. The image the strikers created of the Republicans as the guardians of privilege—much more sharply edged than the general public's view—is not likely to fade quickly.

The communitarian unselfishness, on the other hand, may diminish. Historians of civic virtue have concluded that people are most willing to make sacrifices in the face of danger, particularly if there is a commonly understood enemy.[7] During the strike, the participants were members of a highly motivated community with a shared goal and a perceived enemy—Colt management and the strikebreakers. The daily mini-confrontations on the picket line may have been as important in keeping alive the community's self-identity as in venting anger. As is apparent from the open-ended interviews, the strikers felt they had one story to tell, with only minor variations. A shared narrative—particularly one filled with perceptions of courage and villainy—is ideal to maximize solidaristic values.

If the reestablishment of routine did not have some effects on the strikers' political beliefs, much that was written here would be wrong. At a minimum, the highs and lows of collective battle will be missing. A study of union activists in Britain found that their experiences in the 1926 general strike "do indeed appear to have had a dramatic and permanent effect on their subsequent value-systems and behaviour."[8] Whether that will be true in the Colt strike or other "democratic moments" must await further study.

But it would be a mistake to dismiss these periods as meaningless if there is no sustained increase in selflessness or some other acquired value. Zolberg points out that while "moments of madness" do not (and of course cannot) produce achievements matching the utopian thinking they unleash, they may leave substantial accomplishments in their wake. He cites universal manhood suffrage, the right to an education, and the right to leisure as by-products of the periods he surveys.[9] Mill generalized in the same vein but more broadly: there are some periods of history in which "the mind of the people was stirred up from its foundations," during which people unused to engaging in debate over basic values did so. It is to those periods he attributes "every single improvement which has taken place either in the human mind or institution."[10] While the Colt events took place on a greatly reduced scale, they did produce substantial changes. The ownership of the company changed hands and in some respects—notably the employees' share of the stock and seats on the board—is structurally different from before. In the difficult period which followed, the union zealously guarded these changes. A sudden vision that "everything is possible" will not last, because it cannot be true. But the duration and strength of that vision may help bring about the improbable. It did at Colt.

TYPICALITY

My purpose here—apart from the worthwhile task of simply chronicling the Colt strike—has been to explore the theoretical questions outlined in Chapter 1 through this case study. But every case has its distinctive elements and may provide something less than a pure microcosm. What might be idiosyncratic here?

The set of events I am generalizing to is not strikes as a whole, most of which never come close to the magnitude of this one. The real comparison is with those other situations mentioned throughout as democratic moments. The potentially distinguishing feature of this one are obvious—its scale (confined to about a thousand people) and its specific realm (labor conflict). While its length and intensity are comparable to only a very small handful of strikes, some of the folklore of the conflict was undoubtedly influenced by labor idioms. Historical language and practice typical of labor, actively and capably transmitted by the local leaders, undoubtedly gave some shape to strikers' values. I have suggested that the solidarity and communalism which developed represented a challenge to the prevailing "core value" of individualism. But it is also a historical counterideology generated by labor and parties representing it, exemplified by the famous lament, "What force on earth is weaker than the feeble force of one?" and the rejoinder, "Solidarity forever." This historical labor emphasis on collectivity is compatible with my argument that new norms developed, but its existence does suggest that norms might differ substantively from those described here when the conflict is on some terrain other than work.

There may be other idiosyncratic elements. Like solidarity, distributive justice had been an ongoing concern of labor. It could be that the centrality of this issue might mark this particular nonnormal situation but not others unconnected to labor. There was an irreducible element of truth to Reibeling's "rational striker" analysis. The conflict had a definable beginning and specific goals; much of what happened is understandable as an attempt to reach those goals and bring the conflict to a conclusion. The situation was thus more focused than others discussed as democratic moments—the Paris Commune, the Populist movement, the opening of the Berlin Wall—and more similar to normal interest-group activity.

But these potentially distinguishing features reemphasize how closely the sentiments developed in this strike echo those in a variety of other nonnormal political settings. There is a remarkable similarity in what observers (including professional social scientists) report: a heightened sense of dignity and self-worth; an increase in forms of altruistic behavior; a sudden sense of the relevance and immediacy of politics; and an increased willingness to consider alternatives to prevailing institutional arrangements. Such observers as Gustave Le Bon, who equated these democratic impulses with dangerous anarchy, have noted these qualities in horror.[11] Enthusiastic participants caught up in the sweep of events often proclaim the revealed truth they have seen.[12] Political scientists using the most sophisticated methodological tools—Pierce and Converse on the May–June 1968 events in France—produced a picture of the changes in those who took part which nearly parallels the one here of the Colt strikers: homogenization, increased importance of the left-right political axis, and an increase in political efficacy. The conclusion they drew from their study is strikingly parallel: "Mass protest does wonders to concentrate the mind."[13]

That the description of how citizens experience these abnormal periods is so similar amid such a welter of different methodologies, different eras, and different observer sympathies makes clear that there is some commonality. It also suggests that the transformation of political thinking during the Colt strike shares a great deal with what has occurred in other extraordinary political events.

THE DOMINANT IDEOLOGY DEBATE

I began by suggesting that the study of nonnormal political periods might provide useful commentary on the debates about ideological hegemony. The heart of the debate—to simplify again—is whether popular passivity in the face of powerlessness is best understood as pragmatic or normative acceptance. Studying abnormal periods cannot resolve the debates, but it can provide an important window on some aspects of them. The central claim I have made here—one I believe is consonant with the claims of others who have studied these episodes—is that the political reasoning of participants changes in some measurable and dramatic ways. I have given reasons in the previous chapter why I think these changes have value, but valuable or not, the essential fact is that they have occurred. A conservative leader of the American Revolution disapprovingly characterized an analogous transformation: "The mob begin to think and reason. . . . It is with them a vernal morning, they are struggling to cast off their winter's slough; they bask in the sunshine."[14] If awakening, learning, "casting off," and trying out alternatives are typical of these periods, the bounded character of political thinking in normal times stands out in relief. Moore's argument that people have a perilous capacity for getting used to things gains credence; the Colt strikers apparently felt that some of what they had previously gotten used to now looked questionable when viewed from this new vantage point.

This lends some aid and comfort to hegemony theory, at least in the softer Mill-influenced version I have been employing throughout. Political thinking ordinarily bends toward the customs and prejudices of an age, and those prejudices will inevitably be supportive of existing arrangements of power and resources. This takes place not because of the dissemination of propaganda by the privileged but through the spontaneous process of adaptive preference formation.[15] Democratic moments temporarily dislodge people from the circumstances in which the adaptation takes place and create a political discourse with new elements. Some of that discourse may well comprise sentiments widely held but strategically kept out of view (as Scott maintains); some may be a search for a solution to ordinary problems in unusual times; but some is brought about by the intoxicating "holiday from normal society" itself. In explaining the excited public dialogue of these periods, recognition of a previously prevailing orthodoxy—a dominant ideology—must be part of the equation.

*Colt is more than a company, it is an institution, which since 1836 has been inextricably a part of the American adventure.*
—Official Colt historian R. L. Wilson

The difficulties the new company and returning strikers faced did not end with the settlement. The economic climate in which the new owners operated was the one that Reibeling had predicted: declining military purchases, a downturn in civilian purchases, and greater restrictions on the types of weapons that could be manufactured.[16] The number of jobs in the gun industry in Connecticut declined from a Vietnam-era high of almost 10,000 to a twentieth-century low of 2,500 in 1991. Colt faced an additional problem—the purchase of the division involved enormous borrowing, and the huge debt created uncertainty for potential large-scale military purchasers. The new company filed for Chapter 11 bankruptcy on March 19, 1992, and every industry analyst forecast eventual closure unless the company moved south.

But a cooperative effort of the new management team, the state, and the union forestalled disaster for several years while they sought a buyer. No large-scale concessions were sought from the union in this period. A wage increase scheduled in 1992 was deferred on the condition that the company stay out of bankruptcy. When that did not happen, the deferred wages became one of the many claims against the company's assets. The union took the same approach to the $3.5 million owed to the members in the original settlement—it maintained the claim, but deferred payment.

Negotiations with a financier to lead the company out of bankruptcy collapsed in late 1993. The public culprit was a group of unsecured creditors who objected to a plan which would have reimbursed them less than seventy cents on the dollar. But the union was also unenthusiastic because the new ownership would have eliminated their seats on the board and taken away the employees' 11.5 percent share of stock ownership. The union dragged its feet, though it did not publicly oppose the sale.[17] That, combined with the hostility of the small creditors, killed the sale and left the company's future in peril.

But at the same time, the company took steps to improve its operations. It hired a new production management team, began to offer new weapons, and consolidated its operations in West Hartford, abandoning its historic but antiquated facility under the dome in Hartford (but with no reduction in workforce).[18] In 1994 a new purchaser was located and the company emerged from Chapter 11. The union traded its deferred wages and the $3.5 million claim for its 11.5 percent stock ownership, essentially making an investment in the new company. The new group welcomed the union's participation on the board, now two seats on a board of nine. This was widely heralded as a "second end" to the strike, one that was in some ways even more unexpected than the first.

When I asked Wheeler whether the process of negotiation had gone differently than it would have with the prestrike owners, he pointed out that the union still had guarded its interests carefully and in the end had done quite well. But he added that the union leadership and membership looked on making concessions in this period in a more conciliatory light than they would have previously: "No doubt about it. New management, new cooperation, new attitude."[19]

In the spring of 1989, long before the NLRB ruling and when the buyout seemed like a remote possibility, a union official remarked off-handedly to me, "Wouldn't it make a hell of an ending to this thing if we wound up winning our case and buying the company?" I told him that if that happened I would drop the idea of a book and work on a movie script. Since the union wound up owning only *part* of the company, I decided to stay with the book. But in a sense the conflict did take on the aura of an epic. At times the organization of strike details, the maneuvering among complicated labor laws, the occasional bickering at meetings, and the constant burden for strikers of making ends meet for four years overshadowed cooperation and sacrifice as the most outwardly noticeable qualities of the striking body. But at other times—for instance, in observing union tributes to the thirty-seven members who died during the course of the strike—it seemed that this was a group which understood that its part in the "American adventure" had been an unusual and dramatic one. It was their democratic imagination that impressed me from my first encounters with the Colt strikers. While it may be intangible, it is as real as any measurable benefits. I will let one of the strikers explain it. He is in his mid-fifties, worked at Colt for twenty-three years before he was fired during the period employees worked without a contract, and had a serious bout with cancer during the first year of the strike (he is recovering and has gone back to work):

> I can shave this face in the morning. You got to live with yourself. That's really what you got. Some things can't be bought. You got to tell yourself you can't be bought. Maybe that's what's wrong with the country. . . .
>
> I remember what Walesa said in Poland. He said, "You can stop us, you can stop Solidarity, but you can't stop us here [taps his heart]." You can't take that away from people. It'll always stay there. What can Colt do to me? Colt can't do anything to me now. I don't even worry about them. Because I got it right here. I got what I want right here.

# Appendix A

Qualitative interviewing is open to criticism on a number of grounds. One is the non-comparability of individual sessions. Since most of the questions are not repeated verbatim, and since some of the questions are particular to a specific interview, it can be argued that the responses are not directly comparable. There is no doubt that this is at least partly true. Nonetheless, those who employ this method argue that it is a risk worth taking for the information that the interviews can reveal. In these responses I looked for repeated stories (what I called strike folklore), instances of unanimity or near-unanimity, the categories strikers created to evaluate events, the intensity of views, and the degree to which strikers felt the experience had changed their lives and ideas. I refer readers to others (Robert Lane, *Political Ideology,* Jennifer Hochschild, *What's Fair?* Craig Reinarman, *American States of Mind*) who have made a case for the measuring instruments used in qualitative interviewing and make no further defense of them here.

Nonrandomness is another potential problem in data drawn from qualitative interviewing done with relatively small groups. As I describe below, the group I assembled for these interviews is admittedly not drawn randomly from the population of strikers. There are two ways of mitigating that problem, assuming as I do that there is substantial value to be gained from extended interviews. One is to attempt to simulate randomness through an informed and common-sense effort to piece together a fairly representative sample. The other is to moderate the claims made about the findings. I have tried to do both. Neither is a magic wand which removes the difficulties or makes precision possible. But the measures I took and describe here lead me to conclude that the information taken from these interviews is not seriously misleading.

In the text I have said there were "about" forty interviews, not because I do not know exactly how many interviews I conducted but because I cannot state that number in a single brief and usable form. The circumstances of the interviews varied so widely that no single description of "interview with striker" fits all. There were thirty-five interview sessions, not including the informational interviews with Phil Wheeler, Bob Madore, Rick Reibeling, "Barbara Johnson," Louise Simmons, and Susan Howard. The interviews were all tape-recorded and varied in length from one to four hours. In nine of these sessions, there was more than one participant. Eight of those involved spouses of Colt workers (six wives and two husbands). Those spouses were often more than just peripherally involved—one, for example, had been arrested and hit with a nightstick; one was an ex-supervisor at Colt who refused to return to work even though the company offered to triple his salary; one had worked at the Colt credit union; and one emerged as a public spokesperson, making TV appearances and writing letters to local newspapers. No spouse—not even those less actively involved—seemed begrudging about the commitment to the strike made by the employee, but of course there is at least a potential difference of tone and feel between strikers and supportive spouses that makes equating them as "interviewee" imprecise. One particularly exciting (and excited) interview took place at the strike headquarters. Four strikers joined the person I had been scheduled to meet. This is one example of the difficulty of counting precisely; while all five contributed, some of them came late or left early.

Forty-nine people were interviewed altogether (apart from the informational interviews); forty of those were Colt employees. Fourteen were female, nine were black or Hispanic. Ten had served as union officials above the rank of steward, although some of those held no position at the time of the strike. One had been hired in the ten-month in-plant strike and another had gone back to work briefly during the strike before rejoining the picket lines. Six employees were fired in the early stages of the in-plant strike; I interviewed four of them. Prior to the strike there were five Colt employees doing full-time work for the union. While I talked with four of these, they remain as background information and are not cited in the text. Most of the interviews were done at people's homes; a smaller number were done at the Local 1199 office near the Hartford picket line or at the strike headquarters.

The most obvious peril I faced at the outset was that the people who would volunteer for the interviews might be largely the most committed and articulate strikers. I used several methods to try to compensate. In my original speech at a union meeting soliciting interviews, I stressed the importance of talking to people other than the strongest union supporters and promised anonymity. My words were: "Even if you just sat at home and waited to see what happens, you've got a story and I want to hear it." Of course, that strategy was not foolproof, and the group which signed up at the meeting no doubt was highly unrepresentative. In the course of each interview, I asked people for suggestions of other candidates and took special note of those who seemed to be farthest from the circles of the most committed. Those interviews were somewhat more difficult to arrange; it took delicate negotiating, for instance, to interview the striker who had once returned to work.

The end result was a set of interviews which is still disproportionately drawn from hard-core supporters of the strike but includes a much wider spectrum of views. As a test of the possible disproportionality, I coded each interviewed striker as either activist or simple participant. Then I showed the list of interviewees to Barbara Johnson and asked her to do the same without telling her how I had coded them. We agreed on eleven interviewees as activists, and fifteen appeared on one or the other list. That is a fairly high number out of forty, but it also shows that the interview set went well beyond the union's inner circle. The purpose of qualitative interviews is to examine cognitive maps more closely than surveys permit, and these are sufficient for that purpose.

For the most part, I have not provided a great deal of identifying material in the text when I quote from interviews. Only when such information is useful for interpreting a specific quote—as is occasionally true of the age or work experience of a respondent—have I indicated it. The story of the strike culture is its homogeneity, observable from both the open-ended interviews and the written survey. Information which is essential in many other settings—race, gender, and type of job, for instance—is less important here. That, in fact, is instructive itself. The strike had displaced and obscured most of the normal divisions.

# Appendix B

Basic Questionnaire for Qualitative Interviews

1. How long have you worked at Colt? What kinds of jobs have you had?
2. Before any of this began—before the ten months [preceding the strike]—what was it like to work there? Would you say there was good communication between the company and the employees?
3. Now tell me about the ten-month period. What was it like? Did you see any change on the part of the company? Was there any change on the part of the union? [follow-up] Did people do anything to try to respond?
4. Okay, then the strike started. What do you remember from the first day? Was there a lot of picketing at first?
5. In some situations like this that I have heard of, people sometimes help each other out. Would you say that has been true here? Do you feel there has been a sense of togetherness in the strike? In spite of how long it's been, only about two hundred went back in. Why do you think so few have gone back?
6. When a strike goes on this long, some parts of the government get involved, or maybe they should if they haven't. I'm going to ask you about a few of them. I just want you to tell me what you thought of how they did. The Hartford and West Hartford police? Local elected officials? Congresspeople? The courts?

7. Now I want to ask you a few questions about whether or not you think you've changed any during the strike. Do you think you've changed your attitudes any toward other employees? Toward Colt management? Toward labor-management relations as a whole? Do you think it's a fair system?

8. What would it be like to work here without a union?

9. Imagine that you win and you are ready to go back in. What would you like to see on that first day you go back?

10. If you had the power and there was one thing you could change in the system of industrial relations in our country, what would it be?

# Appendix C

These are all the responses to the question: "What would it be like to work here without a union?"

Hah! You couldn't work there ten minutes without a union.

The foreman would push everyone like a slave. If you don't have no union, you don't have no respect. The foreman says, "Polish my shoes!" If you don't polish his shoes, they fire you.

I would not work there without a union.

Oh shit. Whew! It would be a sweatshop.

Buddy, if you didn't kiss nobody's butt, you'd be in a whole lot of trouble.

It would be hell, really. It would be like those ten months. Without a contract, they were treating people bad.

Unbearable. After you get kicked a few times, you get tired of it.

You'd have to ask the scabs.

I'd be scared. We'd get pushed around and they'd shove you anywhere they wanted. No union, I can't work.

They'd do whatever they wanted.

Whew! You might not last a week. They might as well have a gun to a person's head.

I couldn't work without a union. No. They would try to get away with a lot of things.

I couldn't work there. It would be a slave camp.

Probably the same as those ten months—hell.

I'd be out of there by now. They'd probably force me to retire.

Couldn't do it. No possible way. You have to have peace and quiet. You can't have interference.

Unbearable. They would do anything they could to save money. Safety and quality would go right down the tubes.

I wouldn't, no way. With a union, at least next week you got a job. It isn't like walking down a dark hall. You got procedures, there's no brown-nosing.

Without a union, you're like a log floating down the river. Nothing to grab on to.

It's not pretty. Based on those ten months, it would be one hell of a place to work.

Terrible, no doubt.

# Appendix D

I want to repeat here my thanks to the union leadership for helping me with this survey, especially since they had no way of knowing in advance whether the results would be useful for their goals. The circumstances of the survey were not laboratory ideal, and they created some possible problems for interpretation. The measures I have taken to address those problems will form the bulk of this appendix. But the task of trying to do quantitative research in nonnormal times is inherently difficult. It would be unusual to find circumstances in which to do research on those occasions without encountering severely limiting conditions. I think the usefulness of the data is worth the risk.

After I began to consider the possibilities of doing a survey at a union meeting, I thought over questions I might ask but decided to wait in constructing the questionnaire until I had mentioned the idea to union leadership. They were almost too cooperative; when I asked then-president Madore about the survey, he not only had no objection but said that the upcoming meeting—in four days—would be the only one for the foreseeable future at which it could be done. So I hurriedly wrote the questionnaire and got pencils and cardboard backing for the strikers to use in filling it in. I decided to ask questions in four broad areas: participation in union activities, attitudes toward workplace democracy, orientation toward well-known political figures, and evaluations of the distribution of wealth and opportunity in the United States. By agreement with

Madore, I limited the questionnaire to two sides of a single sheet. This meant that I had to forgo many useful questions under each subtopic. In light of the short amount of time I had to construct the survey, and with the possibility in mind that I might want to compare the strikers' answers to those others have given, I borrowed some questions directly from other sources, particularly Kay Schlozman and Sidney Verba, *Insult to Injury,* and James Kluegel and Eliot Smith, *Beliefs About Inequality.*

The first potential problem based on the circumstances of the survey involves relation of site to sample. Would it not be logical to assume that even the fairly large group at union meetings might contain an overrepresentation of those most committed to the goals of the strike? While that is a reasonable supposition, there are several factors which offset that bias, and one important measure I took to correct it.

There were 1,050 employees on the day of the strike. By the time of the survey, approximately 225 had gone back in to work, and 35 had died. That meant there were roughly 790 potential strikers left. The union's financial secretary pointed out that another 40 had simply drifted away, largely those who had been hired during the in-plant strike and had moved on to other jobs once the strike began. That left 750 people to constitute what the financial secretary called the "striking family." That matched Barbara Johnson's records from the hardship fund.

The weekly union meetings were unusually large affairs, generally drawing between 300 and 400 people during the period I observed them. One reason for the large turnout was the social atmosphere the strike engendered, as described in Chapter 3. But another reason was that these meetings served as the place where strikers picked up their weekly strike pay. That meant there was a significant dilution of the self-selection process. Many members were there principally to pick up their checks. By a stroke of good luck, the union leadership had made a forceful appeal to members to attend meetings the week before I conducted the survey. That resulted in a large influx of non-regulars at the next meeting; attendance was about 450. That further diluted self-selection. By a stroke of bad luck, I had not attended the earlier meeting, did not expect the larger crowd, and brought only 300 questionnaires.[1] I left 25 surveys with the financial secretary to distribute to people who worked during union meeting time and picked up their paychecks at the union hall. I got back 23 usable responses from those. I distributed the remaining 275 in the union hall and got back 230, for a total of 253 usable responses.

In order to assess the representativeness of the group that met that day, the most important question to answer is not how many people were there, but what types of people were *not* there. The union accepted two excuses for handing out checks to those who did not attend—a part-time job during meeting time or physical disability, which in an older workforce like this was not an insignificant problem. It was from these groups that the financial secretary collected 23 surveys. There also was a small number of strikers who had taken full-time jobs and were thus (by virtue of making more than $150 a week) ineligible for strike pay. While I recognized an occasional person in this category attending union meetings anyway, obviously most of those people could not attend due to time conflicts. While any missing group will bias a sample, this group's absence would bias it severely only if we can assume that full-time job holders were less committed to strike goals than part-time job holders or those without a job. Two pieces of demographic information support the representativeness of those at the meeting. Both Reibeling and Johnson gave the average age at that point as 52; the average of my sample was 52.7. Reibeling's estimate of seniority was 20.5 years; my sample averaged 20.3. Nonetheless, despite the double dilution of self-selection, it is likely that there would have been a slight overrepresentation of activists among the 450 people at that meeting, and therefore the 253 in my sample. The problem can be demonstrated by this question. Is it reasonable to think that activists were as high a proportion of the 300 people who were not there as of the 450 who were? Even though I knew by eyeballing that some of the strike's most fervent partisans rarely came due to jobs or illness, the answer is still clearly no.

Fortunately, I included a question which gave me an opportunity to compensate for that bias. Some of the most committed activists participated in the Community-Labor Alliance (CLA). This was a group initiated by other labor officials in the city which met throughout the strike and was composed of varying numbers of Colt union officials, city labor council members, strike supporters, and rank-and-file strikers. It was a step of some magnitude for a striker who was not a union official to attend nighttime meetings where strike strategy and demonstrations were discussed. CLA participation is a good operational indicator of hard-core activism. One of the survey questions asks whether people have been to a CLA meeting "never," "once," or "many times." I added together the last two categories to arrive at a total of 63 people who claim to have been to at least one CLA meeting. No doubt there is some slight overreporting (or confusion) here. Barbara Johnson and another nonstriking member of the CLA estimated the number of strikers who had been to at least one CLA meeting at between 50 and 60, and there may have been a few of those who were not at the union meeting at which the survey was taken. But most hard-core activists were there—that is what might give rise to the suspicion of a biased sample in the first place—and overreporting of "good citizen" activity is simply a fact of survey life.

By cross-tabulating those who had been to at least one CLA meeting with each question, I obtained a subsample of activists and nonactivists. That is why I lumped together the two positive answers to the CLA question—I was generous in assigning people to the "activist" category in order to correct the potential bias in the sample. A complete profile of the questions and data from the whole sample and two subsamples appears in Appendix F. Here is a condensed overview. There are differences between the nonactivists' sample and the whole sample, but the more important story is that those differences were small. The differences run in the expected direction; that is, the nonactivists were slightly less supportive of the strike, less active, and less supportive of goals and policies normally associated with unions than the sample as a whole. In short, the nonactivists' answers are somewhat to the "right" of the sample as a whole. In the first twenty questions, seventeen differences were in this expected direction. But none was statistically significant at .05, and only three were borderline (significant by stretching things a bit to $p < .1$).[2]

The last five questions on redistribution and opportunity reveal a slightly different pattern and are handled separately, as explained in Chapter 5. In order to maximize the possibility of difference between samples, I also compared the sample of nonactivists with the sample of activists. The differences between these two subsamples are predictably larger (nine are significant at .05, all in the expected direction). Where the differences between the subsamples tell an interesting story, I have called them to the reader's attention. But my purpose in creating these two subsamples is not principally to compare them but to negate the potential bias in the survey. This overview supports an important generalization: there is not a single substantive conclusion I would draw based on the whole sample that I have to alter by using the subsample of nonactivists. In order to provide the most accurate representation of the strikers as a whole, and also in order to present the most compelling case, *I have used the nonactivist subsample throughout the text except where otherwise noted.* The N's in the tables refer *only* to the nonactivists rather than the number of respondents as a whole. I have no doubt that this is an overcorrection. Activists are part of the striking body and the numbers presented in the text eliminate them completely. But that is a more tolerable bias, because it means that statements about change and commitment to the strike will have a tougher test to pass.

People may still have objections to the sample. While there may be steps I could have taken to improve the process, readers need to keep in mind that it was done quickly, with severe limitations on time and space, without money to entice respondents, and without the luxury of continuously adding to the sample as in telephone surveys. The overriding fact is that it was done. Insistence on meeting "standard" interviewing format would have ensured that it would not be done, and that would have been a valuable opportunity lost.

# Appendix E

The direct comparison of the electoral choices of strikers and other Connecticut union members is imprecise for reasons unrelated to the representativeness of the sample of strikers. The Institute for Social Inquiry figures are taken from a random sample of all Connecticut union members. The sample to which they are being compared is by definition taken only from *strikers,* not the entire Colt workforce as it existed on January 23, the day before the strike. About 225 of those employed on that day went back to work and were therefore not part of the group whose opinions are recorded here. In almost every case, that is not a major issue, since the book is concerned with the attitudes of strikers. But it is important in Chapter 4. It is not just possible but highly likely that a greater percentage of those who went back to work were predisposed to vote Republican and to evaluate Republicans favorably. This is based not on any knowledge of the returnees' views but on common sense. There is a certain constellation of attitudes about individualism, unions, the ethics of working during a strike, and Republican orientation which fits together logically and undoubtedly in some predictive relation. My argument in Chapter 4 is that the enormous difference between the Democratic vote and unfavorable evaluations of Reagan given by Colt strikers and other Connecticut union members is due to a reorientation of political thinking caused by the conflict. But could it be nothing more than a reflection of the fact that many of those predisposed to think Republican were siphoned out of the sample because they had returned to work? Was the sample a self-selected overrepresentation of those who were more inclined to have disliked Reagan more *before* the strike?

In all likelihood self-selection makes the differences between the two groups compared in the chapter appear greater than they would have been had the whole workforce remained on strike. But the Democratic majority among strikers is so large that a few simple tests show that the difference with other union members is not artifactual. If I make the stringent assumption that the returnees, had they stayed on strike, would have voted for Bush in exactly the same proportion that strikers voted for Dukakis, and if they had voted at the same rate as the strikers, the figures would have been 73 percent for Dukakis and 27 percent for Bush. Under the preposterously demanding assumption that *every single person* who returned to work would have voted for Bush, 72 percent still would have voted for Dukakis. Either figure is still a sizable increase from the 55 percent of union members in the state as a whole who voted Democratic, a difference which in both cases is significant at .01. And it is far-fetched to believe that either of these demanding assumptions is in fact accurate. While it is likely that the returnees were more Republican than those who remained on strike, their socioeconomic status and UAW membership does not suggest they would have been as uniformly Republican as the strikers became Democratic.

The evaluations of Reagan follow a similar pattern. Combining the two unfavorable ratings gives Reagan a "negative" of 96 percent from the strikers, compared with 54 percent from other union members. Adopting the two assumptions above, and assuming that as many returnees would have abstained from answering the question as strikers, the negatives would have been 75 percent if returnees were the mirror opposite of the strikers and 74 percent if they all had given Reagan favorable ratings. That is still a difference from other union members which is significant at .01. And again, the assumptions are likely to overcorrect the bias grossly.

This should establish that the strike caused a movement of participants' views. But why use numbers in the chapter which I admit here are likely to overstate the differences? There is no precise way to calculate the predispositions of the returnees. The numbers in the appendix simply show that *no* estimate of the political attitudes of the returnees changes the basic conclusion. The numbers given in the chapter provide the only hard and fast information—what the political attitudes of the strikers were three years into the strike. They argue that the striking "family" had reached an extraordinary unity in its view of national politics. The comparisons and this appendix argue that the unity deepened during the strike.

# Appendix F

The data below are taken from 253 returned questionnaires (see Appendix D for details). There were four additional questions in the original survey. Respondents were asked their age, which averaged 52.7 ($N$=199), and length of service, which averaged 20.3 years ($N$=115). There was a question about whether the interests of management and workers are opposed, but I worded the response categories so ambiguously that I disregarded the results. Then there was the question about participation in the Community-Labor Alliance, which I used to divide activists from nonactivists (Appendix D). Other than those, all the information taken from the survey appears below. Here are some preliminary points:

A. Twenty-five respondents did not turn the page over to its second side. That accounts for most of the fall-off in $N$'s beginning with question 13.

B. Significance tests are given for the differences between the nonactivists and the whole sample and for the differences between nonactivists and activists. The test of significance is a difference of proportion test using a normal distribution. The reason I present significance as lenient as .1 is substantive. Since one possible objection to the survey is that it oversamples activists, I want to show that even with very tolerant standards, there is little difference between the nonactivist sample and the sample as a whole.

C. The nonactivists and the activists do not add up to the sample as a whole. That is because 57 people either skipped the question of whether they had been to a Community-Labor Alliance meeting or answered "don't know." I could have created a non-activist sample out of all those who did not answer "yes" to that question, on the very plausible assumption that the real activists would have remembered those meetings. That would have had the benefit of increasing the nonactivist N's. But I excluded those who did not answer from either subsample, which creates a purer group of nonactivists, making the similarities with the sample as a whole more meaningful.

*Whole* means the entire sample of 253; *Non* means the nonactivist subsample of 133; *Act* means the activist subsample of 63. N's specific to each question are also given (missing data excluded). An asterisk next to the nonactivist subsample indicates a significant difference between the nonactivists and the sample as a whole; a dagger next to the activist subsample indicates a significant difference between the activists and nonactivists. In a table with neither symbol, there is no significant difference. The test is only for one response category in each question, which I selected for its substantive interest. It will be noted below each question which particular category is being tested. All numbers are percentages.

1. During the strike, have you ever picketed more than the required four hours?

|  | No, never | Once or twice | Many times |
|---|---|---|---|
| Whole (229) | 5.4 | 17.4 | 77.2 |
| Non (124) | 5.6 | 23.3 | 71.0 |
| Act (56)† | 0 | 10.7 | 89.3 |

Tested for "many times."
†p < .05

2. During the strike, did you ever go to any of the union's other rallies?

|  | No, never | Once or twice | Many times |
|---|---|---|---|
| Whole (224) | 5.8 | 28.1 | 66.1 |
| Non (126) | 5.6 | 33.3 | 61.1 |
| Act (57)† | 1.8 | 22.8 | 75.4 |

Tested for "many times."
†p < .05

3. *During the strike,* have you ever written or spoken to a government official such as a state representative or congressman?

|  | No, never | Once or twice | Many times |
|---|---|---|---|
| Whole (222) | 50.9 | 36.9 | 12.2 |
| Non (125)° | 59.2 | 34.4 | 6.4 |
| Act (57)† | 42.1 | 36.8 | 21.1 |

Emphasis in original. Tested for "many times."
°p < .1
†p < .05

4. *Before the strike,* did you ever write or speak to a government official?

|  | No, never | Once or twice | Many times |
|---|---|---|---|
| Whole (214) | 73.4 | 20.1 | 6.5 |
| Non (126) | 82.5 | 14.4 | 3.2 |
| Act (57)† | 50.9 | 31.6 | 17.5 |

Emphasis in original. Tested for "many times."
†p < .1

5.  During the ten-month period without a contract, employees sometimes wore yellow T-shirts to work to show solidarity. Did you ever do this?

|  | No, never | Once or twice | Many times |
|---|---|---|---|
| Whole (227) | 15.9 | 17.6 | 66.5 |
| Non (125) | 19.2 | 20.0 | 60.8 |
| Act (60)† | 10.0 | 15.0 | 75.0 |

Tested for "many times."
†p < .05

6.  During the ten-month period, employees also sometimes walked around the plant during lunch singing union songs. Did you ever do this?

|  | No, never | Once or twice | Many times |
|---|---|---|---|
| Whole (221) | 27.6 | 18.1 | 54.4 |
| Non (127) | 34.6 | 17.3 | 48.0 |
| Act (56)† | 12.5 | 16.1 | 71.4 |

Tested for "many times."
†p < .05

7.  Did you vote in the 1988 presidential election?

|  | Yes | No |
|---|---|---|
| Whole (236) | 86.9 | 13.1 |
| Non (128) | 86.7 | 13.3 |
| Act (59) | 89.8 | 10.2 |

Tested proportion directly.

8.  If you voted, who did you vote for?

|  | Bush | Dukakis |
|---|---|---|
| Whole (203) | 7.4 | 92.6 |
| Non (113) | 7.1 | 92.9 |
| Act (53) | 9.4 | 90.6 |

Tested proportion directly.

9.  On the whole, how would you rate Ronald Reagan as president?

|  | Poor | Only fair | Good | Very good |
|---|---|---|---|---|
| Whole (221) | 71.5 | 22.2 | 5.0 | 1.3 |
| Non (122) | 71.1 | 24.8 | 4.1 | 0 |
| Act (56) | 78.6 | 16.1 | 5.4 | 0 |

Dichotomized negative and positive categories, then tested proportions.

10.  Besides picketing, do you ever spend any other time with Colt employees?

|  | No | Once in a while | A great deal |
|---|---|---|---|
| Whole (209) | 31.3 | 43.3 | 25.5 |
| Non (120)* | 35.8 | 46.7 | 17.5 |
| Act (55)† | 21.8 | 34.5 | 43.6 |

Tested for "a great deal."
*$p < .1$
†$p < .05$

11.  Compared to the time when you were working, have you gotten to know other employees better?

|  | No | About the same | A little more | A lot more |
|---|---|---|---|---|
| Whole (199) | 6.0 | 14.6 | 28.6 | 50.8 |
| Non (104)* | 7.0 | 17.5 | 34.2 | 41.2 |
| Act (54)† | 3.7 | 13.0 | 22.2 | 61.1 |

Tested for "a lot more."
*$p < .1$
†$p < .05$

12.  In a situation like this, people sometimes try to help each other out. Has that gone on in this strike?

|  | No | Once in a while | A great deal |
|---|---|---|---|
| Whole (205) | 7.7 | 25.8 | 66.5 |
| Non (117) | 6.8 | 23.1 | 70.0 |
| Act (54) | 1.9 | 26.4 | 71.8 |

Tested for "a great deal."

13.  Circle the phrase which describes your feelings about the other strikers:

|  | Don't know them | Some are friends | We are like brothers and sisters |
|---|---|---|---|
| Whole (140) | 10.0 | 27.9 | 62.1 |
| Non (81) | 13.6 | 33.3 | 53.0 |
| Act (39)† | 5.1 | 15.4 | 79.5 |

Tested for "brothers and sisters."
†$p < .1$

14. Have you ever thought about going back in as an individual?

|  | No, never | Early in the strike | Late in the strike |
| --- | --- | --- | --- |
| Whole (171) | 91.8 | 5.8 | 2.3 |
| Non (102) | 91.2 | 5.9 | 2.9 |
| Act (45) | 91.1 | 6.7 | 2.2 |

Tested for "never."

15. What is the most important reason you have remained a striker?

|  | Back pay | Want my job back | Respect for other strikers |
| --- | --- | --- | --- |
| Whole (177) | 10.7 | 43.5 | 45.8 |
| Non (95) | 10.5 | 41.1 | 48.4 |
| Act (52) | 13.5 | 42.3 | 44.2 |

Tested for "respect."

16. If you had to take another job, how important would it be to you that there was a union there?

|  | Not at all | Somewhat important | Very important |
| --- | --- | --- | --- |
| Whole (209) | 7.2 | 17.7 | 75.1 |
| Non (117) | 7.7 | 22.2 | 70.1 |
| Act (54) | 5.6 | 13.0 | 81.5 |

Tested for "very important."

17. Some people say that employees should have a voice in work decisions. Others disagree. How much say should employees have over the way work is done?

|  | None | A little | Some | A lot |
| --- | --- | --- | --- | --- |
| Whole (200) | 3.0 | 8.5 | 36.0 | 52.5 |
| Non (112) | 3.6 | 6.3 | 40.2 | 50.0 |
| Act (56) | 1.8 | 10.7 | 28.6 | 58.9 |

Tested for "a lot."

18. How much say should employees have over the quality of work?

|  | None | A little | Some | A lot |
| --- | --- | --- | --- | --- |
| Whole (192) | 3.1 | 6.2 | 23.4 | 67.2 |
| Non (110) | 3.6 | 4.5 | 23.6 | 68.2 |
| Act (51) | 2.0 | 5.9 | 23.5 | 68.6 |

Tested for "a lot."

19.  How much say should employees have over selection of supervisors?

|  | None | A little | Some | A lot |
|---|---|---|---|---|
| Whole (189) | 17.5 | 13.8 | 39.7 | 29.1 |
| Non (109) | 19.3 | 13.8 | 45.0 | 22.0 |
| Act (50)† | 16.0 | 12.0 | 36.0 | 36.0 |

Tested for "a lot."

† p < .1

20.  How much say should employees have over what a company does with its profits?

|  | None | A little | Some | A lot |
|---|---|---|---|---|
| Whole (192) | 16.1 | 13.5 | 35.9 | 34.4 |
| Non (114) | 13.2 | 16.7 | 38.6 | 31.6 |
| Act (51)† | 13.7 | 9.8 | 29.4 | 47.0 |

Tested for "a lot."

† p < .1

21.  How good a chance do you think a person has to get ahead today, if the person works hard?

|  | Little chance | Some chance | A good chance | A very good chance |
|---|---|---|---|---|
| Whole (203) | 28.1 | 29.6 | 20.7 | 21.7 |
| Non (118) | 30.5 | 28.8 | 19.5 | 21.2 |
| Act (52) | 26.9 | 30.8 | 21.2 | 21.2 |

Added nether-end categories, added middle categories, formed a "strong views, weaker views" dichotomy, then tested proportions.

22.  Circle your feeling about this statement: America is the land of opportunity where everyone who works hard can get ahead.

|  | Strongly disagree | Disagree | Agree | Strongly agree |
|---|---|---|---|---|
| Whole (194) | 12.9 | 33.0 | 33.0 | 21.1 |
| Non (111) | 9.0 | 36.9 | 35.1 | 18.9 |
| Act (52)† | 24.5 | 28.3 | 24.5 | 22.6 |

Added nether-end categories, added middle categories, formed a "strong views, weaker views" dichotomy, then tested proportions.

† p < .1

23.  How much chance does the child of a factory worker have to become a business executive or a professional?

|  | No chance at all | A slight chance | Some chance | A good chance |
|---|---|---|---|---|
| Whole (180) | 16.9 | 34.9 | 28.6 | 19.6 |
| Non (103) | 15.2 | 39.0 | 32.4 | 13.3 |
| Act (49)† | 17.3 | 28.8 | 25.0 | 28.8 |

Added nether-end categories, added middle categories, formed a "strong views, weaker views" dichotomy, then tested proportions.

† p < .05

24.  Circle your feeling about this statement: The government should tax the rich heavily in order to redistribute wealth.

|  | Strongly disagree | Disagree | Agree | Strongly agree |
|---|---|---|---|---|
| Whole (187) | 4.8 | 16.0 | 38.5 | 40.6 |
| Non (108) | 4.6 | 20.4 | 43.5 | 31.5 |
| Act (49)† | 4.1 | 10.2 | 32.7 | 53.1 |

Added nether-end categories, added middle categories, formed a "strong views, weaker views" dichotomy, then tested proportions.

† p < .05

25.  Circle your feeling about this statement: There should be a top limit on income so that no one can earn more than $200,000 a year.

|  | Strongly disagree | Disagree | Agree | Strongly agree |
|---|---|---|---|---|
| Whole (183) | 19.1 | 41.0 | 23.5 | 16.4 |
| Non (103) | 16.5 | 42.7 | 26.2 | 14.6 |
| Act (49) | 26.5 | 40.8 | 18.4 | 14.3 |

Added nether-end categories, added middle categories, formed a "strong views, weaker views" dichotomy, then tested proportions.

# Notes

## 1. The Times That Try Men's Souls

1 The former view is discussed by Aristide Zolberg, "Moments of Madness," and Michael Nelson, "'Pentecost' on the Pacific," the latter by a tradition of writers extending from Thucydides on the civil war in Corcyra to Crane Brinton on Jacobinism as a fever.

2 Lawrence Goodwyn, *The Populist Moment: A Short History of the Agrarian Revolt in America*. Here is his evocative description of the democratic spirit of that movement: "When a farm family's wagon crested a hill en route to a Fourth of July 'Alliance Day' encampment, and the occupants looked back to see thousands of other families trailed out behind in wagon trains, the thought that 'the Alliance is the people' took on transforming possibilities. Such a movement . . . instilled hope in hundreds of thousands of people who had been without it" (p. 34).

3 *Slavery: A Problem in American Institutional and Intellectual Life.*

4 William Gamson, Bruce Fireman, and Steven Rytina, *Encounters with Unjust Authority*, p. 108.

5 *Plato's Republic*, pp. 82–83. Plato proposed telling everyone that the reason people were awarded different roles was that they were originally fashioned from different metals. He was somewhat doubtful that his fable would succeed, however. When he

asked, "Can you suggest any device which will make our citizens believe this story?" his straight man replied that it would not be likely to work in the first generation.

6 Nicholas Abercrombie, Stephen Hill, and Bryan S. Turner, *The Dominant Ideology Thesis;* Robert Jessop, *Traditionalism, Conservatism, and the British Political Culture;* Frank Parkin, *Class Inequality and Political Order;* and Larry Spence, *The Politics of Social Knowledge.*

7 *Injustice: The Social Bases of Obedience and Revolt,* pp. 458–459.

8 Ibid., p. 188.

9 Ibid., p. 69. For other variations on the dominant ideology theme, see Joan Cocks, *The Oppositional Imagination;* Jennifer Hochschild, *What's Fair?;* James Kluegel and Eliot Smith, *Beliefs About Inequality;* Murray Edelman, *The Political Spectacle;* and Frank Parkin, *Class Inequality.* These authors come from a variety of disciplines, employ widely different methodologies, and are not always even discussing the same subject; nonetheless, they seem to agree on the point at issue.

10 *Domination and the Arts of Resistance,* p. 3. The substance of what he says here about a "hidden transcript" is similar to arguments in his earlier writings about a "little tradition" of resistance which coexists with a more visible "big tradition" of ostensible value consensus ("Protest and Profanation: Agrarian Revolt and the Little Tradition").

11 Michael Adas, "From Footdragging to Flight: The Evasive History of Peasant Avoidance Protest in South and Southeast Asia."

12 Abercrombie et al., *Dominant Ideology,* p. 159.

13 *The State of the Masses,* chapter 9. See also Guenther Lewy, *False Consciousness,* and Nelson Polsby, *Community Power and Political Theory,* 2d ed.

14 Hamilton and Wright, *State,* pp. 88–89.

15 The most extreme well-known example was life in Nazi concentration camps, which were little but a form of organized brutality. Camp authorities were nonetheless faced with the problem of moving prisoners around from task to task and therefore needed at least elementary methods of social organization. For the way in which prisoners reacted to those routines, see Bruno Bettelheim, *The Informed Heart,* and Viktor Frankl, *Man's Search for Meaning.*

16 Henri Lefebvre, *The Explosion: Marxism and the French Revolution,* p. 13.

17 Scott, *Domination,* chapter 4. He calls this the "thin theory" of hegemony. Max Weber provided this early formulation: "Every highly privileged group develops the myth of its natural superiority. Under conditions of stable distribution of power . . . that myth is accepted by the negatively privileged strata" (*Economy and Society,* p. 953).

18 Peter Berger and Thomas Luckmann, *The Social Construction of Reality;* Jon Elster, *Sour Grapes;* Don Zimmerman and Melvin Pollner, "The Everyday World as a Phenomenon."

19 *Federalist Papers,* no. 49.

20 *The Essential Works of John Stuart Mill,* p. 318.

21  *Everyday Life,* p. 15. But I should add that one does not have to subscribe to hegemony theory at all to believe that the stability of institutional arrangements will play a role in mass beliefs. Cohesion and the specific pattern of mutual obligations will condition anyone's set of expectations as well as the costs of opposition, including the likelihood and severity of coercion.

22  Earl Thorpe, "Chattel Slavery and Concentration Camps"; Orlando Patterson, "Quashee." These are both in Ann Lane, ed., *The Debate Over Slavery: Stanley Elkins and His Critics.* Eugene Genovese, "Rebelliousness and Docility in the Negro Slave: A Critique of the Elkins Thesis," in the same volume, takes issue with both positions; Genovese argues that a single slave can move from Sambo to Nat Turner without ever having struck a false pose.

23  *Domination,* p. 4.

24  The maximalists are usually leftists of some kind. But the pulls of daily problem solving are sometimes said to defuse right-wing radicalism as well: "Such unloved but potent social forces in the 1950s as consumerism and suburbanization may in some ways have helped cool the fires of McCarthyism. . . . Perhaps the suburbs, with the centrifugal force of privatization and 'togetherness,' encouraged a blandness that, though maddening to young 1960s radicals, also frustrated right-wing extremists" (Richard Fried, *Nightmare in Red,* p. 192).

25  *State,* pp. 402–403.

26  This is not so much a specific formulation by a particular writer as an extrapolation based on market-oriented theories of interest. A brief but revealing aside in Polsby's *Community Power* makes that point directly. If pluralists found little dissatisfaction among blacks in New Haven in the 1950s, and if there were riots in the 1960s, this must (Polsby's term is an ironic *may*) mean that grievances accumulated later, not that the initial findings missed something (pp. 171–172).

27  Scott, *Domination,* p. 223.

28  "Moments of Madness." Sidney Tarrow borrows that term to describe the 1967–1970 period of conflict in Italy, during which "themes of autonomy and resistance to authority were widely diffused" (*Democracy and Disorder,* p. 215).

29  "Moments of Madness," p. 187. Zolberg notes how often observers of these special periods stress these sentiments in their reports. Confirming evidence comes from this account of the opening of the Berlin Wall: "If 'revolutionary' describes, among other things, a state of mind, a mass psychology in which people of all kinds become involved in events outside their own day-to-day existence, in which social questions become immediate and personal, in which awareness is heightened, energies liberated, creativity emerges from nowhere and is apparent everywhere, then the month between October 9 and November 9 was a revolutionary month" (Peter Marcuse, "Letter from the German Democratic Republic," p. 32).

30  *Thelma and Louise,* Metro-Goldwyn-Mayer, 1991.

31  The last two conditions are important to distinguish democratic moments from simple chaos. In *Thelma and Louise* both Thelma and her husband had their worlds

torn apart; while she confronts questions of gender and power, he descends into increasingly bewildered incomprehension.

32 Michael Goldfield, *The Decline of Organized Labor in the United States,* p. 195, provides an account which makes the increased dedication by management and its hired consultants to antiunion activity into the primary explanation for the declining percentage of unionized employees in the workforce. See also Jonathan Rosenblum, *The Copper Crucible,* for a description of the strategy behind the use of replacement workers.

33 As examples: the air traffic controllers, Phelps Dodge, Hormel, Clinton Corn, Jay Maine. The first and last of these, as well as the general trend of Reagan-era labor setbacks, were subjects of constant discussion among the Colt strikers.

34 A British study of mass participation in labor conflict concluded that being on strike was a bore: "Waging the class struggle can be intensely depressing" (Kenneth Roberts, *The Fragmentary Class Structure,* p. 97).

35 Virtually all of the information I present was gathered before the events which led to the strike's successful conclusion. The inferences I draw would not have changed in any meaningful way had the strike failed. My deemphasis of the strike's success is based on two factors. First, I think that the success was idiosyncratic and does not presage a reborn labor movement. The same management tools of hardballing and then threatening striker replacement were enough to panic the Caterpillar strikers into retreat in the spring of 1992. Second, the subsequent bankruptcy cast a shadow of ambiguity on the strikers' victory, although the newly created company was able to fight its way out.

36 *Slavery.*

37 Goffman, *Asylums.*

38 Richard Pfeffer, *Working for Capitalism.* See Lendler, *Just the Working Life,* chapters 2 and 4, on my reasons for making use of this formulation.

39 Robert Dahl, *A Preface to Economic Democracy;* Ronald Mason, *Participatory and Workplace Democracy;* Carol Pateman, *Participation and Democratic Theory.*

40 See David Halle, *America's Working Man,* and Reeve Vanneman and Lynn Cannon, *The American Perception of Class,* for an estimation of the extent of a cohesive vision among industrial employees.

41 Hamilton and Wright, *State,* chapter 6 for the first; Karen Sacks, *My Troubles Are Going to Have Trouble with Me,* and Donald Nonini, "Everyday Forms of Popular Resistance," for the second; and Michael Burawoy, *Manufacturing Consent,* and Youseff Cohen, *The Manipulation of Consent,* for the third.

42 Something like this very nearly happened in the Iranian revolution. There was a political scientist doing research in the slums of south Teheran in the late 1970s just as that area was becoming a center of the anti-Shah mobilization. Unfortunately, his project ended just as the mobilization reached its peak. See Farhad Kazemi, *Poverty and Revolution in Iran,* for the useful results.

43 *Injustice,* p. 188.

## 2. Irrepressible Conflict

1 Phil Wheeler, interview with author.

2 Madore was not originally from the firearms division but had become identified with Wheeler and the strike.

3 Richard Reibeling, interview with author.

4 See Hamilton and Wright, *State,* particularly pp. 91–94, for an argument that surveys are superior to field studies and other forms of nonquantitative data; see Fantasia, *Cultures of Solidarity,* pp. 5–8, for the reverse. Neither book categorically dismisses the usefulness of the unfavored method, but each expresses a clear preference for the one it employs.

5 At times the data are best interpreted when this timing is kept in mind; I will try to bring that to the reader's attention as I proceed.

6 Simmons went on to be elected to Hartford City Council. Her research on the Colt conflict is presented in "Organizational and Leadership Models in Labor-Community Coalitions" and *Organizing in Hard Times.*

7 One of the tasks Johnson took on, with the union's support, was the organization of small stress-management groups for the strikers. The impressions she conveyed from them provided additional insight into the ways in which strikers were interpreting events.

8 Robert L. Wilson, *Colt, an American Legend,* p. 10.

9 Ibid., p. 136.

10 Wilson estimates Colt's personal income at $1 million in 1860 and 1861 (p. 111).

11 Glenn Weaver, *Hartford,* p. 80.

12 The company purchased the patent for the first machine gun (as well as the automatic pistol carrying his name) from John Browning. When the army was slow to express interest in the machine gun, the Colt general manager shrugged it off: "In the meantime, there's all of South America" (Ellsworth Grant, *The City of Hartford 1784–1984,* pp. 30–32).

13 Ibid., p. 93.

14 For a discussion of the weaknesses of 7a, see James Atleson, *Values and Assumptions in American Labor Law,* chapter 2, and Christopher Tomlins, *The State and the Unions,* chapter 4. Both stress the inability of the labor board created by that law to enforce its rulings with sanctions.

15 *Hartford Courant,* March 14, 1935.

16 *Hartford Courant,* March 20, 1935. Republican Senator Joseph Nye, who headed that committee, spoke at a union rally in support of recognition. Colt was the sole supplier of machine guns at that point, and the government took an active interest in the strike from the beginning.

17 The timing of the end of the strike carried some unfortunate ironies for the employees. One argument the company had made was that even the minimal rights extended to workers by 7a of the NRA were suspect. Grant quotes President Stone as telling the NRA administrator, "And you know as well as I that there's a serious question as to whether the whole NRA is constitutional" (*City of Hartford,* p. 128). One

week before the strike ended the Supreme Court indeed ruled against it, but one month later, the much stronger Wagner Act was passed.

18 Much of my account of the events of 1941 and 1948 comes from a tape made by Gunning on July 20, 1982. The tape was made available to me by Gunning's daughter, Meg Whinnem.

19 Gunning's distrust was partly based on experience. He had been a production worker at another plant in Hartford which the IAM had tried to organize in 1927–1928. Craft workers struck and production workers were not invited to join the strike.

20 Gunning tape.

21 "I knew little of the question of the National Labor Relations Board and the company apparently knew less about it" (Gunning tape).

22 John Mueller, "The UE-IUE Conflict in Bristol, Connecticut"; Susan Howard, "The UE-UAW Struggle at Colt's." While Howard's paper was done for an undergraduate class on labor history, it is written with a good professional reporter's trained eye for accuracy and confirmation. She also made use of the Gunning tape and an interview with Gunning's wife.

23 Mueller, "The UE-IUE Conflict." He describes in detail a contest between the UE and the IUE at the E. Ingraham Company in Bristol in which the main IUE handbill was titled "Americanism or Communism: You Must Choose." The vote on disaffiliation from the UE was so close that two ballots were needed.

24 *Hartford Times,* May 15, 1948. Colt also charged in that letter that the record of the local UE during World War II was one of "factionalism, bitter internal strife and constant interruption of production." That was particularly disingenuous. When there was a brief walkout over an arbitration ruling cutting wages in May 1943, the general secretary of the UE sent this telegram to the local: "The small faction that is provoking this undisciplined action is harming the welfare of thousands of Colt workers. . . . The interruption of production . . . cannot be tolerated and violates this international union's no-strike policy" (Grant, *City of Hartford,* p. 165). Of course, the attitude of a union in which Communists played a role as they did in the UE might be expected to be different at the the beginning of the Cold War than it had been during World War II.

25 His preferred position was to stay in the UE and oppose leftist policies, according to his wife (Howard interview with Anna Gunning). That position was stated publicly by Sid Gunning in a letter to the *Hartford Times,* May 15, 1948.

26 Gunning tape.

27 This process is described in Ronald Schatz, *The Electrical Workers,* pp. 178–180.

28 *Hartford Times,* June 3, 1948.

29 Mueller, "The UE-IUE Conflict," p. 13. The spin I have put on these events is consonant with the Gunning tape, his wife and daughter's recollections, the newspaper record, and the interpretations of the two people who wrote about them, Howard and Mueller. A more cynical interpretation might be that it was a velvet raid by the UAW. Even if that were true, the essential effects remain—no internal division and

no florid anti-UE or anticommunist rhetoric. One more fact tends to substantiate the account as written. The two strongest UE supporters became part of local leadership after Gunning moved up to join the UAW staff.

30 Ray Boryczka, "Militancy and Factionalism in the United Auto Workers Union, 1937–1941."

31 The causes of that fiasco have been variously given as failure to modernize, the poor quality of information transmission, and even the age of the president (Grant, *City of Hartford,* pp. 162–167; Wilson, *Colt,* pp. 272–273). The armory stopped making weapons completely and survived only because it had previously diversified into dishwashers.

32 Grant, *City of Hartford,* pp. 187–189. The company also used a facility in Rocky Hill, Connecticut, for a time to cope with the increased demand.

33 Wheeler interview.

34 Ibid.

35 Ibid. Because Wheeler and the others fired were grieving their dismissals, they retained their union positions.

36 Wheeler interview; *Hartford Courant,* April 1 and 3.

37 Richard Reibeling, interview with author. His explanation for the declining market share was that Colt made the top-of-the-line commercial gun and that people bought cheaper as well as fewer guns.

38 Reibeling interview.

39 What happened to the $1.8 million is an interesting sidebar to the strike. At first the offer was unconditional and Colt said it was interested. Then the Hartford Redevelopment Agency attached the stipulation that Colt be required to guarantee it would continue to employ 140 city residents at its Hartford plant. The company balked and appealed to the city council, complaining about ex post facto conditions. But by then the strike had started and the council said the money would be available only when the labor dispute was settled. The company replied that the city could keep its money.

40 The "cash cow" concept is discussed in Barry Bluestone and Bennet Harrison, *The Deindustrialization of America,* pp. 149–151. The accusation that Colt Industries was draining resources from the firearms division is not exclusive to the union. It was repeated by Worth Loomis, briefly CEO of the poststrike company, in a talk at Trinity College, and by firearms industry analyst David Guthrie, quoted in "State's Big Stake in Colt Clouds Debate on Guns," *New York Times,* July 5, 1992.

41 The choice of terms in describing those who work during strikes is a matter of contention. Unions, of course, call them scabs. Management calls them replacement workers, which is also their legal name. The fact that American labor law permits companies to hire new permanent employees is not a compelling argument that a writer must follow suit and adopt that language. I will use the term *strikebreaker,* because that is most precisely what those who cross picket lines are doing. Union members seem to understand the political nature of language: there was a sign at a

bar near the Hartford plant which strikers frequented which read "Scabs are *not* replacement workers."

42 Paul Levy, "Unidimensional Perspective of the Reagan Labor Board," gives these examples of what the new board found acceptable: "an employer's declaration from the outset that he demanded a $35 per week reduction in wages and if the employees would not accept that position they simply 'don't work here anymore'; an employer's refusal to continue bargaining while referring the union to its attorney, who in turn refused to return telephone calls; an employer's withdrawal of an offer only after the union had accepted it; and an employer's demands that were known to be unacceptable in order to induce its employees to conduct a hopeless strike or to abandon collective bargaining" (pp. 332–333).

43 See Tom Balanoff, "The Cement Workers' Experience," pp. 6–8, for a description of the forced strike as a management weapon; also Rosenblum, *Copper Crucible,* for a description of the first prominent use of that strategy.

44 Wheeler and Reibeling interviews. I should point out for the sake of accuracy that Reibeling was claiming that this had *always* characterized union-management relations at Colt, not that it had come to do so recently. On the other hand, these were certainly *his* perceptions, and he had been in a position to translate those judgments into policy only since becoming head of labor relations in 1983.

45 Wheeler interview.

46 Reibeling interview.

47 Ibid.

48 At the NLRB hearing, the company lawyer asked Wheeler, "Do you recall Mr. Reibeling telling you that with regard to the zero wage increase and the healthcare contribution that he was not 'playing around'?" Wheeler: "I think it was said" (p. 374).

49 UAW Local 376 to Reibeling, February 18, 1985.

50 Reibeling to Wheeler, February 26, 1985. Most of the italics are mine; Reibeling underlined the word *not.* In his interview with me, Reibeling explained that he meant the proposal was not based on short-term financial loss but on long-term market conditions. However, the company did not take the occasion of that exchange to clarify that point or to restate those conditions in response to the union's request. Employees regarded Reibeling's words as a taunt.

51 The precise wording at the bottom of the proposal was "NOTE: If this proposal is accepted and ratified prior to April 1, 1985, the Company will renew its lease for the Huyshope Avenue [Hartford] facility. If the proposal is not accepted and ratified . . . the Company offers to start negotiation concerning the relocation issue involving the military manufacturing facility."

52 I have no reason to doubt that Reibeling was accurately describing Colt Industries policy, but less than a year later Colt did increase a final offer to its Chandler-Evans division, located on the same block as Colt. The initial offer had been the same, but management relented on the two red flag issues, zero raises and copayment. When I asked Reibeling about that, he granted that there was some flexibility under some

conditions. "Let's face it. The [parent] company was not interested in having two divisions on strike, so I'm sure there was some strategic thinking."

53 Wheeler and Howard interviews; *Hartford Courant,* March 30, 1985.

54 A number of questions were asked about this speaker at the NLRB hearing, but his identity was never specified beyond "a black guy from a UAW local in the Midwest."

55 *Hartford Courant,* March 30, 1985.

56 Reibeling: "The union's decision to work without a contract came as something of a surprise to us. . . . We thought that given Wheeler's history, not only at Colt but at other companies, that he would strike. . . . We weren't really sure what was going to happen." Interview.

57 Atleson, *Values and Assumptions,* chapter 3; Tomlins, *The State,* pp. 240–241.

58 There is a large set of activities in which employees may engage that is neither illegal—in violation of any criminal statutes—nor protected from company retaliation by suspension or termination (Atleson, *Values and Assumptions,* pp. 46–48).

59 The administrative law judge found that one worker fired in the ten-month period was terminated so that the company could impress on employees the fact that it could act arbitrarily ("Decision," p. 60). The fired employee was generally active but did not hold any union position.

60 The phrase "running the plant backward" is taken from an article of that title by Jack Metzgar. While Metzgar was advocating pressuring the company through an in-plant strategy, he carefully sought to describe activity he believed to be protected. This strategy is roughly similar to the British union strategy of "working to rule."

61 A plant official could not cite any case of an employee who had been disciplined for turning down overtime prior to this time (NLRB Hearing, p. 2974). He later brought up the unrelated example of an employee who was disciplined after agreeing to work and then not showing up. Of course, the company had never faced such a massive refusal to work overtime, either.

62 "Decision," pp. 6, 37.

63 The judge is speaking in legal terms. Readers will have to make their own decisions about whether collective resistance by employees not sanctioned by American labor law should be termed misconduct.

64 NLRB Hearing, pp. 5049, 5063.

65 Company lawyer at NLRB hearing: "Mr. Reibeling suggests that the union is making certain information requests as a means of harassment rather than in connection with good faith bargaining." Wheeler: "Definitely not" (p. 234). Company lawyer: "Did you know on April 1, 1985, Mr. Wheeler, that an employer could not unilaterally implement a proposal without being at an impasse?" Wheeler: "I thought that was the case" (p. 419). Lawyer: "You knew, Mr. Wheeler, that if you just kept asking for information you could avoid impasse. Didn't you?" Wheeler: "We weren't at an impasse" (424).

66 The company's purpose in not letting employees make further credit union deductions was to prevent covert dues payments. When there is no contract, the union cannot receive its dues through a checkoff, and some employees used the credit

union as a surrogate. As with some other company practices in that period, it returned small-arms fire with a bazooka.

67 Howard interview.

68 Wheeler interview.

69 Howard interview.

70 Reibeling interview.

71 The company eventually worked its way back up to 925 employees. There were about 250 union members who returned, almost all of them in the first year.

72 NLRB Hearing, p. 1633.

73 NLRB Hearing, p. 2004.

74 *Hartford Courant,* March 8, 1986.

75 For an account of the formation and activities of the Community-Labor Alliance, see Simmons, *Organizing,* pp. 44–56.

76 NLRB Hearing, p. 2580.

77 The union made a unilateral offer to return to work on August 24, 1986. The company refused and the state ruled it a lockout.

78 The record which the NLRB reviewed in deciding not to bring that charge consisted in part of notes of negotiation meetings provided by the company. The union produced evidence in the later NLRB hearing that those notes had been edited extensively, and the administrative law judge threw the notes out as evidence (NLRB Hearing, pp. 3754–4105). Union leaders felt that had they spotted the editing earlier, they would have been able to sustain the surface bargaining charge.

79 "Decision," p. 63.

80 At first I had trouble understanding why the company would fire strikers it had already replaced. But even an unfavorable ruling would have left the strikers with the right to be called back when jobs became available. Management said it would not reemploy these seventeen because of strike misconduct. The judge ruled that while some had committed acts of strike misconduct, all were entitled to full rights because of "disparate treatment"—strikebreakers had committed similar acts and not been disciplined, and "condonation"—the company had absent-mindedly included these people in "come back to work" telegrams after they had been fired.

81 The union claimed the Armed Services Committee told Colt to settle the strike.

82 Press release, Local 376, May 3, 1989.

83 In the resolution of an unfair labor practice strike, those hired after the strike are dismissed, although the union members who crossed the picket line are not.

84 The state is permitted to invest up to 3 percent of its pension money in programs offering social and economic benefit. The main debate which ensued was not around the value of intervening in the market, but the propriety of subsidizing the production of guns.

## 3. *A Rather Substantial Commitment*

1 This is particularly true of some of the early "crowd psychology" studies, defining that genre widely enough to include both Gustave Le Bon and Crane Brinton.

There is the added temptation when one has a potful of stirring quotes by participants, as I do here, and as most observers of popular conflict will, to blur the difference between what is representative and what sounds dramatic.

2 This is the conclusion of authors as diverse as Philip Converse, "The Nature of Belief Systems in Mass Publics," and Moore, *Injustice.* Converse speaks to this optical
illusion in the sometimes overlooked final pages of his article, particularly pp.
249–254, in which he dissects the followership of the highly ideological Nazi and
abolitionist movements.

3 That is why Zolberg pointed to the need for resolving the crowd into individuals
("Moments of Madness," p. 207).

4 Reibeling, interview with author. Later in this chapter, Reibeling will be presenting
a more complex and sophisticated assessment of employee attitudes.

5 These arguments are offered in addition to what to many should be the clincher:
that these workers were in fact still on strike and that this must have revealed a preference for striking rather than the alternatives. The individual strikers were free to
return to work at any point.

6 Although some members were critical of that decision by union leadership, they
were careful to place that in context of overall support for and even admiration of
the job the leaders had done. An example: "That's one mistake the union made, not
to strike [at that point]. And God bless the union, I've been on strike for three years,
and I'll stay on strike for three more years if I have to."

7 Howard, interview with author. I had a personal experience which confirmed the
openness Howard is describing and also suggested that the union leadership felt it
had nothing to hide from outsiders. Madore addressed two classes of mine at
Mount Holyoke College and issued a blanket invitation to students—not all of
whom were sympathetic to the strikers—to come to union meetings.

8 That is, they might have applied to unions the cost-cutting strategy of retrospective
evaluation. This is more normally used in assessing voting decisions (Morris Fiorina, *Retrospective Voting in American National Elections*), but the virtual absence
of negative retrospective judgments here seems remarkable.

9 *Sit-Down: The General Motors Strike of 1936–1937,* especially chapter 6.

10 Ibid., p. 157.

11 Ibid., p. 132. The quotation is taken by Fine from oral history.

12 As is this characterization of the cooperative spirit in the British miners' strike of
1984 by Huw Beynon, *Digging Deeper,* p. 192: "Since the strike, the communities
have been reactivated, the food kitchens have drawn people together and ended
their isolation. Many families have had luxury goods re-possessed and although they
have felt a loss at first, they quickly realize how easy it is to survive without them.
Bourgeois notions of individualism and materialism which have slowly been woven
into working class life have been pulled apart by the strike. Now, so much everyday
experience revolving around food, money, friendships and support are shared experiences. Any personal difficulty now becomes public and no one goes without attention or support. Miners and their families from other communities who visit the

picket line or attend meetings are welcomed with open arms and treated as com-
rades." Even though this and many similar observations made about the emergence
of these sentiments during times of sharp conflict are open to criticism as being
merely anecdotal, it is worth noting the persistence of *fraternité* in these accounts.

13  While this view has been challenged—see, for instance, Jane Mansbridge, "The
Rise and Fall of Self-Interest in the Explanation of Political Life"—it remains the
default position of mainstream political science. It also underlies the notion of
working class "instrumentalism" said by a team of British sociologists to be central
to modern working class consciousness (John H. Goldthorpe and David Lockwood,
*The Affluent Worker,* p. 49).

14  Or, as it is both technically and commonly called, free riding. "Even if all of the individuals in a large group are rational and self-interested, and would gain if, as a
group, they acted to achieve their common interest or objective, they will still not
voluntarily act to achieve that common or group interest" (Mancur Olson, *The
Logic of Collective Action,* p. 2). Approaching the same problem from a different
angle, Craig Calhoun points out that the common assumption that increased class
consciousness will inevitably lead to greater commitment to collective action is
flawed. A greater consciousness of obstacles and the strength of opposing forces
might just as logically lead to inaction (*The Question of Class Struggle,* p. 136).

15  Robert Bellah, Richard Madsen, William Sullivan, Ann Swidler, and Steven Tipton,
*Habits of the Heart,* and Kluegel and Smith, *Beliefs About Inequality,* are two
among many overviews of American individualism; Jennifer Hochschild, *What's
Fair?* shows how individualism is especially pronounced in the economic domain;
and Kay Schlozman and Sidney Verba, "Unemployment, Class Consciousness, and
Radical Politics: What Didn't Happen in the Thirties," show that it can survive a
substantial dose of negative personal experience.

16  James Q. Wilson, *Political Organizations,* pp. 172–174.

17  Pfeffer, *Working for Capitalism,* and Richard Balzer, *Clockwork,* note this tendency. Burawoy, *Manufacturing Consent,* attributes it to the games employers create and employees adopt to define the parameters of fairness in a work day. See especially p. 82, where he describes the employees' notion of "being screwed" as
actions on the part of management which prevent them from fulfilling their daily
quota.

18  Hamilton and Wright, *State,* p. 69.

19  See Appendix A for the question. Of course, these evaluations were made after two
years of striking, and what I was getting from people was their memory of how they
had felt about work. No doubt, some part of the nostalgia for the pre-1985 times is
explained by what Alvin Gouldner called "The Rebecca Myth"—a past made better
than it looked at the time by virtue of comparison with an undesirable present (*Patterns of Industrial Bureaucracy,* pp. 79–83).

20  Extended break times and individualized rule application are often an implicit part
of what is regarded as fair. Alvin Gouldner characterizes these as comprising a pat-

tern of "indulgencies," which, when removed, come to symbolize a betrayal of trust (*Wildcat Strike: A Study in Worker-Management Relationships,* p. 18).

21  "Strikers," Connecticut Public Television documentary. The lawyer argued that the union had engaged in an unprotected organized slowdown.

22  While it would be safe to assume that among those who returned the level of protest activity during that period was lower, it is not at all the case that everyone who became a strikebreaker had refused to take part. The NLRB testimony alone turned up several strikebreakers who testified that they had refused overtime.

23  Interview with author. One reason Howard was able to accumulate such valuable information was that she received calls from employees during work tipping her off about forthcoming events.

24  NLRB Hearing, pp. 6007–6008.

25  "Small group discussions can do something that surveys and private interviews cannot: They can reveal inchoate attitudes that people are usually reluctant to express unless they are validated or reinforced by others" (Samuel Popkin, *The Reasoning Voter,* p. 45).

26  This is the Christmas incident Howard reported in Chapter 2; the retelling of it from the inside illustrates both how important it was to employees and how accurate Howard's observations were.

27  NLRB Hearing, p. 2697. The company's legal and public explanations also amounted to a claim of one-sided war, this one waged by the union against a management which was trying to get on with business as usual while under duress. The administrative law judge's ruling rejected that interpretation. It was a two-sided war, with both sides viewing the contract and the requirements of the National Labor Relations Act in somewhat the way Oliver North viewed the Boland Amendment.

28  I explored these interactions in *Just the Working Life,* particularly chapter 4, on "Industrial Non-Democracy."

29  William Gamson, Bruce Fireman, and Steven Rytina, *Encounters with Unjust Authority,* chapter 10.

30  "I saw when people were about ready to go on strike, nobody made withdrawals. I saw right then that they were serious. You had people from the old country [Italy], from Puerto Rico, from Portugal, from Poland. Half couldn't speak English well. I saw then that people were going to be able to carry this thing off" (interview with author).

31  Scott, *Domination,* p. 209.

32  Michael Nelson, "'Pentecost,'" p. 141.

33  Fantasia, *Cultures,* pp. 87–88.

34  As alleged most famously by Le Bon in *The Crowd.* The question of the rationality of people's behavior during such periods will be discussed further in Chapter 6. See Ray Boryczka, "Militancy and Factionalism in the United Auto Workers Union, 1937–1941," p. 15, for a description of how quickly the Flint sit-down euphoria faded.

35 Some of the evidence is summarized in Steven Peterson, *Political Behavior,* chapter 7.

36 Staughton Lynd, *The Fight Against Shutdowns,* p. 124. Terry Buss and C. Richard Hofstetter reinforced Lynd's observations using quantitative methods in "Powerlessness, Anomie, and Cynicism: The Personal Consequences of Mass Unemployment in a Steel Town."

37 The UAW permitted people to make up to $150 a week and remain eligible for strike benefits.

38 When I compared the activists with the nonactivists, there were slightly more activists (p < .05, test of distribution between proportions using normal distribution) who participated many times in nonrequired picketing. There were also more activists who reported going to rallies, but the difference was not significant.

39 Reibeling, interview.

40 That term is neither mine nor Reibeling's; it belongs to Goldthorpe and Lockwood, *The Affluent Worker,* p. 179. They argued that labor militancy did not contradict the thesis of "instrumentalism." Workers might simply see their best chance at achieving individual goals as acting in unison.

41 Fantasia, *Cultures,* chapter 5.

42 Bernard Karsh, *Diary of a Strike,* p. 125.

43 There is considerable irony in the fact that it took being torn away from from work for these relationships to be cemented, given that Marxists and syndicalists have often argued that assembling workers together under a single roof would produce an active sense of common interests.

44 Michael Burawoy points to the "fragmenting and individuation life on the factory floor" (*The Politics of Production,* p. 33) and discusses how interpretation of work and employee resistance is often patterned by a subdivided labor process. The Colt employees here seem to be expressing some gratification at breaking out of relationships strongly influenced by job and department boundaries.

45 This was one of several instances in which I used comments from the open-ended interviews to create one of the response categories in the fixed-answer survey. Since using something similar to strikers' own words might be suggesting the "proper" answer, it is possible that the degree of solidarism as indicated by these responses is overestimated. But I think there is offsetting value in using strikers' own words to create response categories. There will be a bias only if "we are like brothers and sisters" becomes common linguistic currency and is understood as the "good citizen" answer. It probably was, but only within the confines of the strike. It is not normal working-class language. Vanneman and Cannon point out that one of the reasons for the picture of American workers as "class unconscious" is that they have no inherited language of class, and "It is expecting too much to presume that workers should develop this vocabulary *de novo*" (*The American Perception of Class,* p. 107). The Colt strikers have developed that vocabulary. They still had to *choose* that answer, and the number who did has meaning, but the production of a "good citizen" language of solidarity in this conflict is additionally important.

46  The classic exposition of this is in Samuel A. Stouffer, et al., *The American Soldier.*

47  Fantasia, noting such exchanges in the Clinton Corn strike, concluded from them that "rigid conceptions of private property gave way to a more collective sense" (*Cultures,* p. 208). I do not think mutuality challenged private property on a conceptual level. The fact that strikers saw each other as a part of a family led them to employ norms about private property similar to those in a family.

48  Johnson also pointed out that symptoms of social deterioration sometimes associated with a group facing hardship over a protracted period, such as divorce and alcoholism, had not increased over the four-year period: "It is not showing what you would expect, which is a peaking of stress-related factors." She contrasted that with studies of unemployment in the New England area which showed both those categories sharply up among the long-term unemployed. This is her analysis: "Stress is a matter of control. You can have a lot of stress, but if you have control of that stress, you can manage it. This was their decision. For right, for wrong, for indifferent, it was their decision." Interview with author.

49  James Q. Wilson argues that even those union members who become involved in a crisis situation—whom he calls "crisis activists"—are not likely to do so for reasons of ideological commitment: "Their involvement in the union is instrumental, not expressive or social" (*Political Organizations,* p. 173).

50  He didn't. His picture appeared in the *Hartford Courant* the day the NLRB verdict was announced, joyously embracing a supporter.

51  Fine, *Sit-Down,* p. 281.

*4. A General Attention to Public Affairs*

1  Kay Schlozman and Sidney Verba studied the political inactivity of the unemployed, first constructing a set of steps which were necessary to translate personal hardship into political activity: the hardship must be perceived as such; there must be a perception that government is a relevant body to act on the problem; a group which is affected must perceive itself as a group; policy preferences must be formulated; and the resources for political action must be present or developed (*Injury to Insult,* p. 13).

2  Jennifer Hochschild, *What's Fair?;* Robert Lane, "Market Justice, Political Justice."

3  That is a theme of some of the most prominent works of contemporary political science: Paul Lazarsfeld, Bernard Berelson, and Hazel Gaudet, *The People's Choice;* Angus Campbell, Philip Converse, Warren Miller, and Donald Stokes, *The American Voter;* Converse, "The Nature of Belief Systems in Mass Publics." The evidence was reviewed and updated by Eric R. A. N. Smith in *The Unchanging American Voter;* he found "no credible evidence for any but trivial changes in sophistication either in the 1960s or at any other time from the 1950s to the present" (p. 8). Smith goes on to say that the public's lack of political knowledge is so well documented that pollsters have stopped asking questions to test it (p. 159).

4  Converse, "Belief Systems," p. 255.

5  Stephen Bennett, *Apathy in America,* pp. 27–28.

6 Norman Nie, Sidney Verba, and John Petrocik, *The Changing American Voter.*

7 Robert Lane, *Political Ideology;* more recently, Hochschild, *What's Fair?;* Craig Reinarman, *American States of Mind.*

8 Harry Wray, "Comment on Interpretations of Early Research into Belief Systems."

9 The retrospective voting school, pioneered by V. O. Key, *The Responsible Electorate,* expanded by Fiorina, *Retrospective Voting in American National Elections.*

10 Benjamin Page, *Choices and Echoes in Presidential Elections;* Roderick Hart, *The Sound of Leadership;* Walter Dean Burnham, *Current Crisis in American Politics,* but also throughout his writing. Page discusses the deliberate ambiguity of politicians, which raises the information costs and thus makes politics most accessible to elites; Hart focuses on the increased use of commercial marketing strategies for campaigns and the resultant debasement of political debate; Burnham has written extensively about the exclusion of much of the electorate due to the absence of a labor- or class-based party. What they have in common is that they reverse the more standard assumption of responsibility for public ignorance.

11 Nobody quite promotes ignorance as a virtue, but Joseph Schumpeter, *Capitalism, Socialism, and Democracy,* does not see it as an unalloyed vice; it keeps the public from excessive meddling in affairs of state.

12 Even those who argue that citizens have enough information about the most important questions to vote wisely (Key) or that party identification contains substantial issue content (Fiorina) do not allege that most people possess a great quantity of information or even a great interest in government. They argue that people do not *need* a great deal of information to choose rationally.

13 Herbert Gans, *Middle American Individualism,* p. x.

14 I must add a caveat. It has been argued that everyday concerns are *themselves* political and that notions of politics and democracy which do not recognize that are elitist. Benjamin Barber makes that argument in the preface to *Strong Democracy:* "I am less anxious in this book to call for new political behavior than I am to get Americans to call what they are already doing *political* behavior. I am less concerned to expand democracy than to expand our understanding of what counts as democratic" (p. xiv). Whether one agrees with this expanded view of politics or not, there remains a distinctive category of governmental decision making, and it is still useful to learn how distant citizens find it. It may be perfectly appropriate to call the Colt strike a political act and still be impressed with how it increased people's attentiveness to government.

15 *State,* p. 373. Similar themes are explored by Richard Brody and Paul Sniderman, "From Life Space to Polling Place: The Relevance of Personal Concerns for Voting Behavior."

16 Robert Lane, "Government and Self-Esteem."

17 In a variation on this theme, the employees who took part in the Flint sit-in constructed and carried out such quasi-governmental functions as rule making, security, and education (Fine, *Sit-Down*).

18 "Moments," p. 196.

19 *Reconstruction,* p. 163 and p. 316.

20  Leon Litwack, *Been in the Storm So Long,* p. 507.

21  Goodwyn, *The Populist Moment,* p. 282. Emphasis in original.

22  "Empowerment" seems to me a reasonable translation of the more technical term "political efficacy."

23  Roy Pierce and Philip Converse, "Attitudinal Sources of Protest Behavior in France: Differences Between Before and After Measurement." Participants included both students—who primarily demonstrated—and workers—who primarily struck. The political differences between the two groups became less pronounced during the course of events, while the differences between both and bystanders grew.

24  Ibid., p. 310.

25  NLRB v. MacKay Radio and Telegraph, cited in Atleson, *Values and Assumptions,* p. 23.

26  Katherine Stone, "The Post-War Paradigm in American Labor Law." The government is never really out of the bargaining process. Through property law and policing power, it ensures that the fight will be an unequal one. But it is not overtly involved on a regular basis.

27  Brody and Sniderman, "Life Space": "Whatever may be the case elsewhere, it does seem that in America comparatively few personal problems are 'politicized'" (p. 360).

28  Interview with author.

29  Interview with author.

30  Kennelly's speech began, "I'm not happy to be here" and described the whole conflict as unfortunate. She was not regarded by most strikers as being either highly sympathetic or especially helpful.

31  Those arrested included three state representatives and a Hartford city councilwoman. The councilwoman was a Republican; all the others mentioned in the paragraph were Democrats.

32  In the end, of course, the company did not prove to be so impregnable. Is this vindication for the argument that the power of business is presumed to be greater than it actually is? Possibly. But it took an improbable combination of factors for the strike to turn out to be successful: a skilled leadership, a committed rank and file, legal blunders on Colt's part, a reasonably sympathetic judge, and the decision by the company to sell the division. Had any one of these not been present, the strike would have ended in defeat for the union.

33  Space limitations in the written survey prevented me from asking whether strikers considered government intervention appropriate.

34  One of the widely repeated stories was about a "magic lot"—a single pallet of well-produced guns which strikers claimed was moved around from station to station whenever government inspectors showed up, to disguise the inferior quality being produced generally.

35  Some strikers with an understanding of hardball electoral politics attributed O'Neill's lack of interest to the UAW's support for O'Neill's opponent for the 1986 nomination.

36 *Hartford Courant,* October 10, 1986.

37 An entire book has been devoted to a study of disorders created in strike line policing. David Waddington et al., *Flashpoints: Studies in Public Disorder.*

38 The term "strikebreaker" could not be accurately applied to all those going to work.
Some of those were managerial personnel, who do not usually replace the work of
the strikers. The anger of the picketers was directed toward those crossing the line
in roughly this pecking order: (1) the former union members (whom they called
"superscabs"); (2) the managerial personnel perceived as the cause of the situation;
(3) the newly hired replacement workers; (4) the other white-collar workers, a few
of whom the strikers knew to be at least mildly sympathetic.

39 An excerpt from the hearing helps communicate the mood. A supervisor who noticed a flat tire as he left the parking lot was asked why he drove through the picket
line without checking the tire. "It would have been insanity. There's no way to get
out of your car with those strikers out there, the attitude that they had and the—just
the general tenor of the line was so abusive that to get out of your car at that point
would have been ridiculous" (NLRB Hearing, p. 4179).

40 Interview with author.

41 Fantasia, *Cultures,* p. 195.

42 The union went to court and won back her right to appear on the picket line.

43 This does not mean that those arrested were satisfied that justice was done. Some
pointed to the dropped charges as an illustration of the injustice of the original arrest. It does mean that the anger was directed toward police and company, not the
courts.

44 Twenty interviewees had been observers, eleven others had been witnesses, and
five had no contact with the proceedings. There were some for whom I had no information.

45 "Protest and Profanation: Agrarian Revolt and the Little Tradition."

46 NLRB Hearing, p. 1814.

47 Ibid., p. 637.

48 Ibid., p. 5660.

49 Ibid., p. 5847.

50 Waddington, *Flashpoints,* p. 163.

51 NLRB hearing, p. 4808. It was actually a supervisor who made the original false
claim. I heard these two stories so often that I just wrote "secretary" and "tires" in
my notes from the tapes whenever strikers brought them up.

52 The notion of "subversion" works to legitimate institutions by dismissing even the
most hostile of outcomes as the result of a corruption of rules rather then of the nature of the rules themselves.

53 Michael Goldfield, *The Decline of Organized Labor in the United States,* p. 195.
Thomas Geoghegan, *Which Side Are You On?* makes the same point humorously,
but insightfully.

54 This was the resolution that Reibeling said was passed "in a process which was
highly irregular."

55 Interview with author.

56 Brody and Sniderman in "Life Space" tested for an "activation effect"— the possibility that citizens are propelled into political motion by a "socially-located" problem (p. 350). Using voter turnout as the dependent variable, they found no evidence that such an effect exists. The thrust of their conclusion about the effect seems consonant with the broader usage I am making of it. Steven Peterson, *Political Behavior,* reached the same conclusion: "Stressful situations are related to diminution in interest, efficacy, and action" (p. 68).

57 It was the 1938 MacKay decision which made that possible. It is fair to say that the strategy of replacing strikers grew in popularity during the Reagan era and that changes in interpretation of case law were favorable to that strategy.

58 See, for instance, Michael Huspeth and Kathleen Kendall, "On Withholding of Political Voice: An Analysis of the Political Vocabulary of a 'Non-Political' Speech Community."

59 In describing strikers as reorganizing a worldview through the lens of their conflict, I am both relying on and stretching slightly Benjamin Barber's notion of citizenry in *Strong Democracy.* His citizens debate and formulate ideas on the basis of generalized civic interest. But at times he discusses broad based popular movements such as the Grange (p. 237) and the Populists (p. 269)—both organized around particularized interests—as examples of how citizenship can be enhanced in a fashion somewhat similar to my usage here.

60 Joan Huber and William Form, *Income and Ideology;* James Kluegel and Eliot Smith, *Beliefs About Inequality.*

61 *The Captive Public,* particularly pp. 40–46.

62 For a contrasting view, see Sidney Tarrow, *Democracy and Disorder,* pp. 67–70. He points out that in the tumultuous Italian politics of 1967–1970, conventional forms of protest and political participation reinforced each other. Centrifugal forces in the form of ideological challenges also arose within the most dominant and codified bodies of thought in Italy, Marxism and Catholicism.

*5. Horatio Alger to Robin Hood*

1 Nelson, "'Pentecost,'" p. 154.

2 *The Marx-Engels Reader,* pp. 172–173.

3 *Prison Notebooks,* p. 333. Scott argues that the promises extended by any regime become the basis for criticizing its performance, and thus conflict occurs within the hegemonic framework rather than over it. "The crucial point . . . is that the very process of attempting to legitimate a social order by idealizing it *always* provides its subjects with the means, the symbolic tools, the very ideas for a critique that operates entirely within the hegemony. . . . The most common form of class struggle arises from the failure of a dominant ideology to live up to the implicit promises it necessarily makes" (*Weapons of the Weak,* p. 338). Emphasis in original.

4 Abercrombie, et al., *The Dominant Ideology Thesis,* p. 26. The authors also argue that all but the most conspiratorial of dominant ideology theories give "no adequate

account of the *generation* of appropriate ideology" (p. 27); emphasis in original. I make no claims about generation in this chapter, although the book as a whole is built around the theme that the reification of dominant institutions and processes plays the decisive role in the process. Cocks describes how this can be in *The Oppositional Imagination:* "We must recognize an element of sheer givenness on the part of a regime of truth and blind habit on the part of those who think, desire, and act within its terms. This is so even with respect to regimes specifying terms of mastery and servitude as fundamental identities of social life" (p. 188).

5 Other than behavior; there is certainly enough truth to Scott's argument about hidden transcripts to make it obligatory to look away from the public stage, where powerful and powerless interact.

6 This is a long-standing contention of the "American exceptionalist" school. It also has an interesting shadow version on the left in the Jay Lovestone and Earl Browder tendencies in the American Communist Party. The left version is explored in Leon Samson, "Americanism as Surrogate Socialism."

7 This is my interpretation of the conclusions reached by Seymour Martin Lipset and William Schneider, *The Confidence Gap*, particularly on pp. 88–89, where they explore the paradox of a public's approving of the principles of free enterprise and political competition but disapproving of what appear to be the normal workings of those processes.

8 Kluegel and Smith, *Beliefs*, p. 11.

9 Edward Greenberg, *Workplace Democracy*, p. 144. He borrows the term "possessive individualism" to encapsulate the core ideology. The borrowing is from C. B. MacPherson's *The Political Theory of Possessive Individualism.*

10 Schlozman and Verba, *Injury to Insult*, p. 131.

11 Greenberg, *Workplace Democracy*, pp. 143–147.

12 Calvin Exoo, "Polling a People of Paradox," p. 86.

13 Interview on "Strikers," Connecticut Public Television.

14 It would have been preferable here, as elsewhere, to have had a survey taken before 1985 to compare to the strikers' answers given after the conflict began. Since that was not available, and since I knew when I gave the written survey that I might want to compare the answers I received with answers given by people in more normal circumstances, I took the questions for the tables in this chapter directly from previous surveys, which will be cited within the relevant tables.

15 "Some antipathy toward the poor and hence toward welfare may be 'natural,' inherent in the dominant ideology belief in individualism—which holds the poor responsible for their own position through their blameworthy personal characteristics" (Kluegel and Smith, *Beliefs*, p. 157).

16 This anti-Rawlsian strain within American core values is confirmed by Kluegel and Smith, *Beliefs:* "Our respondents predominantly agree with the statement that incomes should not be more equal because it would prohibit dreaming of becoming a success" (p. 109).

17  Hochschild, *What's Fair?* p. 142; Kluegel and Smith, *Beliefs,* p. 168.

18  Lane, "Market Justice"; Hochschild, *What's Fair?* chapter 6. This is the basis for Ralph Nader's famous quip that the only thing Americans distrust more than a car made by General Motors is a car made by the government.

19  *Injury,* p. 202.

20  Ibid., p. 220. Even in the case of a group facing a great deal of hardship—those who had been unemployed for a period of seven to eleven months—only 58 percent advocated heavy taxation of the rich (p. 211).

21  Kluegel and Smith, *Beliefs,* p. 165.

22  The survey was by Civil Service Inc., cited in Everett Carll Ladd, *The American Polity,* p. 67. I used the figure $200,000 because I wanted to correct for inflation but keep a round number. Although the questions I use for comparison are not identical, there is no doubt of the general drift of the previous findings: Ladd added that "every asking of this question since the 1930s has produced this same basic result."

23  The authors make no claim as to whether these views about the distribution of opportunity match reality. But they do point out with a touch of irony that some versions of the extent of opportunity are almost incoherent; for instance, the claim that "the average American considers him or herself 'better than average' in terms of his or her prospects to get ahead" (*Beliefs,* p. 52). This might be called the Lake Wobegon syndrome; for more examples, see Robert Lane, *The Market Experience,* p. 225.

24  Schlozman and Verba, *Injury,* p. 109.

25  Ibid., p. 111.

26  Jane Mansbridge provides an overview of some of the rethinking in "The Rise and Fall of Self-Interest in the Explanation of Political Life."

27  David Sears and Jack Citrin, *Tax Revolt: Something for Nothing in California,* pp. 140–141.

28  Aaron Beck, *Depression: Causes and Treatment,* p. 283.

29  For debate over the usefulness of schema theory, see Pamela Conover and Stanley Feldman, "How People Organize the World: A Schematic Model," and James Kuklinski, Robert Luskin, and John Bolland, "Where Is the Schema? Going Beyond the 'S' Word in Political Psychology."

30  David Sears and Carolyn Funk, "Self-Interest in Americans' Political Opinions," p. 165. On the same topic, see also Jack Citrin and Donald Green, "The Self-Interest Motive in American Public Opinion."

31  Joanne Martin, "When Expectations and Justice Do Not Coincide: Blue Collar Visions of a Just World," p. 331. The author pointed out (p. 330) that the questionnaire "encouraged consideration of radically different imaginary alternatives."

32  Nor is it just confined to Americans. My theme has been that stable institutions create their own legitimacy, and that part of that process is the reduction of flexible thinking about alternatives. It may also be, however, that the range of debate in this

country is unusually narrow. "Their political ideals are at the very core of national identity. Americans cannot abandon them without ceasing to be Americans in the most meaningful sense of the word." Samuel Huntington, *American Politics: The Promise of Disharmony,* p. 63.

33 Paul Sniderman, *A Question of Loyalty,* p. 151. His study has particular force because the specific "disaffecteds" he surveyed were in the Bay Area in the early 1970s—surely as hardened a group of disaffecteds as could be found.

34 It might seem that the very tangible factors mentioned here are at odds with my earlier notion of learning-through-breakdown-in-routine. I think they are not warring concepts. These new patterns of socialization and new sources of information would never have emerged had the conflict not ruptured old behavior patterns.

35 *Domination,* p. 223. The union leadership strongly discouraged racial epithets and showed the movie *Matewan* at one of its weekly meetings to discuss the importance of racial unity.

36 The United States is one of the few advanced industrial countries in which strikers may be permanently replaced. Efforts to amend MacKay through the legislative process ended first with a George Bush veto, then with a Republican filibuster. The proposed legislation would have permitted temporary, but not permanent, replacements.

37 Sniderman, *Loyalty,* p. 151.

38 What is not apparent in the transcription is the speaker's intensity. His decibel level increased steadily throughout the answer.

39 An invaluable and unsentimental description of workday subordination from the inside is Charles Spencer's *Blue Collar.* Greenberg in *Workplace Democracy* provides an excellent capsule summary: "Within the business firm, the rights of free speech, free association, election of leadership, and general control of collective policy—so central to most definitions of the democratic polity—are not generally considered to be in effect. It is widely assumed by all parties concerned—employees and business managers, union and government officials—that the wage relationship that forms the core of economic life in capitalism axiomatically implies an unequal and hierarchical relationship within the firm" (p. 29).

40 For arguments along those lines, see Donald Wells, *Empty Promises,* and Rick Fantasia, Dan Clawson, and Gregory Graham, "A Critical View of Worker Participation in American Industry." I worked as a production worker in a Procter and Gamble plant in which the central purpose in the initiation of a "participation" plan was to get departmental employees involved in deciding how jobs were to be eliminated.

41 Interview with author. Reibeling also said that the union disapproved of those meetings.

42 While it is only conjecture, it is worthwhile considering whether that was in fact a plus in the ways strikers thought of workplace democracy—that is, *had* the company implemented some of the "quality-circle" programs, it might have discredited industrial democracy by associating it with a hated regime. Of course, real participation might also have made the strike unnecessary.

43 Witte was invited in to analyze the experiment. The findings are reported in *Democracy, Authority, and Alienation.* He found no consistent pattern of change in the survey conducted after the program began. The Colt activist subsample here is not different enough to warrant separate listing. They were more in favor of participation, but by margins that were not statistically significant.

44 Rudy Fenwick and Jon Olson, "Support for Worker Participation: Attitudes Among Union and Non-Union Workers."

45 Thomas Kochan, Harry Katz, and Nancy Mower, "Worker Participation and American Unions," p. 277.

46 This is a classical populist package. Earlier I suggested that it also resembled European or even Scandinavian social democracy. What ordinarily differentiates the two is attitudes toward the use of central government. Ronald Reagan's anti-Washington, antigovernment rhetoric drew on one prominent strand of populist thinking. I think Chapter 4 indicates that the strikers were neither wholly populist nor wholly social-democratic in their orientation toward the potential usefulness of government in promoting justice.

47 Carol Pateman, *Participation and Democratic Theory;* Ronald Mason, *Participatory and Workplace Democracy.*

48 The language of "inadmissible ideas" comes from Goodwyn, *The Populist Moment.*

49 Drew McCoy, *The Last of the Fathers: James Madison and the Republican Legacy,* p. 270.

50 Samuel Popkin, *The Rational Peasant,* p. 247. Sometimes the motivating condition is physical separation. That is captured best by Peace Corps volunteer–turned country and western singer–turned mystery writer Kinky Friedman: "Sometimes you can see things more clearly when they're not there. Most of the great books about human freedom, for instance, were written in prison. From my own personal experience, I have put a black pill of opium into a cup of coffee, drunk it down, stood at the edge of the Borneo jungle staring out across the South China Sea, and seen America more lucidly than at any time in my life. This was made possible partly by the drug, but mostly, I believe, by the physical absence of America" (*Frequent Flyer,* p. 135).

## 6. Reconstructing the Political Spectacle

1 In *Rivethead,* autoworker-author Ben Hamper describes that sense of permanence from the perspective of a third generation "shoprat." The phrase "like a rock" has also become famous in television commercials for Chevrolet trucks. The implications are interesting and relevant. On one level it is simply intended to call attention to the no-frills durability of the product. But it also implies durability on another level—a harkening back to the mom–apple pie–Chevrolet (literally) "better times," a sense which is amplified by the nostalgia-drenched heartland Americanism in the voice of singer Bob Seger.

2 Cocks, *The Oppositional Imagination,* p. 191. Ironically, she is referring here to members of the dominant group, for whom this kind of mobility is more easily avail-

able. Another route she proposes is "the getting of critical consciousness through the hard living of life" (p. 193), which is the special province of the less privileged. In this strike, the two paths intertwined.

3 *Injustice*, p. 480.

4 I should point out that this portrait of Russian workers in the revolutionary years as nonideological is not unanimous; for contrary views see Victoria Bonnell, *Roots of Rebellion*, chapter 10; Steven Smith, *Red Petrograd;* and Reginald Zelnick, "Passivity and Protest in Germany and Russia: Barrington Moore's Conception of Working-Class Responses to Injustice."

5 The need for and role of noneconomic incentives in collective action is discussed in Olson, *The Logic of Collective Action*, pp. 60–65, and Wilson, *Political Organizations*, pp. 39–51. Olson (p. 123) specifically rejects the notion that hardship caused by the dislocations inherent in the free market are enough to override the free-rider problem. Thus there is no reason to expect organized demands for remedies as a conventional response. From this perspective, the Colt strike was distinctly abnormal.

6 "Varieties of Altruism," p. 54.

7 One can cram strike behavior back into a rational actor box by defining a sense of well-being in collective activity to be part of individual interest. But then all it would mean is that when people do things, they have some reason. The only activity excluded would be by lunatics.

8 *Domination*, p. 209.

9 Ibid., p. 225. Scott explicitly contrasts his conclusions about "moments of madness" with Zolberg's. Whereas Zolberg talked about these periods as an "intensive learning experience," Scott says, "The process, then, is more one of recognizing close relatives of one's hidden transcript rather than of filling essentially empty heads with novel ideas" (p. 223).

10 Ibid.

11 This wording is taken from Judith Shklar, *The Faces of Injustice*, p. 45.

12 The phrase is applied by Fantasia, *Cultures*, to the Clinton Corn strike of 1979.

13 W. Lloyd Warner and J. O. Low, *The Social System of the Modern Factory: The Strike, A Social Analysis*, quoted in Karsh, *Diary*, p. 3. If the use of "men" to mean all humans sounds particularly grating here, make the translation necessary for a book (from which the quotation is taken) written in 1947.

14 "Radical self-transformation can yield a narcissistic and nefarious denial of politics itself: a war on tolerance, a disdain for limits, an assault on compromise, a contempt for mundanity" (Benjamin Barber, "The Dangers of Self-Transformation in Revolutionary Political Practice," p. 2).

15 James Madison, *Federalist Papers*, 63.

16 "Any idea of moderation was just an attempt to disguise one's unmanly character; ability to understand a question from all sides meant that one was totally unfitted for action. Fanatical enthusiasm was the mark of a real man" (*The Peloponnesian War*, p. 242).

17 *The Anatomy of Revolution,* pp. 17–22.

18 *Strike,* p. 21.

19 Jeffrey Young, *Cognitive Therapy for Personality Disorders.*

20 P. 295. Mill also talked about the special need to hear views representing "the neglected interests the side of human well-being which is in danger of obtaining less than its share" (p. 297).

21 The consensual view is described in Robert Shalhope, *The Roots of Democracy.* The case for inclusion is made most forcefully by James Madison in "Notes on Suffrage."

22 The quintessential "bad man" is Stackolee, a mythological African-American character who murdered fellow gamblers, raped women, defied white authority, and eventually chased the devil out of hell (Bruce Jackson, *"Get Your Ass in the Water and Swim Like Me,"* pp. 43–55).

23 *Domination,* p. 49.

24 Our interview was conducted a year before the strike ended, and therefore her remarks were not influenced by the successful conclusion.

25 Political thinkers as scornful of finding virtue in the public as Alexander Hamilton ("Take mankind in general, they are vicious") and Gouverneur Morris nonetheless admitted that human nature could "rise above itself" at critical moments, particularly in war (Gerald Stourzh, *Alexander Hamilton and the Idea of Republican Government,* p. 78, for the former; Ralph Ketchum, *James Madison,* p. 119, for the latter).

26 Shelley Burtt, "The Politics of Virtue Today: A Critique and A Proposal," p. 365.

27 This might be debatable around the edges—that is, one might prefer that people not draw lessons from their experience which are deeply antidemocratic or racialist. Even these can have some value if they articulate grievances which might otherwise be unheard. In any case, the strikers' views have not veered in either of those directions.

28 Language taken from Stephen Bennett, "Americans' Knowledge of Ideology, 1980–1992," p. 274.

29 Bruce Ackerman, *We the People,* chapter 9.

## 7. A Vernal Morning, and the Day After

1 Language taken from Richard Flacks, *Making History.*

2 Ackerman, *We the People,* chapter 1.

3 Robert Lane, "From Political to Industrial Democracy," p. 641. Ironically, he points to the example of an industrialist who offered to sell his plant to the employees if they would invest about $3,000 each. They refused, being unwilling to assume the risk. The Colt strikers made just such an investment, although collectively, not individually, after they returned to work.

4 The famous phrase from Joseph Schumpeter, *Capitalism, Socialism, and Democracy.* Lane, *The Market Experience,* points to the acceptance of contingency as a step toward cognitive complexity, and therefore one of the benefits of the market.

5 Richard Couto, "The Memory of Miners and the Conscience of Capital: Coalminers' Strikes as Free Spaces," p. 15.

6 As an example, Michael Mann, *Consciousness and Action Among the Western Working Class*, chapter 6. Zolberg cites one reason that the argument that democratic moments are chimerical always looks like hard-headed realism: "Even those who record the joy of living at a good time almost always take it back" ("Moments," p. 205).

7 Thomas Pangle, *The Spirit of Modern Republicanism*, p. 57; Paul Rahe, *Republics Ancient and Modern*, p. 698. Pangle quotes Jefferson on the source of civic virtue: "Calamity was our best physician" (p. 375).

8 Patricia Fosh, *The Active Trade Unionist*, p. 67.

9 "Moments," p. 206.

10 *The Essential Works of John Stuart Mill*, p. 285.

11 Daily life, according to Le Bon, regulated existence invisibly; crowd members were temporarily free of that regulation and also "freed from the sense of their insignificance and powerlessness" (*The Crowd*, p. 34). He viewed that as a dangerous development.

12 For example, the oft-repeated comment by participants in the campus sit-ins in the late 1960s that they "learned more in a few weeks [of the protest] than in four years of college."

13 Pierce and Converse, "Attitudinal Sources," p. 315.

14 Gouverneur Morris, quoted in Max Mintz, *Gouverneur Morris and the American Revolution*, p. 44. This famous quotation is usually taken as evidence of the low esteem in which some founders held the populace ("poor reptiles" in his next phrase). What is more interesting is that Morris here deplores not principally the innate stupidity of "the mob" but precisely what Zolberg applauds—the utopian strains which occur during a sudden awakening, and beckoning of a "vernal morning."

15 The term is from Jon Elster, *Sour Grapes*. "It *is* a massive fact of history that the values and beliefs of the subjects tend to support the rule of the dominant groups, but I believe that in general this occurs through the spontaneous invention of an ideology by the subjects themselves, by way of dissonance-reduction, or through their illusionary perception of causality" (p. 147).

16 Colt brought out a single-shot rifle called the Sporter which became the subject of a great deal of gun control debate. Opponents claimed it could easily be converted into a semiautomatic "assault weapon." When Connecticut passed a stiff gun control law in 1993, it exempted the Sporter by name. But the congressional ban on assault rifles made it illegal. Colt later replaced it with a single-shot rifle called the Match Target.

17 Phil Wheeler, reinterview with author, August 16, 1995.

18 The hiring of the new production management team was described in Leonard Felson, "Connecticut, Inc. / Colt Comfort."

19 Wheeler, reinterview.

*Appendix D*

1 I should explain that I also had underestimated how many people came to more normal-sized meetings. I counted chairs and noses and came up with about 300. I did not take enough account of people drifting in and out the back of the hall. The president and financial secretary convinced me that 350 was more accurate, and I confirmed that by counting more systematically at future meetings.

2 Test for difference between two proportions.

# Bibliography

Abercrombie, Nicholas, Stephen Hill, and Bryan S. Turner. *The Dominant Ideology Thesis*. London: Allen and Unwin, 1980.

Ackerman, Bruce. *We the People*. Cambridge: Harvard University Press, 1991.

Adas, Michael. "From Footdragging to Flight: The Evasive History of Peasant Avoidance Protest in South and Southeast Asia." *Journal of Peasant Studies* 13, 2 (1986): 64–86.

Allen, Sheila, and Diana Barker, eds. *Dependence and Exploitation in Work and Marriage*. New York: Longman, 1976.

Atleson, James. *Values and Assumptions in American Labor Law*. Amherst: University of Massachusetts Press, 1983.

Bahro, Rudolph. *The Alternative in Eastern Europe*. London: Verso, 1978.

Balanoff, Tom. "The Cement Workers' Experience." *Labor Research Review* 7 (1985): 5–34.

Balzer, Richard. *Clockwork: Life In and Outside an American Factory*. Garden City, N.Y.: Doubleday, 1976.

Barber, Benjamin. *Strong Democracy: Participatory Politics for a New Age*. Berkeley: University of California Press, 1984.

————. "The Dangers of Self-Transformation in Revolutionary Political Practice." Paper prepared for American Political Science Association convention, 1992.

Beck, Aaron. *Depression: Causes and Treatment*. Philadelphia: University of Pennsylvania Press, 1967.

Bellah, Robert, Richard Madsen, William Sullivan, Ann Swidler, and Steven Tipton. *Habits of the Heart: Individualism and Commitment in American Life*. Berkeley: University of California Press, 1985.

Bennett, Stephen. *Apathy in America, 1960–1984: Causes and Consequences of Citizen Political Indifference*. Dobbs Ferry, N.Y.: Transnational Publishers, 1986.

———. "Americans' Knowledge of Ideology, 1980–1992." *American Politics Quarterly* 23, 4 (1995): 259–278.

Berger, Peter, and Thomas Luckmann. *The Social Construction of Reality: A Treatise in the Sociology of Knowledge*. New York: Doubleday, 1966.

Bettelheim, Bruno. *The Informed Heart: Autonomy in a Mass Age*. New York: Free Press, 1960.

Beynon, Huw, ed. *Digging Deeper: Issues in the Miners' Strike*. London: Verso, 1985.

Bierhoff, Hans Werner, Ronald Cohen, and Jerald Greenberg, eds. *Justice in Social Relations*. New York: Plenum, 1986.

Bluestone, Barry, and Bennet Harrison. *The Deindustrialization of America: Plant Closings, Community Abandonment, and the Dismantling of Basic Industry*. New York: Basic, 1982.

Bonnell, Victoria. *Roots of Rebellion: Workers' Politics and Organizations in St. Petersburg and Moscow, 1900–1914*. Berkeley: University of California Press, 1983.

Boryczka, Ray. "Militancy and Factionalism in the United Auto Workers Union, 1937–1941." *Maryland Historian* 8 (1977): 13–25.

Brinton, Crane. *The Anatomy of Revolution*. New York: Random House, 1960.

Brodner, Steve. "Shot from Guns: Colt Workers in Their Own Words." *Northeast Magazine*, August 1989: 9–17.

Brody, Richard, and Paul Sniderman. "From Life Space to Polling Place: The Relevance of Personal Concerns for Voting Behavior." *British Journal of Political Science* 7 (1977): 337–360.

Burawoy, Michael. *Manufacturing Consent: Changes in the Labor Process Under Monopoly Capitalism*. Chicago: University of Chicago Press, 1979.

———. *The Politics of Production: Factory Regimes Under Capitalism and Socialism*. London: Verso, 1985.

Burnham, Walter Dean. *The Current Crisis in American Politics*. New York: Oxford University Press, 1982.

Burtt, Shelley. "The Politics of Virtue Today: A Critique and a Proposal." *American Political Science Review* 87 (1993): 360–368.

Buss, Terry, and C. Richard Hofstetter. "Powerlessness, Anomie, and Cynicism." *Micropolitics* 2 (1983): 349–377.

Calhoun, Craig. *The Question of Class Struggle: Social Foundations of Popular Radicalism During the Industrial Revolution*. Chicago: University of Chicago Press, 1982.

Campbell, Angus, Philip Converse, Warren Miller, and Donald Stokes. *The American Voter.* New York: John Wiley and Sons, 1960.

Cheal, David. "Hegemony, Ideology, and Contradictory Consciousness." *Sociological Quarterly* 20 (1979): 109–117.

Citrin, Jack. "Comment: The Political Relevance of Trust in Government." *American Political Science Review* 68 (1974): 973–988.

Citrin, Jack, and Donald Green. "The Self-Interest Motive in American Public Opinion." *Research in Micropolitics* 3 (1990): 1–28.

Cocks, Joan. *The Oppositional Imagination: Adventures in the Sexual Domain.* London: Routledge, 1989.

Cohen, Youseff. *The Manipulation of Consent: The State and Working-Class Consciousness in Brazil.* Pittsburgh: University of Pittsburgh Press, 1989.

Conover, Pamela, and Stanley Feldman. "How People Organize the World: A Schematic Model." *American Journal of Political Science* 28 (1984): 95–126.

Converse, Philip. "The Nature of Belief Systems in Mass Publics." In *Ideology and Discontent,* ed. David Apter. New York: Free Press, 1964.

Couto, Richard. "The Memory of Miners and the Conscience of Capital: Coalminers' Strikes as Free Spaces." Paper prepared for American Political Science Association convention, 1991.

Dahl, Robert. *A Preface to Economic Democracy.* Berkeley: University of California Press, 1985.

Dawley, Alan. *Class and Community: The Industrial Revolution in Lynn.* Cambridge: Harvard University Press, 1976.

Edelman, Murray. *Constructing the Political Spectacle.* Chicago: University of Chicago Press, 1988.

Elkins, Stanley. *Slavery: A Problem in American Institutional and Intellectual Life.* Chicago: University of Chicago Press, 1959.

Ellerman, David. "The Employment Relation, Property Rights, and Organizational Democracy." In *International Yearbook of Organizational Democracy,* ed. Colin Crouch. New York: J. Wiley and Son, 1983.

Elster, Jon. *Sour Grapes: Studies in the Subversion of Rationality.* Cambridge: University of Cambridge Press, 1983.

Exoo, Calvin. "Polling a People of Paradox." *New Political Science* 16/17 (1989): 179–189.

Fantasia, Rick. *Cultures of Solidarity: Consciousness, Action, and Contemporary American Workers.* Berkeley: University of California Press, 1988.

Fantasia, Rick, Dan Clawson, and Gregory Graham. "A Critical View of Worker Participation in American Industry." *Work and Occupations* 15 (1988): 468–488.

Felson, Leonard. "Connecticut, Inc. / Colt Comfort." *Connecticut Magazine* 58 (1995): 39–43.

Fenwick, Rudy, and Jon Olson. "Support for Worker Participation: Attitudes Among Union and Non-Union Workers." *American Sociological Review* 51: 505–522.

Fine, Sidney. *Sit-Down: The General Motors Strike of 1936–1937.* Ann Arbor: University of Michigan Press, 1969.

Fiorina, Morris. *Retrospective Voting in American National Elections.* New Haven: Yale University Press, 1981.

Flacks, Richard. *Making History: The Radical Tradition in American Life.* New York: Columbia University Press, 1988.

Foner, Eric. *Reconstruction: America's Unfinished Revolution, 1863–1877.* New York: Harper and Row, 1988.

Fosh, Patricia. *The Active Trade Unionist: A Study of Motivation and Participation at Branch Level.* Cambridge: Cambridge University Press, 1981.

Frankl, Viktor. *Man's Search for Meaning: An Introduction to Logotherapy.* New York: Pocketbooks, 1963.

Fried, Richard. *Nightmare in Red: The McCarthy Era in Perspective.* New York: Oxford University Press, 1991.

Friedman, Kinky. *Frequent Flyer.* New York: Berkley, 1989.

Gamson, William. *Talking Politics.* New York: Cambridge University Press, 1992.

Gamson, William, Bruce Fireman, and Steven Rytina. *Encounters with Unjust Authority.* Chicago: Dorsey, 1982.

Gans, Herbert. *Middle American Individualism: The Future of Liberal Democracy.* New York: Free Press, 1978.

Genovese, Eugene. "Rebelliousness and Docility in the Negro Slave: A Critique of the Elkins Thesis." In *The Debate Over Slavery,* ed. Ann Lane. Urbana: University of Illinois Press, 1971.

Geoghegan, Thomas. *Which Side Are You On? Trying to Be for Labor When It's Flat on Its Back.* New York: Farrar, Straus, Giroux, 1991.

Ginsberg, Benjamin. *The Captive Public: How Mass Opinion Supports State Power.* New York: Basic, 1986.

Goffman, Erving. *Asylums: Essays on the Social Situation of Mental Patients and Other Inmates.* New York: Anchor, 1961.

Goldfield, Michael. *The Decline of Organized Labor in the United States.* Chicago: University of Chicago Press, 1987.

Goldthorpe, John H., and David Lockwood. *The Affluent Worker in the Class Structure: Industrial Attitudes and Behaviour.* Cambridge: Cambridge University Press, 1968.

Goodwyn, Lawrence. *The Populist Moment: A Short History of the Agrarian Revolt in America.* New York: Oxford University Press, 1978.

Gouldner, Alvin. *Wildcat Strike: A Study in Worker-Management Relationships.* New York: Harper and Row, 1954.

——— . *Patterns of Industrial Bureaucracy: A Case Study of Modern Factory Administration.* New York: Free Press, 1984.

Gramsci, Antonio. *Selections from Prison Notebooks,* ed. Quinten Hoare and Geoffrey Nowell Smith. London: Wishart, 1971.

Grant, Ellsworth. *The City of Hartford, 1784–1984: An Illustrated History.* [Hartford:] Connecticut Historical Society, 1986.

Greenberg, Edward. *Workplace Democracy: The Political Effects of Participation.* Ithaca, N.Y.: Cornell University Press, 1986.

Habermas, Jurgen. *Legitimation Crisis.* Boston: Beacon, 1973.

Halle, David. *America's Working Man: Work, Home, and Politics Among Blue-Collar Property Owners.* Chicago: University of Chicago Press, 1984.

Hamilton, Richard, and James Wright. *The State of the Masses.* New York: Aldine, 1986.

Hamper, Ben. *Rivethead: Tales from the Assembly Line.* New York: Warner, 1991.

Hart, Roderick. *The Sound of Leadership: Presidential Communication in the Modern Age.* Chicago: University of Chicago Press, 1987.

Heller, Agnes. *Everyday Life.* London: Routledge, 1984.

Hill, Christopher. *The World Turned Upside Down: Radical Ideas in the English Revolution.* New York: Viking, 1972.

Hiller, E. T. *Strike.* Chicago: University of Chicago Press, 1928.

Hochschild, Jennifer. *What's Fair? American Beliefs About Distributive Justice.* Cambridge: Harvard University Press, 1981.

Holahan, David. "High Noon at Colt." *Connecticut Magazine,* July 1988: 84–89.

Howard, Susan. "The UE-UAW Struggle at Colt's." Unpublished paper.

Huber, Joan, and William Form. *Income and Ideology.* New York: Free Press, 1973.

Huntington, Samuel. *American Politics: The Promise of Disharmony.* Cambridge: Harvard University Press, 1981.

Huspeth, Michael, and Kathleen Kendall. "On Withholding of Political Voice: An Analysis of the Political Vocabulary of a 'Non-Political' Speech Community." *Quarterly Journal of Speech* 77 (1991): 1–19.

Jackson, Bruce. *"Get Your Ass in the Water and Swim Like Me": Narrative Poetry from Black Oral Tradition.* Cambridge: Harvard University Press, 1974.

Jencks, Christopher. "Varieties of Altruism." In *Beyond Self-Interest,* ed. Jane Mansbridge. Chicago: University of Chicago Press, 1990.

Jessop, Robert. *Traditionalism, Conservatism, and the British Political Culture.* London: Allen and Unwin, 1974.

Karsh, Bernard. *Diary of a Strike.* Urbana: University of Illinois Press, 1982.

Kazemi, Farhad. *Poverty and Revolution in Iran: The Migrant Poor, Urban Marginality, and Politics.* New York: New York University Press, 1980.

Ketchum, Ralph. *James Madison: A Biography.* New York: Macmillan, 1971.

Key, V. O. *The Responsible Electorate: Rationality in Presidential Voting, 1936–1960.* Cambridge: Harvard University Press, 1966.

Kluegel, James, and Eliot Smith. *Beliefs About Inequality: Americans' Views of What Is and What Should Be.* New York: Aldine, 1986.

Kochan, Thomas, Harry Katz, and Nancy Mower. "Worker Participation and American Unions." In *Challenges and Choices Facing American Labor,* ed. Thomas Kochan. Kalamazoo, Mich.: W. E. Upjohn Institute for Employment Research, 1984.

Kuklinski, James, Robert Luskin, and John Bolland. "Where Is the Schema? Going Beyond the 'S' Word in Political Psychology." *American Political Science Review* 85 (1991): 1342–1355.

Ladd, Everett Carll. *The American Polity: The People and Their Government.* New York: W. W. Norton, 1987.

Lane, Ann, ed. *The Debate Over Slavery: Stanley Elkins and His Critics.* Urbana: University of Illinois Press, 1971.

Lane, Robert. "Government and Self-Esteem." *Political Theory* 10, 1 (1982): 5–31.

———. *Political Ideology: Why the American Common Man Believes What He Does.* New York: Free Press, 1982.

———. "From Political to Industrial Democracy." *Polity* 17 (1985): 623–648.

———. "Market Justice, Political Justice." *American Political Science Review* 80 (1986): 383–401.

———. *The Market Experience.* Cambridge: Cambridge University Press, 1991.

Laurie, Bruce. *Working People of Philadelphia, 1800–1850.* Philadelphia: Temple University Press, 1981.

Lazarsfeld, Paul, Bernard Berelson, and Hazel Gaudet. *The People's Choice: How the Voter Makes Up His Mind in a Presidential Campaign.* New York: Columbia University Press, 1968.

Le Bon, Gustave. *The Crowd: A Study of the Popular Mind.* New York: Penguin, 1977.

Lefebvre, Henri. *The Explosion: Marxism and the French Revolution.* New York: Monthly Review, 1969.

Lendler, Marc. *Just the Working Life: Opposition and Accommodation in Daily Industrial Life.* White Plains, N.Y.: M. E. Sharpe, 1990.

Levy, Paul. "The Unidimensional Perspective of the Reagan Labor Board." *Rutgers Law Journal* 16 (1985): 269–390.

Lewy, Guenther. *False Consciousness: An Essay on Mystification.* New Brunswick, N.J.: Transaction, 1982.

Lichtenstein, Nelson. "Auto Worker Militancy and the Structure of Factory Life." *Journal of American History* 67 (1980): 335–353.

———. *Labor's War at Home: The CIO in WW II.* New York: Cambridge University Press, 1982.

Lipset, Seymour Martin, and William Schneider. *The Confidence Gap: Business, Labor, and Government in the Popular Mind.* Baltimore: Johns Hopkins University Press, 1987.

Litwack, Leon. *Been in the Storm So Long: The Aftermath of Slavery.* New York: Vintage, 1979.

Ludtke, Alf. "Organizational Order or Eigensinn?" In *The Rites of Power: Symbolism, Ritual, and Politics in the Middle Ages,* ed. Sean Wilentz. Philadelphia: University of Pennsylvania Press, 1985.

Lukes, Steven. *Power: A Radical View.* London: Macmillan, 1974.

Lynd, Staughton. *The Fight Against Shutdowns: Youngstown's Steel Mill Closings.* San Pedro, Calif.: Singlejack, 1982.

McCoy, Drew. *The Last of the Fathers: James Madison and the Republican Legacy.* New York: Cambridge University Press, 1989.

MacPherson, C. B. *The Political Theory of Possessive Individualism: Hobbes to Locke.* Oxford: Oxford University Press, 1962.

Madison, James. "Notes on Suffrage." *Letters and Other Writings,* vol. 4, ed. William Rives and Philip Fendall. Philadelphia, 1821.

Madison, James, Alexander Hamilton, and John Jay. *The Federalist Papers.* New York: Mentor, 1961.

Mann, Michael. *Consciousness and Action Among the Western Working Class.* London: Macmillan, 1973.

Mansbridge, Jane. "The Rise and Fall of Self-Interest in the Explanation of Political Life." In *Beyond Self-Interest,* ed. Jane Mansbridge. Chicago: University of Chicago Press, 1990.

Marcuse, Peter. "Letter from the German Democratic Republic." *Monthly Review,* 42 (1990): 30–62.

Martin, Joanne. "When Expectations and Justice Do Not Coincide: Blue Collar Visions of a Just World." In *Justice in Social Relations,* ed. Hans Werner Bierhoff, Ronald Cohen, and Jerald Greenberg. New York: Plenum, 1986.

Marx, Karl. *The German Ideology.* In *The Marx-Engels Reader,* ed. R. C. Tucker. New York: W. W. Norton, 1978.

Mason, Ronald. *Participatory and Workplace Democracy: A Theoretical Development in Critique of Liberalism.* Carbondale: Southern Illinois University Press, 1982.

Metzgar, Jack. "Running the Plant Backwards." *Labor Research Review* 7 (1985): 35–44.

Mill, John Stuart. *The Essential Works of John Stuart Mill.* New York: Bantam, 1965.

Mintz, Max. *Gouverneur Morris and the American Revolution.* Norman: University of Oklahoma Press, 1970.

Moore, Barrington. *Injustice: The Social Bases of Obedience and Revolt.* White Plains, N.Y.: M. E. Sharpe, 1978.

Mueller, John. "The UE-IUE Conflict in Bristol, Connecticut." Unpublished paper.

Nelson, Michael. "'Pentecost' on the Pacific: Maritime Workers and Working-Class Consciousness in the 1930s." *Political Power and Social Theory* 4 (1984): 141–182.

Nie, Norman, Sidney Verba, and John Petrocik. *The Changing American Voter.* Cambridge: Harvard University Press, 1979.

Nonini, Donald. "Everyday Forms of Popular Resistance." *Monthly Review* 40, 6 (1988): 25–36.

Olson, Mancur. *The Logic of Collective Action: Public Goods and the Theory of Groups.* Cambridge: Harvard University Press, 1971.

Page, Benjamin. *Choices and Echoes in Presidential Elections.* Chicago: University of Chicago Press, 1978.

Pangle, Thomas. *The Spirit of Modern Republicanism: The Moral Vision of the American Founders and the Philosophy of Locke.* Chicago: University of Chicago Press, 1988.

Parkin, Frank. *Class Inequality and Political Order: Social Stratification in Capitalist and Communist Societies.* New York: Praeger, 1972.

Pateman, Carol. *Participation and Democratic Theory.* Cambridge: Cambridge University Press, 1970.

Patterson, Orlando. "Quashee." In *The Debate Over Slavery,* ed. Ann Lane. Urbana: University of Illinois Press, 1971.

Peterson, Steven. *Political Behavior: Patterns in Everyday Life.* Newbury Park, Calif.: Sage, 1990.

Pfeffer, Richard. *Working for Capitalism.* New York: Columbia University Press, 1979.

Pierce, Roy, and Philip Converse. "Attitudinal Sources of Protest Behavior in France: Differences Between Before and After Measurement." *Public Opinion Quarterly* 54 (1990): 295–316.

Plato. *Plato's Republic,* trans. G. M. A. Grube. Indianapolis: Hackett Publishing, 1974.

Polsby, Nelson. *Community Power and Political Theory: A Further Look at Problems of Evidence and Inference,* 2d edition. New Haven: Yale University Press, 1980.

Popkin, Samuel. *The Rational Peasant: The Political Economy of Rural Society in Vietnam.* Berkeley: University of California Press, 1979.

———. *The Reasoning Voter: Communication and Persuasion in Presidential Campaigns.* Chicago: University of Chicago Press, 1991.

Rahe, Paul. *Republics Ancient and Modern: A Classical Republicanism and the American Revolution.* Chapel Hill: University of North Carolina Press, 1992.

Reddy, William. "The Textile Trade and the Language of the Crowd at Rouen, 1752–1871." *Past and Present* 74 (1977): 62–89.

Reinarman, Craig. *American States of Mind: Political Beliefs and Behavior Among Private and Public Workers.* New Haven: Yale University Press, 1987.

Roberts, Kenneth. *The Fragmentary Class Structure.* London, Heineman, 1977.

Rosenblum, Jonathan. *Copper Crucible: How the Arizona Miners' Strike of 1983 Recast Labor-Management Relations in America.* Ithaca, N.Y.: ILR Press, 1995.

Rude, George. *The Crowd in History: A Survey of Popular Disturbances in France and England, 1730–1848.* New York: Wiley, 1959.

Sabel, Charles. *Work and Politics: The Division of Labor in Industry.* Cambridge: Cambridge University Press, 1982.

Sacks, Karen. *My Troubles Are Going to Have Trouble with Me: Everyday Trials and Triumphs of Women Workers.* New Brunswick, N.J.: Rutgers University Press, 1984.

Samson, Leon. "Americanism as Surrogate Socialism." In *Failure of a Dream? Essays in the History of American Socialism,* ed. John Laslett and Seymour Martin Lipset. Garden City, N.J.: Anchor, 1974.

Schatz, Ronald. *The Electrical Workers: A History of Labor at General Electric and Westinghouse, 1923–1960.* Urbana: University of Illinois Press, 1983.

Schlozman, Kay, and Sidney Verba. "Unemployment, Class Consciousness, and Radical Politics: What Didn't Happen in the Thirties." *Journal of Politics* 39 (1977): 291–323.

———. *Injury to Insult: Unemployment, Class, and Political Response*. Cambridge: Harvard University Press, 1979.

Schumpeter, Joseph. *Capitalism, Socialism, and Democracy*. New York: Harper and Row, 1962.

Scott, James. "Protest and Profanation: Agrarian Revolt and the Little Tradition." *Theory and Society* 4, 1 (1977): 1–38, and 4, 2 (1977): 211–246.

———. *Weapons of the Weak: Everyday Forms of Peasant Resistance*. New Haven: Yale University Press, 1985.

———. *Domination and the Arts of Resistance: Hidden Transcripts*. New Haven: Yale University Press, 1990.

Sears, David, and Jack Citrin. *Tax Revolt: Something for Nothing in California*. Cambridge: Harvard University Press, 1985.

Sears, David, and Carolyn Funk. "Self-Interest in Americans' Political Opinions." In *Beyond Self-Interest*, ed. Jane Mansbridge. Chicago: University of Chicago Press, 1990.

Shalhope, Robert. *The Roots of Democracy: American Thought and Culture, 1760–1800*. Boston: Twayne, 1990.

Shklar, Judith. *The Faces of Injustice*. New Haven: Yale University Press, 1990.

Simmons, Louise. "Organizational and Leadership Models in Labor-Community Coalitions." In *Building Bridges: The Emerging Grassroots Coalition of Labor and Community*, ed. Jeremy Brecher and Tim Costello. New York: Monthly Review Press, 1990.

———. *Organizing in Hard Times: Labor and Neighborhoods in Hartford*. Philadelphia, Temple University Press, 1994.

Smith, Eric R. A. N. *The Unchanging American Voter*. Berkeley: University of California Press, 1989.

Smith, Steven A. *Red Petrograd: Revolution in the Factories, 1917–1918*. New York: Cambridge University Press, 1983.

Sniderman, Paul. *A Question of Loyalty*. Berkeley: University of California Press, 1981.

Spence, Larry. *The Politics of Social Knowledge*. University Park: Pennsylvania State University Press, 1978.

Spencer, Charles. *Blue Collar: An Internal Examination of the Workplace*. Chicago: Vanguard, 1977.

Stokes, Susan. "Hegemony, Consciousness, and Political Change." *Politics and Society* 19, 3 (1991): 265–290.

Stone, Katherine. "The Post-War Paradigm in American Labor Law." *Yale Law Journal* 90 (1980–1981): 1509–1580.

Stouffer, Samuel A., et al. *The American Soldier: Combat and Its Aftermath*, vol. 2 of *Studies in Social Psychology in World War II*, ed. Social Science Research Council. [Princeton: Princeton University Press, 1949–1950.]

Stourzh, Gerald. *Alexander Hamilton and the Idea of Republican Government*. Stanford: Stanford University Press, 1970.

Tarrow, Sidney. *Democracy and Disorder: Protest and Politics in Italy, 1965–1975.* New York: Oxford University Press, 1989.

Thompson, E. P. "The Moral Economy of the English Crowd in the Eighteenth Century." *Past and Present* 38 (1967): 76–136.

Thorpe, Earl. "Chattel Slavery and Concentration Camps." In *The Debate Over Slavery,* ed. Ann Lane. Urbana: University of Illinois Press, 1971.

Thucydides. *The Peloponnesian War.* New York: Penguin, 1954.

Tomlins, Christopher. *The State and the Unions: Labor Relations, Law, and the Organized Labor Movement in America, 1880–1960.* New York: Cambridge University Press, 1985.

Vanneman, Reeve, and Lynn Weber Cannon. *The American Perception of Class.* Philadelphia: Temple University Press, 1987.

Waddington, David, Kare Jones, and Chas Critcher. *Flashpoints: Studies in Public Disorder.* London: Routledge, 1989.

Weaver, Glenn. *Hartford: An Illustrated History of Connecticut's Capital.* Woodland Hills, Calif.: Windsor, 1985.

Weber, Max. *Economy and Society.* Berkeley: University of California Press, 1970.

Wells, Donald. *Empty Promises: Quality of Working Life Programs and the Labor Movement.* New York: Monthly Review Press, 1987.

Wilentz, Sean, ed. *The Rites of Power: Symbolism, Ritual, and Power Since the Middle Ages.* Philadelphia: University of Pennsylvania Press, 1985.

Wilson, James Q. *Political Organizations.* New York: Basic, 1973.

Wilson, Robert L. *Colt, an American Legend: The Official History of Colt Firearms from 1836 to the Present.* New York: Abbeville, 1985.

Witte, John. *Democracy, Authority, and Alienation in Workers' Participation in an American Corporation.* Chicago: University of Chicago Press, 1980.

Wray, J. Harry. "Comment on Interpretations of Early Research into Belief Systems." *Journal of Politics* 41 (1979): 1173–1184.

Young, Jeffrey. *Cognitive Therapy for Personality Disorders: A Schema-Focused Approach.* Sarasota, Fla.: Professional Resource Exchange, 1990.

Zimmerman, Don, and Melvin Pollner. "The Everyday World as a Phenomenon." In *Understanding Everyday Life*, ed. Jack Douglas. Chicago: Aldine, 1970.

Zolberg, Aristide. "Moments of Madness." *Politics and Society* 2, 2 (1972): 183–207.

# Index

# DATE DUE

| | | | |
|---|---|---|---|
| | | | |
| | | | |
| | | | |
| | | | |
| | | | |
| | | | |
| | | | |
| | | | |
| | | | |
| | | | |
| | | | |
| | | | |
| | | | |
| | | | |
| | | | |
| | | | |
| | | | |
| | | | |
| | | | |
| | | | |
| | | | |
| | | | |

DEMCO 13829810